Bratzel & Rout, Latin American History

DISCARD

DEDICATED TO

Charles C. Cumberland

&

David C. Bailey

who in many ways are still our mentors

Selected Reading Lists and Course
Outlines from American Colleges
and Universities

Latin American

History

edited by John F. Bratzel and Leslie B. Rout Jr.
Michigan State University

 **Markus Wiener Publishing, Inc.**

ISBN 0-910129-38-X
Library of Congress Card No. 85-040725
Printed in America

TABLE OF CONTENTS

II. TOPICAL COURSES IN LATIN AMERICAN HISTORY AND CULTURE

A. Pre-hispanic Cultures

B. People and Personalities of Latin America

C. The Military in Latin America

D. Women in Latin America

E. Blacks in Latin America

INTRODUCTION

When we first began this project, we assumed that it would be mainly used as an aid by new faculty. We hoped that young Ph.Ds would look at the books assigned, the reading lists proffered, as well as the assignments given by more established faculty and gain a head start in setting up their own classes. As we studied and organized the material, however, we realized that a book of syllabi was just as valuable for fine tuning courses already in existence. It is instructive for both young and "old" faculty to learn what their colleagues are doing.

We also observed in our perusal of the material a clear sense of commonality in what professors are teaching and requiring. Almost every syllabus emphasizes the necessity to attend class, the evils of late papers, and the need to participate in class discussions. Most courses follow common themes and develop them in similar ways. We also noted that the use of films and map quizzes have become a standard part of many courses.

There were, however, many unique and different features in some of the courses. David Bushnell, following the injunction of Simon Bolivar, teaches his introductory course from the present to the past. Hugh Hamill presents a unique way of stimulating student discussions. Carlos Cortes has an entire course based on film, while Judith Elkins has established one on Jews in Latin America. Finally, who but Bill Beezley would have a "Hawaiian Shirt" Day.

We hope that whether you are just beginning your career or are an old hand that you will closely examine this book. Where possible, we tried to present copies of exactly what materials students receive. In some cases, however, we had to retype material so it could be duplicated. In such cases we tried to keep the same style and format of the original. Because of length requirements, we also dropped some bibliographies from syllabi which were similar to others.

Finally, we would like to thank all those who sent us material. Their contributions should help all of us to become better teachers and scholars.

John F. Bratzel &   East Lansing

Leslie B. Rout, Jr.

I. GENERAL SURVEYS OF LATIN AMERICAN HISTORY AND CULTURE

INTRODUCTION TO LATIN AMERICAN HISTORY

LAH 2020   FALL 1984

Professor Bushnell
Grinter 360

Course objectives: This course does not pretend to summarize the entire history of Latin America in one semester. Instead it will emphasize selected topics, from the Cuban Revolution to the Spanish Conquest of Mexico. (None other than the Liberator Simón Bolívar recommended that the teaching of history begin with things already partly familiar to the student and move from there, in reverse chronological direction, to things more remote.) The student should thereby gain a sense of the variety of Latin American history as well as a preliminary acquaintance with broader historical developments of which the featured topics are in some sense representative.

Course methods: The subject matter of the course will be presented by means of lectures, readings, films and other audio-visual aids, and class discussion. Students will submit one written report and take the exams and quizzes specified below.

Topics and assignments:

1. The Cuban Revolution.

   Films Lucía (Part II) and Portrait of Teresa will be shown in the second week. A three-page (typed double-spaced or handwritten equivalent) report on either of the two films is due on 5 September.

2. Argentine Populism Under Juan D. Perón

   Reading: Fraser and Navarro, Eva Peron

3. The Mexican Revolution

   Film: Mexico, the Frozen Revolution (24 September)

4. Examination covering films, reading, and lectures on first three topics (28 September).

5. Brazilian "Modernization."

   Reading: Amado, Gabriela, Clove and Cinnamon.
   Quiz on lectures and reading for this topic, date to be announced.

6. Political "Instability" in Uruguay.

   Reading: Hudson, The Purple Land.
   Quiz, as on previous topic, date to be announced

3

7. Bolivar and Spanish American Independence

Reading: Bushnell, _The Liberator Simón Bolívar: Man and Image_ (xeroxed selections only)

8. The Conquest of Mexico

Reading: Díaz, _The Conquest of New Spain_

9. Final Examination covering topics 7 and 8 in detail, all other topics at broad-brush level.

Supplementary reading. Students who miss lectures or wish further information on topics that are not fully treated in the course are urged to consult any standard text of Latin American history. For convenience of the class, two of these--Shafer, _History of Latin America_ and Keen and Wasserman, _Short History of Latin America_--will be placed on reserve in Library East.

HISTORY 102
THE LATIN AMERICAN EXPERIENCE

Fall term   Professor Bailey

OBJECTIVES:
   History 102 is a course in general education. The focus is
on the experience of being Latin American, yet each topic ad-
dressed partakes of universal humanistic concerns. The course is
not vocationally oriented nor is it a part of a sequence in
professional training. It is hoped that this general education
course may inspire students to pursue further study of Latin
America in a variety of disciplines; it seeks to provide skills
and techniques which will facilitate this, but the same skills
and techniques will be equally applicable to a wide spectrum of
academic pursuits.
   Specifically, the content deals with identity and evolution
of a culturally and geographically autonomous part of the modern
world. History 102 addresses historical processes that have
placed Latin Americans in their present condition of being both a
part of the western world and at the same time often alien to it.
It takes as its point of departure both the contemporary reality
of Latin America as projected in the news media and other sources, and the experiences and humanistic perspectives of the
students for whom the course is designed.

EVALUATION:
   There will be a midterm and a final examination, both of
which will include (but not exclusively) factual data presented
in lectures and readings. The midterm and final will each count
25% of your grade. The balance of the final grade will be based
on four or five short analytical papers, which will be submitted
at two-week intervals. The papers will be evaluated from the
viewpoint of both content and writing skills, with emphasis given
to the student's ability to understand concepts and develop
ideas.

READING ASSIGNMENTS:
      Michael Coe, The Maya
      Ricardo Pozas, Juan, the Chamula
      Domingo F. Sarmiento, Facundo Quiroga
      Stanley and Barbara Stein, The Colonial Heritage of Latin
         America
      Celso Furtado, The Economic Growth of Brazil from Colonial
         Times to the Present
      José Enrique Rodó, Ariel
      Lee Lockwood, Castro's Cuba, Cuba's Fidel
      David St. Clair, Child of the Dark

5

SCHEDULE:

I. THE INDIAN, PAST AND PRESENT

Week 1. The Indian Past

Cultural origins in America
Rise of the classic civilizations
The archaeological record
Conquest and cataclysm: The coming of the Europeans

Slide presentation: The archaeology of Middle America

Readings: Michael Coe, The Maya

Week 2. The Enduring Indian

Life after conquest: The forging of a caste society
Absorption: The Mestizo
Isolation: The Indian community
The Indian World-view and "modernity"

Readings: Ricardo Pozas, Juan the Chamula

II. RULE BY MEN AND RULE BY LAW: THE CAUDILLO

Week 3. The Search for a System

Independence and the crisis of legitimacy
The failure of constitutional government
The rise of strong-man rule

Readings: From Domingo Sarmiento, Facundo Quiroga

Week 4. The Caudillo and the National State

The evolution of the state apparatus
Presidents and generals
The modern caudillo: Juan Perón and Fidel Castro

Readings: Lee Lockwood, Castro's Cuba, Cuba's Fidel

Tape presentation: Excerpts from Castro's speeches

III. THE STRUGGLE FOR MODERNITY

Week 5. A recipe for Underdevelopment

The economic legacy of Iberian rule
Nineteenth Century: Latin America joins the developing
    West as an unequal partner
Twentieth century: Industrialization, too little and
    too late

6

Readings: From Stanley and Barbara Stein, *The Colonial Heritage of Latin America*

Week 6. *The Revolutionary Road to Modernity*

Mexico's "traditional" revolution, 1910-1940
Cuba's Marxist gamble, 1959-
Brazilian development as a contrast

Readings: Charles C. Cumberland, "Latin America's Twentieth-Century Revolutions"

Slide Presentations: The Mexican Revolution; Cuba Today

IV. THE WORLD OUTSIDE: LATIN AMERICA AS CLIENT AND VICTIM

Week 7. *From Iberian Rule to British Hegemony: The Nineteenth Century*

The willing client: Latin America and the commodity market
Nineteenth-century intervention in Latin America

Readings: From Stein and Stein, *Colonial Heritage*

Week 8. *The Colossus of the North*

The Monroe Doctrine and the Western Hemisphere idea
The United States as hemispheric policeman
"I took Panama": Teddy Roosevelt and his world
Latin America and the United States: The burden of continuity

Readings: Norman Bailey, "The United States as Caudillo"

V. THE SEARCH FOR IDENTITY: ART, LETTERS, AND INTELLECTUALS

Week 9. *Latin Americans as Westerners*

Liberal and conservative thought in the nineteenth century
The lure of positivism

Readings: Juan Bautista Alberdi, "Bases...for the Political Organization of the Argentine Republic

Week 10. *Latin Americans as...Latin Americans*

The literature of nationalism
The literature of social protest
Art and revolution

Readings: Rubén Darío, "Ode to Theodore Roosevelt: José Enrique Rodo, *Ariel*

Slide presentations: Mexican revolutionary mural art

History 335--Humanities 380 (Ibero-Latin American Culture) -- Spring 1983

GENERAL INFORMATION SHEET

Instructor: Dr. J. W. Cooney
Office: Gottschalk Hall 301A, 588-6817
Office Hours: MWF 7:30 AM-7:50 AM. & 10:00 AM - 10:50 AM. If you cannot make these office hours, please arrange an appointment with the instructor. If you cannot reach the instructor on the telephone, leave your name and telephone number with the Secretary of the History Department. She will get in touch with me and I will try to get back to you. Office hours are for you to use.

The purpose of this course is to acquaint the student with the broad sweep of Iberian and Latin American culture. As one will see, this is an ambitious design since the roots of Iberian culture go back to at least 1000 BC, and the Indian heritage of Latin America to much the same date. While certain aspects of this course must be historical in nature, it is the instructor's intention to concentrate on topic matters. You will be given a Topics-Readings Sheet which will present those topics.

Texts: Irving A. Leonard, Baroque Times in Old Mexico. John A Crow, Spain: The Root and the Flower. Jorge Luis Borges, A Personal Anthology. Jorge Amado, Gabriela, Clove and Cinamon. The texts will not replace the lectures, but complement them. Texts will come from both texts and lectures.

General Information: I do not take attendance. Your grade comes solely from the tests and the assigned work. However, remember that at least 50% of my exams come directly from my lectures. Good attendance is simply necessary to get a good grade. If you miss a class, get the notes from a friend, or better, xerox those notes in the library so no one loses possession of notes. I do not give any type of extra credit, or supplementary work. If you have questions during the lectures, raise your hand and I will try to answer you immediately. Do not feel bashful about such questions as others may have the same difficulty.

Pop Quizes: These can and may be given at the discretion of the instructor. I do not give makeups on pop quizes.

Tests: There will be three (3) announced tests--two mids and a Final. They will be about 40% essay, 30 % Identification, and 30% Multiple-Choice, True-False. There will be choices on the essay and Identification Questions. Questions will come from both the lectures and the assigned readings. If I give you specific questions about the texts, you may not have any choice, but be required to answer that particular questions. Pay attention to your readings therefore. Makeups are possible on the mids. You cannot miss the Final. I require bluebooks and blue or black ink. If you do not use these, you will be penalized on the grading of the exam. All answers must be in the bluebook. If you have questions about my grading, see me in my office. I cannot discuss individual exams in the classroom. I will try to get your exams back to you as rapidly as possible. My grading scale for individual exams and for the entire semester is as follows: 87-100 A; 76-86 B; 62-75 C; 51-61 D; 0-50 F. Always check my arithmetic when you get an exam back. It is your numerical total which matters for the final semester grade.

Outside Reading: Each student is required to read one book (not a text) dealing with some aspect of Ibero-Latin American culture. Approximately eight weeks into the semester, that student will deliver to the instructor a review of the book chosen. Students must clear their choice of book with the instructor. A Book Review Sheet is supplied. Students getting less than a B- on the book review will be allowed to redo that review with the possibility to bringing it up to no more than a B-. Fiction is OK but that also must be cleared with the instructor. Typewritten reviews are appreciated but if you do not type well, do it longhand. Longhand will not be penalized.

The instructor would appreciate it if students with difficulties see him early in the semester. With the best will in the world there is little I can do for you the last weeks of the semester. I dislike giving Incompletes as does A & S. If you get one, for whatever reason, it is your responsibility to clear it up, not mine. Students who miss the Final without informing beforehand the Instructor flunk. Plagiarism is grounds for an F and dismissal from school, as is cheating of any nature. If you do not do the book review you can expect no better than a C for the semester, no matter what your exam grades are. I do not post grades at the end of the semester, nor do I mail them out, and I do not inform students of grades over the phone. You will receive your grades from the Registrar in the normal fashion. I only discuss grades in my office.

JWC

History 335--Humanities 380 (Ibero-Latin American Culture)--Spring 1983
Dr. Cooney

READINGS TOPICS SHEET

Texts: Irving a Leonard. <u>Baroque Times in Old Mexico</u>. = L
Jorge Luis Borges. <u>A Personal Anthology</u>. = B
John Crow. <u>Spain: The Root and the Flower</u>. 2= C
Jorge Amado. <u>Gabriela, Cinamon and Clove</u>. = A

The above texts will be used to supplement the lectures and other forms
of presentation. Given the nature of this course, it would be indeed hard
to find any text or small number of texts that would cover the entire gamit
of Iberian and Latin American culture. Remember therefore, that the texts
only supplement the lectures. They do not replace them. Pay as much
attention to the lectures and other forms of presentation as the texts.

1. Orientation. C 1-22

2. Iberia: Geography, Iberians, Celts, Romans, and Moors (Readings only)
   C 23-77.

3. The Reconquest: Church, Warrior, and the Spanish Middle Ages. C 78- 132.

4. Latin America: Geography and the Indian Background. lectures and
   slide presentation.

5. The High Civilizations of Indian America. Lectures and Slides.

6. Iberia and the Renaissance. C 132-160.

7. Portuguese and Spanish Exploration. lecture.

8. Latin America: The Conquest. lectures and slides.

9. Spain: The Counter Reformation, Church Society, and Culture.
   C 161-184.

10. Spain and the Siglo de Oro: Literature and Art. C 185-224. lectures
    and slides.

11. Latin America: Race and Society. L 37-52

12. The Economic Basis of Latin American Colonial Life. lecture

13. Latin American Urban Life and the Woman. L vii-36.

14. Spanish America: Towards an independent Culture. L 53-228.

15. Iberia and the New World: The Enlightenment. C 225-241

16. Enlightenment and Art: The Case of Goya. C 241-243 and slides.

17. The French Revolution, Napoleon, and Latin American independence.
    lectures.

18. Latin American Political Culture and the Question of the "liberator".
    lectures.

19. Criollos and French Culture in Latin America. lectures.

20. Transforming Societies and the "Cult of Progress": The Case of
    Sarmiento. B 24-25, 161-175, 192-193.

21. The Rise of Brazilian Literature. lecture

22. Spain and Culture in the 19th Century. C 243-251.

23. The Generation of 1898. C 252-277
24. 20th Century Spain c 278-320
25. Latin American Society around 1900. lecture.
26. The Triumph of the Latin American Middle Class Artist and Intellectual. B vii-114.
27. Brazil in 20th Century Art, Architecture, Music and Literature. A the entire book.
28. Mexico and Argentina: Two varieties of literary impulse. B 115-210.
29. The Mexican Artistic Renaissance. lectures and slides.
30. The Urbanization of Latin America. lecture
31. Cultural Impulses from Below: Race, Class, Nationalism, and Politics in Latin American Cultureal Life. lectures.
32. Spain: From Franco to the Present. C 321-392.
33. Art and Literature in Spain: 1930 to the Present. lectures.

I will not spend the same amount of time on each topic, but the above should give to you an idea as to the direction of this course. If you are interested in some aspect of Iberian or Latin American culture that you do not see in the above, speak to me. If I deem it important enough I may get the chance to include it in the semester's presentation.

JWC

11

INTRODUCTION TO LATIN AMERICAN HISTORY

LAH 2020   SPRING 1983

Instructor: Neill Macaulay

Time & place: Tue., 4 period (11:15 am-12:05 pm), Thur., 4-5
periods (11:15-1:10); GPA 2306

Course objective: To introduce students to the main currents in
the evolution of Latin American society, politics, and culture
since 1492.

Textbooks:
      E. Bradford Burns, Latin America: A Concise Interpretive
History, 3rd edition
      David G. Sweet & Gary B. Nash, Struggle and Survival in
Colonial America
      Bernal Díaz, The Conquest of New Spain
      Jorge Amado, The Violent Land
      Miguel Ángel Asturias, El señor presidente: The President

Schedule and reading assignments:

Jan. 6:   introduction
      11:   Burns, pp. 2-18
      13:   Sweet & Nash, chapters 7 & 11
      18:   Burns, pp. 19-22; Sweet & Nash, chapter 8
      20:   Burns, pp. 24-27; Sweet & Nash, chapter 9
      25:   Burns, pp. 27-37; Sweet & Nash, chapter 15
      27:   Burns, pp. 37-54; Sweet & Nash, chapter 17
Feb. 1:   Sweet & Nash, chapters 13 & 16
       3:   Burns, pp. 54-59; Sweet & Nash, chapter 14
       8:   Sweet & Nash, chapters 2 & 10
      10:   Burns, pp. 59-61; Sweet & Nash, chapter 18
      15:   Sweet & Nash, chapters 6 & 20
      17:   Burns, pp. 63-79; Sweet & Nash, chapter 5
      22:   no assigned readings
      24:   midterm examination; responsible for all the above
reading plus Díaz, Conquest of New Spain
Mar. 1:   Burns, 81-91
       3:   Burns, 91-108
       8:   Burns, 108-118
      10:   Burns, 120-131
      15:   Burns, 131-144
      17:   Burns, 144-152
      22:   Burns, 154-169
      24:   Burns, 171-180

12

```
Apr.  5:   Burns, 180-198
      7:   Burns, 200-222
     12:   Burns, 222-237
     14:   Burns, 237-262
     19:   Burns, 264-292
     21:   no assigned readings
     27:   final examination; responsible for all reading assign-
ments in Burns since the beginning of the course plus Amado, The
Violent Land, & Asturias, The President.
```

Examinations and quizzes:

1) There will be a two-hour final examination, composed of objective and essay questions, which will account for 50% of the course grade, unless, for any reason, the student fails to take the midterm examination, in which case the value of the final exam will be 80%. While the final exam will be cumulative, material covered after the midterm will receive the greater emphasis. The final exam is scheduled for Wed., Apr. 27, at 3:00-5:00 pm.

2) There will be a fifty-minute examination, composed of objective and essay questions which will account for 30% of the course grade. The midterm exam will be given on Thursday, February 24, at 12:20-1:10 pm (5th period).

3) During the semester there will be twelve unannounced, ten-minute quizzes, each based on the reading assignment for the day of the quiz. The average of the ten highest quiz grades will account for 20% of the course grade. (In other words, the two lowest grades will be dropped in calculating the student's quiz average).

13

HH363 History of Latin America   Associate Professor Masterson
Course Information   Fall 1983

Introduction:

This course is a general survey and synthesis of the history of Latin
America from the Pre-Columbian era to the present day. Through lectures,
readings, discussions, and writing assignments we will analyze and gain
insights into the major political, economic, social, and ideological
developments that have shaped Latin American society. The scope of the
subject mandates that we be selective in this analysis, but we will emphasize themes that will lend unity to our admittedly wide-ranging examination.

Course Mechanics:

Examinations: There will be three exams and the final. One of these
exams will be an objective test over E. Bradford Burns A Short History of
Latin America during the second week of class. The other two term exams
and the final will be primarily essay but will include some short identifications. There will be at least two announced quizzes during the term. I also
reserve the right to give unannounced quizzes if I feel they are necessary.

Written Assignments:

There will be two writing assignments required for this course. The
first will be a 3-5 (typewritten) analysis of Domingo Sarmiento Life in the
Argentine Republic in the Days of the Tyrants. Specific guidelines for this
paper will be distributed well before this assignment is due. The primary
writing exercise for this course will be a 10-page (typewritten) biographical
analysis of a leading Latin American political, military, or intellectual
leader. This assignment will be due the last week of the term and should
reflect substantial research and careful attention to writing and mechanics.
More specific guidelines for this project will also be provided.

Readings:

Consult the class reading schedule for the daily reading assignments.
Note that you will be asked to complete Burns during the first week of
class. This is required to give you a framework for the course. You may
not like it while you are plowing through this material so quickly but you
will be grateful later. Complete all the other assignments before the
scheduled discussion. Much of this material is reasonably complex and you
need to have a good background for our class discussions. Note that I have
placed two additional textbooks on reserve in Nimitz for your further reading
and I have also prepared a list of suggested readings that you will find
useful. Make use of these readings to supplement the assignments when
possible. I will also distribute handouts in class.

Office Hours:

Office: 344 Sampson, Phone x3202

HH363 History of Latin America

Grading:

Final grades will be calculated as follows:

Exam on Burns	100 points	10%
Sarmiento Paper	100 points	10%
Essay Exam I	150 points	15%
Essay Exam II	150 points	15%
Biography Paper	200 points	20%
Final Exam	200 points	20%
Quizzes and Discussion	100 points	10%
	1000 points	100%

Final Grade Determination:

900-1000 points	A
800-899 points	B
700-799 points	C
600-699 points	D
Below 600 points	F

NOTE: All requirements for this course must be met before a passing grade can be given. Any work not completed will result in a failing grade.

UNITED STATES NAVAL ACADEMY
Annapolis, Maryland 21402

H-i 363   History of Latin America   D. M. Masterson
COURSE NUMBER AND TITLE   INSTRUCTOR

FIRST SEMESTER, 1983-84

TEXTS

Keen and Wasserman, **A Short History of Latin America**
E.B. Burns, Latin America: A Concise Intrpretive History
Charles Gibson, Spain in America
Domingo Sarmiento, Life in the ArgentineRepublic in the Days of the Tyrant
John Womack, Zapata and the Mexican Revolution

LESSON SCHEDULE

Week of 24 Aug   Classes begin, Wednesday, 24 August

1. Course Introduction   Burns

2. Latin America: A Proflie; Map Quiz   Burns

Week of 29 Aug

1. The Pre-Hispanic Past I   Burns, K -4
                                                               22

2. The Pre-Hispanic PastII   Burns, KW-23
                                                               32

3. Exam on Burns, Discussion

16

LABOR DAY HOLIDAY, Mon - 5 Sept

Week of 5 Sept

1. The Road to Conquest; Iberian Background   KW-32-49

2. The Conquest of Mexico   KW-50-61

Week of 12 Sept

1. The Conquest Beyond Mesoamerica   KW-61-70

2. The Economic Foundations of Colonial Life   Gibson-48-67

3. State, Church, and Society   Gibson-68-111

End of 4-week marking period - Tue, 20 Sept
4-week grades due Tue, 27 Sept
Preregistration for Second Semester, 22-27 Sept
Football vs Lehigh - Sat, 24 Sept

Week of 19 Sept

1. The Bourbon Reforms   Gibson-112-135

2. Colonial Brazil   KW- 130-143

3. Class and Caste in Colonial Latin America   KW-99-107

Week of 26 Sept

1. Independence: Background   KW-144-149

2. The Liberation Movements   KW-145-161

3. Library Research   Sarmiento

Football vs Air Force, Sat, 8 Oct

Week of 3 Oct

1. The Caudillo and Latin American Society   Sarmiento
                                                             First Paper Due

2. The Struggle for Nationhood: Mexico   KW-200-210

3. The Struggle for Nationhood: Argentina   KW-210-217

17

Columbus Day - HOLIDAY - Mon, 10 Oct
MID-TERM EXAMS - 11-15 Oct (academic reserved period)

Week of 10 Oct

1. The Struggle for Nationhood: Chile   -K.-217-
                                                                          223

2. Exam I

End of Mid-Term Marking Period, Tue, 18 Oct
Football vs Pittsburgh, HOMECOMING, Sat, 22 Oct

Week of 17 Oct

1. The Struggle for Nationhood: Peru   KW-380-396

2. The 19th Century Exception: Brazil   KW-223-233

3. Population and Race in 19th Century Latin America   KW-234-238

Mid-Term Grades due - Tue, 25 Oct

Week of 24 Oct

1. The Literature of Latin American Nationalism   KW-241-259

2. The Revolutionary Response: Mexico   Womack

3. The Revolution Loses its Way   K.i-294-300
   Womack Discussion   Womack

Football vs Syracuse, Sat, 5 Nov

Week of 31 Oct

1. Argentina: The Failure of Democracy   KW-300-314

2. Argentina: The Shadow of Peron   KW-312-325

3. Brazil: The Old Republic   K.i-350-356

Veterans Day - HOLIDAY - Fri, 11 Nov

Week of 7 Nov

1. Brazil: Search for World Power   KW-356-379

2. Revolution From Above: Peru, 1930-1968   K.i-387-398

3. Holiday   18

Week of 14 Nov

1. Peru's "Ambiguous"Revolution Falters   KW-398-403

2. Exam II

3. Socialism and Reaction in Chile   KW-326-349

12-week grades due - Tue, 22 Nov
Registration for Second Semester, 21 Nov-7 Dec
Thanksgiving Day - HOLIDAY - Thu, 24 Nov
No regular academic classes will be held Fri, 25 Nov

Week of 21 Nov

1. Cuba: The Case of Retarded Nationalism   KW-404-415

2. Cuba: The Making of a Revolution   KW-415-422

NO REGULAR CLASSES HELD ON FRI, 2 DEC
Brigade absent, ARMY GAME, Pasadena, Sat, 3 Dec

Week of 28 Nov

1. The Cuban Revolution and Latin America   KW-423-431

2. Uncle Sam's Stepchildren: Central America to the   Woodward
   1960's

3. The Revolutionary Response: Nicaragua   Handout

CLASSES END - Mon, 12 December
EXAMINATIONS BEGIN - Tues, 13 December

Week of 5 Dec

1. El Salvador and the Future   Handout
   Biography Paper Due

2. Latin America and the World Arena

3. Course Review

Exams end and Christmas leave begins - Wed, 21 December
Christmas Holiday, Sun, 25 Dec
New Years Holiday, Sun, 1 Jan 84
Leave Ends - Sun, 8 Jan 84

NOTE:
Midshipmen may depart early on Christmas Leave after completion of their last scheduled
examination or military duty, but in no case earlier than 0800, Tues, 13 Dec 83.

F. Katz, The Ancient American Civilizations

Miguel Leon Portilla, The Broken Spears: The Aztec Account of the Conquest of Mexico

Bernal Diaz del Castillo, The Discovery and Conqeust of Mexico

Stanley and Barbara Stein, Colonial Heritage of Latin America

Francois Chevalier, Land and Society in Colonial Mexico

Hugh Hamill, The Hidalgo Revolt

John Johnson, Simon Bolivar and Spanish American Independence

John Lynch, The Spanish American Revolutions

Tulio Halperin-Donghi, The Aftermath of Revolution in Latin America

E. Bradford Burns, A History of Brazil

James Scobie, Argentina: A City and A Nation

Robert Potash, The Army and Politics in Argentina, 1928-1945

Ramon Eduardo Ruiz, Cuba: The Making of a Revolution

Hugh Thomas, Cuba: The Pursuit of Freedom

Carmelo Mesa Laga, Cuba in the 1970's

M.C. Meyer and W.L. Sherman, The Course of Mexican History

Charles C. Cumberland, Mexico: The Struggle for Modernity

David Werlich, A Short History of Peru

Peter Klaren, Modernization, Dislocation and Aprismo

A.F. Lownthal, The Peruvian Experiment: Continuity and Change Under Military Rule

Fredrick B. Pike, Chile and the United States

Jay Kinsbruner, Chile: A Historical Intrepretation

Fredrick Nunn, Chilean Politics, 1920-1931: The Honourable Mission of the Armed Forces

Franklin W. Knight, The Caribbean

L.B. Rout, The African Experience in Spanish America

RESERVE READING

Ralph Woodward, Central America: A Nation Divided

Thomas Karnes, The Failure of Union: Central America 1824-1975

SCHOOL OF ADVANCED INTERNATIONAL STUDIES
The Johns Hopkins University

INTRODUCTION TO LATIN AMERICAN POLITICS

Professor Roett
Fall 1983-1984

This course is a broad overview of Latin American politics, primarily
in the 20th century. It is an introductory course; those with more advanced
work in Latin American politics should take another course in the politics
sequence to avoid repetition of work previously completed.

There is no written assignment; there will be a final examination in
December. The class will meet Monday morning 8:30 a.m. - 10:30 a.m.

The following books (paperback) are available at the bookstore for
purchase; copies are on reserve in the library, also:

Peter G. Snow, Political Forces in Argentina (rev. ed.)

Riordan Roett, Brazil: Politics in a Patrimonial Society (rev. ed.)

Gary W. Wynia, The Politics of Latin American Development

Juan J. Linz & Alfred Stepan, Eds., The Breakdown of Democratic Regimes:
Latin America

Juan J. Linz, The Breakdown of Democratic Regimes: Crisis, Breakdown, and
Reequilibrium

Arturo Valenzuela, The Breakdown of Democratic Regimes: Chile

Fernando Henrique Cardoso and Enzo Faletto, Dependency and Development in
Latin America

September 12 - Introduction

September 19 - The Game & the Players

Wynia, Pt. I, Chaps. 1-5, pp. 3-130.

Charles W. Anderson, "Toward a Theory of Latin American Politics," in
Howard J. Wiarda, ed., Politics & Social Change in Latin America, pp. 249-65.

Eldon Kenworthy, "Coalitions in the Political Development of Latin
America," in Sven Groennings et al The Study of Coalition Behavior, pp. 103-40.

Michael L. Conniff, "Introduction: Toward a Comparative Definition of Populism," in Conniff, editor, Latin American Populism in Comparative Perspective,
pp. 3-30.

September 26 - Breakdown

Juan J. Linz, The Breakdown of Democratic Regimes: Crisis, Breakdown, and Reequilibrium (Vol. I).

October 3 - Argentina & Brazil - Populism

Wynia, Part II, chap. 6, pp. 133-67.

Peter G. Snow, Political Forces in Argentina, (rev. ed.) chaps. 1 to 6, pp. 1-135.

Riordan Roett, Brazil: Politics in a Patrimonial Society (rev. ed.), chaps. 2 to 5, pp. 24-130.

Thomas E. Skidmore, "A Case Study in Comparative Public Policy: The Economic Dimensions of Populism in Argentina and Brazil,"The New Scholar (1979), pp. 129-66.

October 10 - Argentina, Brazil and Peru - Authoritarianism

Wynia, chp. 8, pp. 207-44.

Peter H. Smith, "The Breakdown of Democracy in Argentina, 1916-1930," Juan J. Linz & Alfred Stepan, eds., The Breakdown of Democratic Regimes: Latin America, pp. 3-27.

Alfred Stepan, "Political Leadership and Regime Breakdown; Brazil," in Ibid., pp. 110-137.

Guillermo O'Donnell, "Permanent Crisis and the Failure to Create a Democratic Regime: Argentina, 1955-66," Ibid., pp. 138-77.

Riordan Roett, chap. 6, Patrimonial Society, pp. 133-70.

Julio Cotler, "Democracy and National Integration in Peru," in A. Lowenthal and C. McClintock, eds., The Peruvian Experiment Reconsidered, pp. 3-38.

Alfred Stepan, The State and Society: Peru in Comparative Perspective, chap. 4, pp. 117-57.

October 17 - Venezuela versus Chile: Different Responses to Democracy

Wynia, chap. 7, pp. 168-206.

Daniel H. Levine, "Venezuelan since 1958: the Consolidation of Democratic Politics," in Breakdown, pp. 82-109.

John D. Martz, "The Party System: Toward Institutionalization,' in Martz and David J. Myers, eds., Venezuela: The Democratic Experience, pp. 93-112.

Arturo Valenzuela, The Breakdown of Democratic Regimes: Chile.

October 24 - The Revolutionary Alternative:

A. Mexico vs. Chile

Wynia, chap. 9 & 10, pp. 245-308.

Lorenzo Meyer, "Historical Roots of the Authoritarian State in Mexico," in Jose Luis Reyna & Richard S. Weinert, eds., Authoritarianism in Mexico, pp. 3-22.

Jose Luis Reyna, "Redefining the Authoritarian Regime," Ibid., pp. 155-71.

Steven E. Sanderson, "Presidential Succession and Political Rationality in Mexico," World Politics XXXV (3), April 1983, pp. 315-334.

Kenneth M. Coleman & C.L. Davis, "Perspective Reform and the Mexican Working Class." LARR, XVIII (1) 1983, p. 3-32.

Barbara Stallings, Class Conflict and Economic Development in Chile, 1958-1973, chap. 4, pp. 76-96 & chap. 6, pp. 125-53.

Arturo Valenzuela, "Political Contraints to the Establishment of Socialism in Chile," in Arturo Valenzuela & J. Samuel Valenzuela, eds., Chile: Politics and Society, pp. 1-29.

October 31 - The Revolutionary Alternative

B. Cuba.

Jorge I. Dominguez, Cuba: Order and Revolution, chaps. 4 to 8, pp. 110-341.

Samuel Farber, "The Cuban Communists in the Early Stages of the Cuban Revolution: Revolutionaries or Reformers?" LARR XVIII (1) 1983, p. 59-84.

November 7 - Authoritarianism and Corporatism

Howard J. Wiarda, "Corporatism and Development in the Iberic-Latin World: Persistent Strains and New Variations," in F.B. Pike & T. Stritch, eds., The New Corporatism.

Phillipe C. Schmitter, "Still the Century of Corporatism?", Ibid.

David Collier, "Overview of th Bureaucratic-Authoritarian Model," chap. 1, 19-32, in Collier, ed., The New Authoritarianism in Latin America.

Fernando Henrique Cardoso, "On the Characterization of Authoritarian Regimes in Latin America," in Collier, ed., Ibid., chap. 2, pp. 33-57.

Albert O. Hirschman, "The Turn to Authoritarianism in Latin America and the Search for Its Economic Determinants," in Collier, ed., chap. 3, 61-98.

Robert R. Kaufman, "Industrial Change and Authoritarian Rule in Latin America: A Concrete Review of the Bureaucratic-Authoritarian Model," in Collier, ed., chapter 5, pp. 165-253.

November 14 - Dependence Theory

Fernando Henrique Cardoso and Enzo Faletto, Dependency and Development in Latin America.

Thomas Angotti, "The Political Implications of Dependency Theory," in R.H. Chilcote, ed., Dependency and Marxism, pp. 124-137.

Colin Henfry, "Dependency, Modes of Production, and the Class Analysis of Latin America," in R.H. Chilcote, ed., Dependency and Marxism, pp. 17-54.

November 21 - Foreign Capital, The State, and Local Entrepreneurs

Alfred Stepan, State and Society, chap. 7, pp. 230-89.

Richard S. Weinert, "The State and Foreign Capital," in Reyna & Weinert, eds., Authoritarian Mexico, pp. 109-28.

Gary Geriffi & Peter Evans, "Transnational Corporations, Dependent Development, and State Policy in the Semiperiphery: A Comparison of Brazil and Mexico," LARR, XVI (3), 1981, pp. 31-64.

Kenneth S. Mericle, "Corporatist Control of the Working Class: Authoritarian Brazil since 1964," in James M. Malloy, ed., Authoritarianism and Corporatism in Latin America, pp. 303-338.

Barbara Stallings, "International Capitalism and the Peruvian Military Government," in A. Lowenthal and C. McClintock, eds., The Peruvian Experiment Revisited, pp. 144-180.

Peter Evans, "Shoes, OPIC, and the Unquestioning Persuasion: Multinational Corporation and U.S.-Brazilian Relations," in Capitalism and the State in U.S. - Latin American Relations. Richard Fagen, Editor, pp. 302-336

November 28 - The Arbiters? The Armed Forces

Gene E. Bigler, "The Armed Forces and Patterns of Civil-Military Relations," in Martz & Myers, eds., Venezuela, pp. 113-33.

David R. Ronfeldt, "The Mexican Army and Political Order since 1940," in A.F. Lowenthal, ed., Armies and Politics in Latin America, pp. 291-321.

Jorge Dominquez, Cuba, chap. 9, pp. 341-78.

Brian Loveman and Thomas M. Davies, Jr., eds., The Politics of Antipolitics: The Military in Latin America , pp. 89-104, 118-41, 174-80, 190-219, 223-41, 251-87.

24

Liisa L. North, "Ideological Orientations of Peru's Military Rulers," in A. Lowenthal and C. McClintock, eds., The Peruvian Experiment Revisited, pp. 245-274.

Victor Villanueva, "Peru's 'New' Military Professionalism: The Failure of the Technocratic Approach," in Stephen M. Gorman, ed., Post-Revolutionary Peru, pp. 157-178.

Miles D. Wolpin, "Military Radicalization in Latin America," Journal of Interamerican Studies and World Affairs, 23(4), November 1981, pp. 395-421.

December 5 - The Roman Catholic Church and Change

Penny Lernoux, Cry of the People, chaps. 10 & 11, pp. 363-448.

Daniel H. Levine, Religion and Politics in Latin America, chaps. 2 & 3, pp. 18-96.

Thomas C. Bruneau, "Basic Christian Communities in Latin America: Their Nature and Significance," in Daniel H. Levine, ed., Churches and Politics in Latin America, pp. 225-236.

Margaret E. Crahan, "Salvation Through Christ or Marx: Religion in Revolutionary Cuba," in Ibid., pp. 238-264.

Phillip Berryman, "What Happened at Puebla," in Ibid., pp. 55-85.

Thomas Whigham
PSY 218
469-1615
office hrs. 6-7 Weds.

LATIN AMERICAN CULTURES

The goal of this course is to provide a basic introduction to Latin American culture. Special emphasis will be placed on the Hispanic, Amerind, and African antecedent , and on the process of cultural synthesis that has occurred since 1492. High culture, as represented in the music, literature, art, and film of Latin America, will also be discussed. Rather than viewing Latin American society as the natural offspring of the Iberian mother countries, I argue that the European conquest began a process of cultural accommodation between Western and non-Western groups. This dynamic interaction between cultures will constitute the essential backdrop for the structure of the course.

REQUIREMENTS:
A midterm and a final examination, 7-10 pages apiece, take-home. These two examinations will account for two-thirds of the course grade, the final third being met be active participation in classroom discussions. Late papers are firmly discouraged.

TEXTS:
Eric Wolf, <u>Sons of the Shaking Earth</u>
Harold E. Davis, <u>Latin American Thought:</u> An <u>Historical Introduction</u>
Carolina María de Jesús, <u>Child of the Dark</u>
Gabriel García Márquez, <u>100 Years of Solitude</u>
V. S. Naipaul, <u>Return of Eva Perón</u> (recommended)

Several other short readings will be handed out in class. All materials are available on reserve in the library.

CLASS SCHEDULE

Jan. 30   Introduction: Some Propositions and Definitions
          Slide presentation.

Feb. 6   The Amerind Heritage
          Wolf, pp. 1-151, Davis, pp. 18-30.

Feb. 13   The Iberian Heritage
          Wolf, pp. 152-256.

Feb. 20   The African Contribution: the beginnings of colonization.

```
Feb. 27   The Colonial World.
          Arzans de Orsua y Vela (handout), Davis, pp. 31-62.

Mar.  6   Independence:  Latin America in the 1800s.
          Davis, pp. 63-149.

Mar. 13   The Place of the Indian in National Culture:   the case
          of Peru.
          Guest speaker.

Mar. 20   City and countryside--an enduring dichotomy?

Mar. 27   Film: Lucía (Cuba, 1969).
          Midterms handed out.

SPRING RECESS

Apr. 10   Variants of political culture.
          Midterms due.

Apr. 17   Women in Latin American culture.
          de Jesús, all.

Apr. 24   Religion and Revolution:   the impact of the 20th
          Century.
          Davis, pp. 150-239.   Naipaul discussed.

May   1   Latin America looks at itself.
          García Márquez, all.

May   8   Film: Los Olivados (Mexico, 1950).
          Finals handed out.

May  15   Some tentative conclusions.
          Finals due.
```

27

Professor Beezley
HA 108   737-2483
Office Hours: 11-12 daily

Textbooks:
Charles Gibson, Spain in America (Harpers)
MacLachlan & Rodríguez, Forging of the Cosmic Race (U. of California)
Miguel León-Portilla, The Broken Spears (Beacon Press)
Irving Leonard, Baroque Times in Old Mexico (U. of Michigan)
Alfred Crosby, The Columbian Exchange (Greenwood)

History 215 is a lecture survey of Latin American history before the era of
independence (1810-1824). It considers the pre-Colombian peoples, European
discovery and conquest of the western hemisphere, and the development of
colonial societies that survived for approximately 300 years.

There will be two hour examinations and a final. The exams are scheduled for
February 9, March 23, and the final exam date assigned by the university. Reading
assignments for the exams are as follows:

first exam: Gibson, chapters 1-3
                               MacLachlan & Rodríguez, chapters 1-4
                               The Broken Spears

second exam   Gibson, chapters 4-7
                               MacLachlan & Rodríguez, chapters 5-8
                               Baroque Times in Old Mexico

final exam   Gibson, chapters 8 & 9
                               MacLachlan & Rodríguez, chapters 9-11
                               Crosby, The Columbian Exchange
Each examination has a value of 100 points.

Students must submit two written essays during the semester. The first assignment
is a critical book review of 3-5 pages due on February 28. Students may select
a volume dealing with colonial Latin America, pre-Colombian socities, or the
expansion of Europe that interests them, with a few exceptions, e.g. no cookbooks,
no travelogue picture books, no junior high books If in doubt, consult the
instructor. The review should include a brief summary of the book's contents,
and a discussion of book's thesis, its arguments, its good and bad points, and
its writing style. The second assignment requires the student to submit a 3-5
page essay. This essay should critically evaluate the following description of the
Spanish colonial experience:
        ...1492. That was simply the year in which sea pirates began to cheat
        and rob and kill....Here is how the pirates were able to take whatever
        they wanted from anybody else: they had the best boats in the world,
        and they were meaner than anybody else, and they had gunpowder....
        They touched this seemingly listless powder with fire, and it turned
        violently into gas. This gas blew projectiles out of metal tubes
        at terrific velocities. The projectiles cut through meat and bone
        very easily, so the pirates could wreck the wiring or the bellows or
        the plumbing of a stubborn human being, even when he was far, far away.
        The chief weapon of the sea pirates, however, was their capacity to
        astonish. Nobody else could believe, until it was much too late, how
        heartless and greedy they were.
Kurt Vonnegut wrote this description of European expansion in the Americas in
His novel, Breakfast of Champions. You may find it helps to substitute "Spaniard"
for "sea pirate." Papers need not be typed. If they are handwritten, the papers

should be written on every other line. One typewritten page equals 250 words, so each assignment calls for 750-1250 words. Each paper has a value of 100 points.

Hawaiian Shirt Day : The examinations require writing two essays for 80 points on each test. It is impossible for anyone to receive a perfect mark of 40 on any of his or her essays. Consequently there are 6 points the student cannot get in the course. To offset this disadvantage, April 12 will be Hawaiian Shirt day. Each student wearing a Hawaii shirt to class will receive 4 points; the two students wearing the most flamboyant shirts (by vote of the class) will receive a total of 6 bonus points each.

Final Grade: The final grade will be calculated accoriding to the traditional percentages. 90% or at least 450 points equals an A; 80% or 400-449 points equals a B; and so forth.

THE B-I-I-I-G CASINO: Each student has the option to join the Big Casino or may be placed in it. A student will have the chance to gamble on the Big Casino on the fifth absence (there are no excused absences), failing to submit a paper on or before the beginning of class on the day the paper is due (no late papers are accepted) or failing to take an examination (no make-ups are permitted). The Big Casino relieves the student of all class requirements; The student gambles his course grade on a three-hour comprehensive final test. The Big Casino exam consists of two hour-long essay questions and 100 short answer (that is, fill-in the blank)questions based on the reading and lectures.

Leon G. Campbell
Office: LibS. 4110 (Ext. 5401)
Office Hours: M 3-5 and by appt.

COLONIAL LATIN AMERICA

Scope: History 160 is the first part of a two-quarter survey of Latin American history from pre-Columbian to modern times. The course deals with the development of the Spanish and Portuguese empires during the Age of Discovery when the New World was explored and occupied. The course concludes with the fall of the American empires with the coming of independence in the first part of the nineteenth century.

The course will emphasize the process of social and economic change that occurred with the intrusion of the Spanish and Portuguese into the lives of the indigenous peoples of the New World. The Aztec and Inca cultures will be studied and attention will be paid to the cultural clash resulting from the Conquest. The nature of colonialism will be explored in detail: the struggle for social justice and economic profit, the reality of race relations, the form and structure of the Spanish State in America, and the ways in which social tensions were managed. I prefer to stress the dynamics of colonialism rather than to narrate simple chronology of events. Many of the lectures are illustrated with slides and other visual materials.

Course Requirements: There are no prerequisites for taking the course.

Required readings: The course text is Charles Gibson, Spain in America (1966), a meaty, paperback treatmeat of the colonial period. To supplement the text, I am also assigning Eric Wolf's Son of the Shaking Earth dealing with the Aztec world before and after Cortes for those particularly interested in Mexico. To illustrate the fascinating story of the Conquest, I have assigned Robert Padden's fast-paced Hummingbird and the Hawk (1970) which dramatizes the struggle between the Aztec and Spanish worlds in 16th Century Mexico. The question of ethnicity and race relations is handled in Magnus Mörner, Race Mixture in the History of Latin America (1967), while Stanley and Barbara Stein's The Colonial Heritage of Latin America (1970) carries the story through independence.

Testing: The final course grade will be based on 1) a midterm examination or a ten-page term paper worth 40%, and 2) a final examination worth 60%. Students have the option of writing two essays with a combined value of 100% of the final grade in lieu of taking a final examination.

The midterm will be held on Thursday, February 19. The final exam is scheduled for Tuesday, March 24, from 3-6 p.m. Both examinations will consist of essay-type questions worth two-thirds of the exam grade, and objective questions (identifications) worth one-third. The latter are taken from terms put on the board during lectures.

The purpose of the term papers is to allow the student to explore
an interesting topic in some detail. The paper must be based on a topic
or question that has been agreed on by the student and the instructor.
Students are free to draw their ideas from any available sources, preferably
from books listed in the Outside Reading List. The essay, however, is not
intended to be solely a research paper but rather a reasoned effort to
explain a historical question on topic of the student's choice, (i.e., why
did the Azted Empire fall? How did women live in colonial Spanish America? etc.)
It need not be footnoted but students must explain the sources of their
information either in the text of the essay or in a short bibliography.
The essays are to be ten (10) pages in length (typed and double-spaced or
the handwritten equivalent).

Essays are due on <u>Thursday, February 19 and Monday, March 23.</u>

Course Schedule

<u>Week</u>	<u>Lecture Topic/Readings</u>
I Jan. 12-16	Introduction Geography of Latin America Wolf, <u>Shaking Earth</u>, vii-20
II Jan. 19-23	The Iberian Peoples, 711-1519 a.d. Gibson, <u>Spain in America</u>, ix-23

	America Before Columbus
	    Mörner, <u>Race Mixture</u>, 1-19
	    Wolf, <u>Shaking Earth</u>, 21-151

III
Jan. 26-30
	The Conquest of Mexico
	    Padden, <u>Hummingbird and Hawk,</u> complete
	    Gibson, <u>Spain in America</u>, 24-29

	The Conquest of Spanish America
	    Gibson, <u>Spain in America</u>, 30-47
	    Stein, <u>Colonial Heritage</u>, vii-26
	    Wolf, <u>Shaking Earth</u>, 152-175

IV
Feb. 2-6
	Spanish Lords of the Land
	    Gibson, <u>Spain in America</u>, 48-67
	    Wolf, <u>Shaking Earth</u>, 176-201

	The Spanish Quest for Order
	    Mörner, <u>Race Mixture</u>, 21-52
	    Stein, <u>Colonial Heritage</u>, 56-81
	    Wolf, <u>Shaking Earth</u>, 202-232

31

V Feb. 9-13	Conquest and Society in Brazil Morner, Race Mixture, 49-52

Race and Miscegenation: The Birth of Mestizaje
Wolf, Shaking Earth, 233-256
Mörner, Race Mixture, 53-74
Gibson, Spain in America, 136-151

VI
Feb. 17-28

The Church and its Powers
Gibson, Spain in America, 68-89

Midterm Examination

VII
Feb. 23-27

The Spanish American Economy: Land
Gibson, Spain in America, 112-135; 151-159
Stein, Colonial Heritage, 28-52

The Mining Economy
Gibson, Spain in America, 91-111

VIII
Mar. 2-6

The Spanish State in America
Gibson, Spain in America, 90-100

IX
Mar. 9-13

Enlightened Despotism 1750-1808
Gibson, Spain in America, 160-181
Stein, Colonial Heritage, 86-119

Defensive Modernization
Gibson, Spain in America, 182-204

X
Mar. 16-20

Independence and After
Gibson, Spain in America, 205-216

Social and Economic Repercussions of Independence
Mörner, Race Mixture, 79-90; 103-109; 139-150
Stein, Colonial Heritage, 124-198

FINAL EXAMINATION:

Tuesday, March 24, from 3-6 p.m.

HISTORY 331
LATIN AMERICA I, THE COLONIAL ERA
FALL 1985

GENERAL CLASS INSTRUCTIONS   PLEASE READ   GENERAL CLASS INSTRUCTIONS

Time: MWF 9:00 - 9:50 AM
Place: Humanities 108
Instructor: Dr. J. W. Cooney
Office and Office Hours: Gottschalk Hall 301 A (588-6817). MWF 8:00-8:50 and 11:00-
11:30 AM. If you cannot make these office hours try to arrange an appointment with Dr. Cooney. If an emergency arises, call the Secretary of the
History Department if you cannot reach me by telephone. Her phone number
is also 588-6817. Leave your name and telephone number. She will get in
touch with me, if at all possible, and I will try to get back to you.

TEXTS: Hubert Herring, A History of Latin America (3rd ed.)
        Irving A. Leonard, Baroque Times in Old Mexico.

The purpose of this course is to acquaint the student with a general view of the
Pre-Columbian Civilizations of Latin America, the European Conquests and subsequent Empires, and the Independence of Latin America. The texts will complement
the lectures, not replace them. Material will be handled in the lectures not
included in the texts, and vice versa.

CLASS INFORMATION

Attendance and Lectures: You are not graded in any fashion for attendance or
lack of same. However, please be aware that much of my tests come from the
lectures and to do well upon them good attendance is necessary. You will be
given a Readings-Topics Sheet which will outline the lectures and Readings in
this class for the semester. At the beginning of each lecture I will place upon
the blackboard various topics, names, etc., which will be dealt with in the
course of that day's lecture. Please take good notes. Those blackboard topics
are designed to aid you in note-taking and also studying for exams. If, in the
course of the lecture, you have a question, immediately raise your hand and I
will break into the lecture to answer your question. If you do miss class, try
to get the notes from a friend, but that friend is advised to get your name and
telephone number. Remember that xerox facilities exist in the library for the
copying of notes if you do not wish to let them out of your hands. Please try
to avoid Incompletes. It is getting harder and harder to get them from A & S.
But if you do receive an Incomplete, it is then your responsibility to get in
touch with the instructor, find out what you have to do to remove it, and then
do it. You have but one semester to remove an Incomplete, then it changes into
an F. I also am forced by College policy to give an F to any student whose
name appears on the Enrollment Sheet but who, for one reason or another, never
attended class. Check your transaction slips that you will receive in the mail
concerning your class enrollment. If you miss the final, and did not inform me
beforehand that you had to miss it because of some emergency, I am also forced
by College policy to give you an F for the class. All withdrawals, normal or
late, are handled by the student. There is no such thing as an administrative
withdrawal. I do not drop you; you must handle the drop procedure and the
paperwork yourself. Failure to withdraw in the correct fashion will result in
an F. Get hold of the Student's Bill of Rights to find out both your responsibilities and rights. Also learn the Grievance Procedure. I do not post or

33

mail grades at the end of the semester. You will be informed of your semester grade by the Registrar in the normal fashion. Neither do I inform you of your grade over the telephone. I do not release grades to anyone but you, unless I receive a dated, signed request from you that I do so. I do not discuss individual grades or exams in the class. If you have questions about these you must see me in my office. Please use the Office Hours if you have difficulties. With all the good will in the world I can do very little for you in the last two weeks of the course (and paradoxically that is generally when I get the most business about difficulties in the course). No extra credit work will be allowed in this class. Everyone has the same responsibilities. I do not engage in panel discussions, Oral Reports, or similar High School nonsense. I am being paid to conduct this class and I am the specialist in this topic. On the other hand, I repeat that if you have questions in the course of the class, be sure to raise your hand immediately and I will try to get to you.

Pop Quizzes: They can be given at the discretion of the Instructor. Generally they are worth ten points each. No makeups on Pop Quizzes, of course.

Map Quiz: At the beginning of the semester each student will be given a list of geographical locations of Latin America and a practice map. Use the maps in your text and atlases, etc. to ascertain these locations. Atlases are found in the Reference Room of the Library. Two weeks into the semester there will be an announced map quiz. You will be given a blank map similar to the practice map and 25 of the geographical locations chosen at random. You will have 15 minutes to complete that map quiz. Makeups are allowed but you must see me within a week of the quiz if you want to take a makeup. This quiz is worth 25 points.

Outside Readings: You will be given a bibliography of books concerned with colonial Latin American History possessed by the U of L library. These books are all in English. By no means, however is this list complete. Students in the course of the semester will read two books of their choice dealing with Colonial Latin American History, and will turn in two book reviews. You will be given a book review sheet guide. The first Book Review is due about seven weeks into the semester; the last one due the last class day of the semester. You are not confined to books on the bibliographical sheet but you must stay within the time period and subject of Colonial Latin America. If you do not complete two (2) Book Reviews you can expect no better than a C in this course regardless of how you do on the other exams. Handwritten reviews are OK, but Blue or Black ink is required. No makeups on Book Reviews. Each is worth 25 points.

Tests: There will be two midterms and a Final. Bluebooks and Blue or Black ink required on all. All will be announced in advance with the topics to be covered on the exam. The mids are 100 points each; the Final 200 points. All tests will be about 50% Essay and 50% Identification. You will be given choices on both Essays and Identifications. Questions will come about 50% from Lectures and 50% from Readings. I give a numerical grade but roughly 87-100 is an A, 77-86 a B, 66-76 a C, 55-65 a D, and below an F. Makeups are allowed but you must see me within one week of the regular exam. No take home exams; no open book tests. No extra credit to make up for a bad test.

Remember to use Office Hours. And in class, in the course of the lectures, if you have questions, raise your hand and I will try to clear up your problem immediately.

If we cannot keep on schedule, the instructor will announce in advance what material the class is responsible for on exams.

TEXTS: Hubert Herring, A History of Latin America (3rd edition)
Irving A. Leonard, Baroque Times in Old Mexico
H = Herring.   L = Leonard.

The texts complement the lectures, they do not replace them. I will be discussing certain things in the lectures not covered in the texts and vice versa. You are responsible for both the readings and the lectures.

1. Introduction, Geography of Latin America, the Pre-Columbian Civilizations (Readings only). H. 3-63.

2. Spain on the Eve of Conquest, The Age of Exploration, Columbus. H. 64-86, 119-128.

3. Other Explorations and the Settlement of the Caribbean. H. 135-136.

4. The Conquest of Mexico. The Conquest of Central America. (Latter topic, readings only) H. 128-135.

5. The Conquest of Peru and Chile; other Conquests. (Readings only) H. 136-149.

6. The African Background and the settlement of Brazil by the Portuguese. H. 87-116, 213-217.

7. Latin America and the Non-Iberian Powers in the 1500's and 1600's (Readings only). Introduction to Land, Labor and Society in the Latin American Empires. H. 150-153, 190-203. L. VII-XI, 21-47.

8. A Racial Society in Spanish America; the same in Brazil. H. 184-189, L. 47-52.

9. The Administration of the Spanish American Empire (Readings only). H. 154-165. L. 1-21.

10. The Church, Society, Education, and Culture in Spanish America. H. 167-183, 204-212. L. 53-171.

11. The Expansion of Colonial Brazil. The Dutch in Brazil (Readings only). The Golden Age of Colonial Brazil. H. 217-233.

12. The Decadence of the Spanish Hapsburgs. Bourbon Reforms in the new Spanish Empire. Pombaline Reforms in Brazil. H. 166, 240-242. L. 172-228.

13. Rumblings of Revolt in the 18th century. H. 237-240, 242-246.

14. Independence Movements in Latin America (Readings only if no time left for lectures). H. 247-286.

Midterms and Finals as announced. Book reviews as announced.
If ever you have any questions concerning this Readings-Topics Sheet, please inquire of the instructor.

H.M. Hamill
Wood Hall 327
486-4466 & 4964

1984

SYNOPSIS:

Office Hours:
MWF 9:00-9:45
11:00-11:45
and by arrangement

   Although this is a survey of Latin American history through to the end of the colonial period, that is to about 1825, it does focus upon a series of related problems. The basic problem is to examine Iberians in America and case studies in the expansion of Europe. The complex civilizations of the Aztecs and the Incas were among the first non-Western cultures to encounter the technology, organization, diseases and life-styles of Europeans. How can we explain the rapid collapse of these Amerindian civilizations and the profound and parallel infusion of Spanish cultural forms into America? Was it entirely that way? What evidence is there of cultural resistance and survival? How does all this help us to understand the intrusion of Western peoples into other non-Western societies? Finally, what is the legacy that the New World societies created over the next three centuries?

   To seek solutions to these and other questions we will study the histories of pre-Conquest Amerindians; the European context of Iberian expansion; the motives and methods of the conquistadores; the impact of disease and other biological factors; psychological confrontations, as between Cortes and Montezuma in 1519-1520; Malinche, the Aztec woman interpreter who filtered that confrontation through her own psyche; post-conquest cultures and immigration; religious syncretism; mestizaje or race mixture; and the development of administrative and socio-economic structures of the colonial world. Brazil appears by way of contrast between Portuguese and Spanish imperial styles. The course ends with those early 19th century rebellions which separated most Latin American territories from their mother countries.

NUTS & BOLTS:

   There will be lectures, discussions both spontaneous and orchestrated, readings, slides, brief papers, maps and examinations.

1. Readings: Assignments are based primarily on paperbacks which you should buy. Reserve readings are also used. A stack list of Recommended Books in the Library will be distributed. A dozen suggested works are for sale in the Co-op.

2. Discussion Papers: There will be three special assignments during the course. These will be short (2 pp.) but carefully prepared critical papers on specific problems (defined in separate handouts). The papers are designed to facilitate controlled classroom discussion. Each paper will be due by a strict deadline before the day of the discussion. This will give me time to evaluate the papers and design a discussion based on your views and insights about the material. Each paper is worth approximately one-sixth of the final grade.

3. Examinations: There will be one hour exam (worth one-sixth) and the final exam (worth one-third of grade). Although objective questions may be used, the emphasis will be on interpretative essays.

4. Maps: Buy two copies of each of the two maps for sale. These will be used with the Lombardi Atlas. You should routinely bring the Atlas to class.

5. Notebooks: I frequently hand out information in class. You will accumulate a lot of maps, lists of terms and places, short readings and announcements. You should use a notebook and/or folder for this course which has ample storage space for looseleaf materials.

I. REQUIRED

Richard Graham, Independence in Latin America (New York: Knopf, 1972).

Delivery
Delayed)   James Lockhart and Stuart B. Schwartz, Early Latin America: A History of
              Colonial Spanish America and Brazil (Cambridge: Cambridge Univ. Press, 1983).

C.L. and J.V. Lombardi, Latin American History: A Teaching Atlas
(Madison: Univ. of Wisconsin Press).

Colin MacLachlan & Jaime Rodriquez, The Forging of the Cosmic Race:
A Reinterpretation of Colonial Mexico (Berkeley: Univ. of Calif. Press, 1980).

Robert C. Padden, The Hummingbird and the Hawk (New York: Harper & Row, 1970).

Two (2) of each map: Mexico & the West Indies (Denoyer Geppert 23167)
                       South America (Denoyer Geppert 25006)

II. Recommended (stocked by Co-op)

Frances F. Berden, The Aztecs of Central Mexico: An Imperial Society
(New York: Holt, Rinehart & Winston, 1982).

Henry F. Dobyns, Their Number Become Thinned: Native American Population
Dynamics in Eastern North America (Knoxville: Univ. of Tennessee Press, 1983).

Nancy M. Farriss, Maya Society Under Colonial Rule (Princeton: Princeton
University Press, 1984).

Charles Gibson, The Aztecs Under Spanish Rule(Stanford: Stanford Univ. Press, 1964

Hugh M. Hamill, Jr., The Hidalgo Revolt: Prelude to Mexican Independence
(Westport: Greenwood Press, 1981). New Intro. & Bibliography. 1st ed. 1966.

James Lockhart & Enrique Otte, eds., Letters and People of the Spanish Indies
(Cambridge: Cambridge University Press, 1976).

Ann M. Pescatello, Power and Pawn: The Female in Iberian Families, Societies
and Cultures (Westport: Greenwood Press, 1976).

David G. Sweet & Gary B. Nash, eds., Struggle and Survival in Colonial America
(Berkeley: Univ. of California Press, 1981).

Tzvetan Todorov, The Conquest of America (New York: Harper & Row, 1984).

Eric Wolf, Sons of the Shaking Earth (Chicago: Univ. of Chicago Press, 1959).

Alfred W. Crosby, Jr., The Columbian Exchange: Biological and Cultural
Consequences of 1492 (Westport: Greenwood Press, 1972).

III. RESERVE: (Indicated by * in the assignments)

E-98-D6-C7   Alfred W. Crosby, The Columbian Exchange: Biological and Cultural
                   Consequences of 1492 (Westport, 1972).

901.981   Gilberto Freyre, The Masters and the Slaves (New York, 1956).
F899
972.03   H.M. Hamill, The Hidalgo Revolt (Gainesville, 1966).
H53-ZH
F-1408-.3   Lewis Hanke, ed., History of Latin American Civilization, Vol. I: The
H322-V,1   Colonial Experience (Boston, 1973). ("Hanke, History" in assignments)

980.0082   Lewis Hanke, ed., Readings in Latin American History, Vol. II. Since 1810.
H625R-V.2   (New York, 1966). ("Hanke, Readings in assignments)

F-1410   Clarence H. Haring, The Spanish Empire in America (New York, 1947).
H25-1963

(folder)   The Harner Thesis: A Collection of readings on Human Sacrifice.

F-1410-H47   Hubert Herring, A History of Latin America (New York, 1968). 3rd ed.
1968
DP-99   Gabriel Jackson, The Making of Medieval Spain (New York, 1972).
J32-1972B
980.082   Benjamin Keen, ed., Readings in Latin American Civilization (Boston, 1967). 2nd e
K25R-1967
378.7281   John Tate Lanning, The Eighteenth-Century Enlightenment in the University
L283E   of San Carlos de Guatemala (Ithaca, 1956).

F-1412-L96   John Lynch, The Spanish-American Revolutions, 1808-1826 (New York, 1973).

(Folder)   Frank J. Moreno, "The Spanish Colonial System: A Functional Approach,"
            Western Political Quarterly, 20 (1967), 308-320. (xerox)

980.01   J.H. Parry, The Spanish Seaborne Empire (London, 1966).
P249S
F-1210-P313 Octavio Paz, The Labyrinth of Solitude: Life and Thought in Mexico.
            (New York, 1961).

(Folder)   John L. Phelan, "Authority and Flexibility in the Spanish Imperial
            Bureaucracy," Administrative Science Quarterly, 5 (June 1960), 47-65.

972-Si58-   Lesley B. Simpson, Many Mexicos (Berkeley, 1971). 4th ed.
1966
HC-125-S76 **Stanley J. Stein and Barbara H. Stein, The Colonial Heritage of Latin
            America (New York, 1970).

F-3429.1A9 **Steve J. Stern, Peru's Indian Peoples and the Challenge of Spanish Conquest:
S75-1982   Huamange to 1640 (Madison, 1982).

(Folder)   Steve J. Stern, "The Rise and Fall of Indian-White Alliances: a Regional
            View of 'Conquest' History," Hispanic American Historical Review 61 (3),
            (August, 1981), 461-491.

F-1210-W6   Eric R. Wolf, Sons of the Shaking Earth (Chicago, 1959).

          ** On Reserve for History 382.

B. An asterisk (*) indicates RESERVE. All works are included in Book Lists.

UNIT I: The INGREDIENTS

pt. 5   What are the questions? Confessions of a GASP (Gringo, Anglo-Saxon, Protestant)

pt. 7   Values: A discussion based on Carlos Fuentes, "Party of One: Latinos
         vs. Gringos" (7 pp.) (Handout) and MacLaughlin & Rodríquez, Forging
         of the Cosmic Race, pp. 1-4. (Hereafter: Cosmic)
           Recommended: *Moyers, "Many Worlds of Carols Fuentes"
                         *Paz, The Labyrinth of Solitude

pt. 10   Unity & Diversity: The Ecological Bases for Society
         Cosmic, pp. 13-66. Lockhart & Schwartz, Early Latin America, pp. 31-57
         (Hereafter: Early). Lombardi, Atlas, study maps pp. 1-7.
         Cosmic, pp. 7-12; Lombardi, Atlas, study maps pp. 1-7; *Simpson, Chs. 1-2
         (21 pp.); *Wolf, Sons ..., pp. 17-20. (handout)

pt. 12-14 1492. Well, why is this date important? The emergence of Amerindian
         Civilizations and Biological Vulnerability.
         Cosmic, pp. 13-66. Lockhart & Schwartz, pp. 31-57 (Hereafter: Early)
         Recommended: *Crosby, Columbian Exchange, Ch. I. Mason, Ancient
         Civilizations of Peru; *Wolf, pp. 48-129.

pt. 17-19 The Incas: Socialist Empire? Military Industrial Complex? Tyranny?
                     None of the Above??
           *Hanke, History, pp. 53-84 Recommended: *Stern, Peru's .., Ch. I.: Metraux,
                                 History of Incas; Wauchope, Pt. III.

T. 17
         OJO! NOTE: Class will meet in the VIDEO THEATER of the LIBRARY (2nd Floor) to
               see the excellent BBC Film "THE INCAS".

t. 21   The Mexica Machine: How do you explain human sacrifiee on a grand scale?
         Padden, Hummingbird and the Hawk, Chs. I-V (99 pp.) Also, be sure to
         read Padden's Preface & Note on Sources & Method, pp. vii-xvi.
         Recommended: Berdan, esp. pp. 99-118; "The Harner Controversy (Folder)
         *Wolf, pp. 130-151; *Hanke, History, pp. 368-377; also books by
         Bernal, Davies, Soustelle, Vaillant; Wauchope, Indian Background, Pts. I,II

ER #1 DUE
CLASS: Monday, Sept. 24 . . . .For Coordinated Discussion on Friday, Sept. 28.

t. 24-26 What made Iberia dynamic and expansionist?
:. 1-3   *Herring, Ch. 3 (28pp.); Early, pp. 3-30; *Parry, Prologue ("The
         Tradition of Conquest"--pp. vary with edition; 11 pp. total);
         *Keen, pp. 40-46.
         Recommended: *Jackson, The Making of Medieval Spain; Elliott,
         Imperial Spain; Payne, A History of Spain and Portugal, Vol. I;
         Vicens Vives, Approaches to the History of Spain (A Catalan's view).

UNIT II: CONQUEST

Oct. 5-8   What was the Context of European Expansion? The Caribbean Phase.
  *Keen, pp. 46-57; *Parry, Ch. 2 (10 pp.); Early. pp. 59-85.
  Recommended: Gibson, Spain in America, pp. 1-23.
  *Hanke, 41-50 (the uncertain impact on Europe), 87-95 (the struggle
  for Justice); Sauer, The Early Spanish Main
  Morison, The European Discovery of America: The Southern Voyages

Oct. 10-12 Were the Conquests Virile or Viral? Epic Histories and Secret Weapons.
  Padden, Chs. VI-XI (122 pp.); *Hanke, History, pp. 131-137 (combat in Peru)
  169-178 (Crosby on Pestilence); *Parry, Ch. IV (15 pp.)
  Recommended: Prescott, Conquest of Mexico and Conquest of Peru
  (the classic epics); Bernal Díaz del Castillo, The Conquest of New
  Spain (Spanish soldier's eye-witness account); Miguel León Portilla,
  The Broken Spears (The Aztecs' view of the disaster); Hemming,
  The Conquest of the Incas (a modern account); *Crosby, Ch. 2.

Oct. 15-17 Why did the Spaniards win against such odds? Did they always win?
  *Simpson, Ch. 3 (11 pp.); Cosmic, pp. 67-76
  Recommended: Gibson, Spain..., 24-47; *Wolf, pp. 152-175;
  Kirkpatrick, The Spanish Conquistadores (for narratives of other
  conquests besides Mexico and Peru).

Oct. 19-22 The Extensions of Conquest
  Early, pp. 86-121; *Stern, "Rise and Fall of Indian-White Alliances" (30 pp.)
  Padden, Ch. II. (15 pp.)
  Recommended: *Hanke, pp. 415-30 (women in Peru), 443-458 (mini-biographies
  of conquistadores; see the larger work: Lockhart, Men of Cajamaraca);
  Spanish Peru, 1532-1560; *Lockhart & Otte, Letters & People, pp. ix-xiii,
  1-61; Céspedes, Latin America: The Early Years.

Oct. 24 (Wednesday):   HOUR EXAMINATION

UNIT III. The Coming of Faction

Oct. 26   From Conquest Culture to Mature Empire: An overview
           Cosmic, pp. 76-91; Early, pp. 122-180.
           Recommended: *Hanke, I, 96-114; *Lockhart & Otte, pp. 63-82, 155-172;
           Gibson, Ch. 3.

Oct. 29, 31   The Conquest of Space: Administration of a vast empire...but HOW?
           Cosmic, pp. 95-143; *Phelan, "Authority and Flexibility...";
           *F.J. Moreno, "Spanish Colonial System..."
           Recommended: *Haring, The Spanish Empire in America, Ch. 408;
           *Lockhart & Otte, pp. 173-210, 247-252; Gibson, Ch. 5.

PAPER #2
DUE IN CLASS   For Discussion on Friday, November 9.
Wed., Nov. 7

Nov. 2   The Conquest of Souls: Syncretism & Churches
           *Hanke, I, 178-186 (Indian contributions to the great monastic
           churches--essay by George Kubler)
           Recommended: *Lockhart & Otte, pp. 211-247, 252-255;
           Gibson, Ch. 4.

Nov. 5, 7   Society & Economy of the Mature Empire
   12,14   Cosmic, pp. 196-248, (society); pp. 144-195 (econ.);
           *Hanke, I, 297-304 (mining bonanza at Potosí); 464-471 (slave revolts)
           Recommended: Early, pp. 253-304 (The Fringe); *Parry, Chs. 11,12,
           6, 13 (colonial trade); *Simpson, chs. 12-16; Elliott, Imperial
           Spain; Leonard, Baroque Times in Old Spain; *Lockhart & Otte, pp. 83-116;
           *Mörner, Race Mixture in History of L.A.; Bowser, African Slaves in
           Colonial Peru; Pescatello, The African in Latin America;
           Rout, The African Experience in Spanish America: Arzans de Orsua &
           Padden, Tales of Potosí; Pescatello, Power and Pawn: Female in Iberian
           ...Societies.

UNIT IV. The Brazilian Contrast

Nov. 16,   Early, 181-252; *Hanke, I, 11-21, 310-319, 431-436, 235-42.
19, 20   Recommended: *Herring, Ch. 12 (20 pp.); *Hanke, I, 215-235, 243-261.
           Hemming, Red Gold: The Conquest of the Brazilian Indians
           *Freyre, The Masters and the Slaves
           Morse, The Bandeirantes
           Schwartz, Sovereignty and Society in Colonial Brazil
           Boxer, The Golden Age of Brazil

UNIT V. Empires in Crisis

Nov. 26, 28   The Bourbon Century: Was it different from the Hapsburg era?
               Early, pp. 305-368
               Graham, Independence, pp. xi-xiii, 3-23
               Cosmic, pp. 251-93
                   Recommended: *Lanning, pp. 342-356 (Enlightenment in Guatemala);
                   *Simpson, Chs. 17-18; *Hanke, I, 356-360, 377-394, 346-354
                   (Science, Sor Juana, & the Inquistion)

Nov. 30   Tensions and Mutinies: Bur Were They Preludes to Independence?
               Graham, pp. 25-70
               *Keen, pp. 172-178 (rebellion of Tupac Amaru II)
               *Hanke, I, 534-544 (Essay by Humphries)
               Recommended: Early, pp. 369-404 (Brazil; *Hanke, I, 471-488,
                   496-518 (criollos, the army, expulsion of the Jesuits)

Dec. 3   The first War for Independence
               Graham, pp. 91-92 (skim pp. 84-89 on Mexico); Early, pp. 405-426
               Cosmic,pp. 294-333
               *Keen, pp. 250-258 OR *Hamill, Hidalgo Revolt, pp. 135-141
               (what it is like to be attacked by 25,000 people with machetes)
               Recommended: *Lynch, Spanish American Revolutions

Dec. 5,7   The Second War for Independence
               Graham, pp. 93-131
               *Hanke, Readings (Not his History), II, 1-10 (Griffin's essay)
               Cosmic, pp. 334-337

PAPER #3
DUE IN CLASS For Discussion on Monday, December 10
FRIDAY, Dec. 7

Dec. 12   The Legacy of Colonialism: How much impact?
               *Hanke, Readings, II, 10-37 (Haigh, Borah, Gibson, Potash)
               *Hanke, History, I, 526-534 (Stein, Powell)
                   Recommended: *Stein & Stein, Colonial Heritage of Latin America
                   *Dealy, the Public Man

HOW TO CHANGE DESULTORY DISCUSSIONS TO STIMULATING SEMINARS
Hugh M. Hamill, Jr.
University of Connecticut

PREMISES: Students learn more from reading when they must write critically
about what they have read. They learn and retain even more if they
talk in a disciplined way about what they have read with others
who have thought about the same problem.

So what else is new?? The problem is how to translate these truisms into a
viable course format.

Most class discussions are like this:

--The teacher and one or two uninhibited students carry on a dialogue;
the other students sit mutely.

--The teacher finally calls on a silent student who "didn't do the reading,
sorry!"

--The teacher lapses into a lecture; the students daydream and doodle.

--When there are only two minutes left, the teacher asks: "Any questions?"
There is only one: "Professor, when are you going to return the exams
we wrote three weeks ago?"

I used to be that teacher. Out of my frustration and despair, however, I
have evolved a solution which engages everyone and leaves both students and
faculty convinced that real learning has occurred. It works in this fashion:

A seminar or section format is employed. Students come to class prepared, and
they all participate in the discussion in a relaxed and confident manner. The
reason they do so is because the class meeting is centered around critical
assessments of the assigned reading required in advance of the session. The
intent of these papers is to ensure that all members of the seminar are prepared to
make the discussions lively and informed as well as to develop individual skills
both written and oral. The papers are expected to be thoughtful and carefully
composed essays. They are not outline notes or uncritical summaries of the
assignment. The creative interjection of other material and individual insights
is encouraged, but these may not be substitutes for reflections on the common
readings. Two pages are required; three are maximum. The papers are due one or
two days before the seminar. In the interval I read, comment on and grade the
papers. I frequently write "R" (for "Raise") in the margins indicating points
students ought to try to interject into the discussion. Having already plotted
a diagram of a controlled discussion based on my own perception of the readings,
I add the names of students beside key ideas in that diagram. I frequently add
new concepts raised by students which had not occurred to me but which enrich
the topic. I return the papers a few minutes before class and give students a
chance to read my comments. Then with the diagram as a guide I conduct a discussion making sure that everyone is included and that all the basic ideas are
covered. Often there is a spirited debate, and the students, secure in having
informed views, frequently pick up the thread of the topic organically. The best
sessions are those in which I have had to use the least guidance. When the discussion spills over into the coffee break, I know it's an especially good day!
One final point: I don't accept late papers; to do so would defeat the purpose
to draw all students into the discussion.

43

LATIN AMERICA FROM INDEPENDENCE TO THE PRESENT

History 216
Professor Beezley   HA 108   737-2483
Office Hours 9:30 to 10:30 daily

The Three Rs of Latin American History

READIN'

Textbooks:
Keen & Wasserman, A Short History of Latin America. 2nd Ed.
Jorge Icaza, Thee Villagers
Oscar Martinez, Fragments of the Mexican Revolution
Robert Armstrong & Janet Shenk, El Salvador: The Face of
    Revolution
William Beezley, "Rocks and Rawhide in Rural Society," University
    of Texas, El Paso, Series on Latin American Topics, No. 1.
Carter Wilson, Crazy February

Assignments and examinations:
There will be three examination on June 3, June 14, and June 26.
These are one-hour examinations with three essay question and 6
items for identification.   Students must write on two essays (40
points each) and identify 5 items (4 points each) on each exam.

First exam: Keen and Wasserman, Short History, chapters 8-11
             Icaza, The Villagers
             Beezley, essay on rural mexico

2nd exam: Keen and Wasserman, Short History, chapters 12-15
             Martinez, Fragments of the Mexican Revolution

Final exam: Keen and Wasserman, Short History, chapters 16-20
             Armstrong & Shenk, El Salvador
             Wilson, Crazy February

'RITIN'

Students must write a 7-10 page essay. This paper should be
prepared in the following manner: students should first read
pages 456-483 in Keen and Wasserman, then go to the Documents
Room in D. H. Hill Library to examine the Foreign Relations of
the United States for the year they are assigned (years will be
assigned the first week of class). For some years there are
several volumes, so students should examine the one on Latin
America, often called Western Hemisphere of the American Republics. After reading through the volume, the student should
briefly relate U. S. relations with Latin America in that year to
the general trends described by Keen and Wasserman, and then
select relations with one Latin American country to discuss in
detail. Papers may be handwritten on every other line of the
page, with 250 words equaling one typewritten page. Papers are
due on June 25.

'RITHMETIC

Each exam and the essay have a value of 100 points. Grades will
be determined by the traditional percentages: 90% and above
equals an A (that is, 360 or more points); 80-89% (or 320 to 359
points) equals a B; 70-79% (280 to 319 points) a C; 60-69% (240
to 279 points) equals a D; fewer than 240 points, no credit.

No one can make a perfect grade (40 points) on an essay question
or on the semester paper; there are about 8 or 9 points that are
impossible for the student to make. Therefore, the following
bonus exists: On May 24, there will be a map quiz on the 20
Latin countries and capitals listed below. A perfect paper will
receive 10 points; 2 or fewer mistakes, 9 points; 4 or fewer
mistakes, 8 points; and 6 or fewer mistakes, 7 points; more than
6 mistakes, no points.

1.	Mexico	Mexico City	2.	Guatemala	Guatemala City
3.	Honduras	Tegucigalpa	4.	Nicaragua	Managua
5.	El Salvador	San Salvador	6.	Costa Rica	San Jose
7.	Panama	Panama City	8.	Cuba	Havana
9.	Colombia	Bogota	10.	Ecuador	Quito
11.	Peru	Lima	12.	Chile	Santiago
13.	Argentina	Buenos Aires	14.	Urugay	Montevideo
15.	Paraguay	Asuncion	16.	Bolivia	Sucre/La Paz
17.	Brazil	Brasilia	18.	Venezuela	Caracas
19.	Haiti	Port-au-Prince			
20.	Dominican Republic	Santo Domingo			

Big Casino: Each student has the option to join the Big Casino
or may be placed in it. A student will have the chance to gamble on
the Big Casino on the fifth absence (there are no excused absences), failing to submit a paper on or before the beginning of
class on the day it is due (no late papers are accepted) or
failing to take an examination (no make-ups are permitted). The
Big Casino relieves the student of all class requirements; the
student gambles his or her course grade on a three-hour comprehensive final test. The Big Casino exam consists of two hour-
long essay question and 100 short answer (that is, fill-in-the-
blank) questions based on the reading and lectures.

SPANISH AMERICA TO WORLD WAR I

I.   The dawn of European colonialism and Spanish
     beginnings in the New World

     A. Europe in the late fifteenth century
         1. World view
         2. Beginnings of scientific advancement and
             informed curiosity
         3. Early European exploration and balance
             between idealism and commercial gain
         4. A wider world: Christopher Columbus and
             Vasco de Gama

     B. Spanish New World beginnings
         1. The Arawaks of the West Indies in 1492
         2. The governorship of Columbus and the seeds of
             colonial exploitation
         3. The moral dilemma of the Indian population
             and the refinement of exploitation
         4. Demographic catastrophe and the lure of the
             mainland

II. The Expansion and consolidation of the Spanish
     Conquest

     A. Mainland Spanish America: resources and
         prospects

     B. The conquest of empire
         1. Composition and motives of the conquerors
         2. The goals of the Crown
         3. The Indian in defeat: legal rights and
             responsibilities

     C. The organization of empire: tribute and labor
         1. The early encomienda
         2. Attempts at reform: the New Laws, 1541-1542
         3. The mature encomienda, 1549-1560
         4. The decline of the encomienda, 1560-1750

     D. The organization of empire: machinery of
         governance
         1. Institutions and goals
         2. The clash between imperial policy and
             colonial reality
         3. State and colonial citizen
             a. Corporation versus individualism
             b. Ethnicity, slavery, and the state
         4. The legacy of colonial governance

46

III. The Church and the Indian

    A. The rationale and structure of the missionary program

    B. Missionary techniques

    C. Missionary accomplishments and failures
       1. Hispanization
       2. Christianization

    D. The Indian and the mature colonial Church
       1. Forms and quality of religious life
       2. The survival of pre-Hispanic beliefs and practices

IV. Spanish America to 1700: external influences and internal developments

    A. Hapsburg foreign policy and the American empire
       1. The reign of Charles V: overview
       2. The reign of Philip II: overview

    B. The English and Dutch in the colonial world to 1609

    C. Internal imperial change and decay
       1. Inflation and the Spanish imperial economy
       2. The institution of forced labor and decline of the Indian population
       3. The rise of the hacienda and debt peonage
       4. Bureaucratic corruption and the legalization of land titles

    D. The end of Iberian colonial monopoly, 1609-1648: overview

    E. Spanish America under the late Hapsburgs
       1. The silver mining boom pauses
       2. Commerical stagnation
       3. Consolidation of the hacienda and debt peonage systems

V. The advent of the Bourbons

    A. A new dynasty with new ideas
       1. Enlightenment thought and imperial policy
       2. Governmental complacency and fear, 1713-1763

    B. Spanish America under the early Bourbons: a formed society and economy

VI. The Bourbon Reforms: origins and implementation

    A. English competition and the challenge of the industrial revolution

    B. Attempts at internal reform in the colonies
       1. The motivations and goals of Charles III and José de Gálvez, 1763-1788: overview
       2. Changes in the bureaucratic apparatus
       3. Church-State relations
         a. The new anticlericalism
         b. The expulsion of the Jesuits
       4. Revival of silver mining
       5. Free trade (comercio libre)
       6. The tobacco monopoly
       7. The establishment of militia

VII. The Bourbon Reforms: effects

    A. Colonial administration

    B. The Church

    C. The mining boom

    D. Free trade and colonial economic development

    E. New and continuing problems
       1. Rising costs of colonial government
       2. Socio-economic unrest
       3. Colonial militarization

VIII. Spanish American Independence

    A. Napoleon and the dynastic crisis of 1808

    B. Traditional explanations for the Independence movement
       1. Colonial resentment over government autocracy and higher taxes
       2. Ideas of the late Enlightenment
       3. Peninsular preferment to government office

    C. Results of recent research
       1. Creole-Spanish rivalry and resentment
       2. Growing Spanish American feelings of separateness and nationalism
       3. Desamortization of Church mortgages
       4. Spanish American perception of fundamental imperial weakness

    D. Independence as a counter-revolution

IX. Spanish America from Independence to World War I

   A. The immediate problems of new nationhood
      1. Economic disruption
      2. Political unpreparedness of upper classes
      3. Boundary disputes and economic rivalries, internal and external
      4. Spanish America and the industrial world

   B. Tentative solutions, 1825-1870
      1. The quest for political legitimacy: constitutions versus the man on horseback
      2. Centralism versus federalism, corporatism versus individualism
      3. Church-State relations
      4. The struggle for economic development

   C. An uneasy peace, 1870-1911
      1. Economic liberalism and political conservatism
      2. Economic progress and the price of dependency
      3. Neglect of socio-economic reform

MODERN AND CONTEMPORARY LATIN AMERICA

LAH 3300
Spring, 1985

Professor Bushnell
360 Grinter

I. Course Objectives

This course does not pretend to be an extensive survey of the history of all Latin American nations in the national period. It seeks instead to acquaint the student in broad outline with the development of the major nations and with fundamental problems whose impact has cut across the histories of substantially all Latin American peoples.

II. Topic Outline

1. The early national period, approximately 1825-1850.
   a. General themes: political adjustments and maladjustments; "liberals" and "conservatives"; the church question; changes and continuity in social and economic structures.
   b. Contrasting national patterns: Mexico, "institutionalized disorder"; New Granada/-Colombia, economic stagnation and political consolidation; Argentina, sectional rivalries and dictatorship; Chile and Brazil, oligarchic adaptability.
2. The heyday of 19th century liberalism, approximately 1850-1880.
   a. The Mexican and Colombian "Reforma."
   b. Argentina after Rosas.
   c. Flowering and decline of the Brazilian monarchy.
   d. Slave emancipation and political autonomy in Cuba.
3. "Order and Progress," approximately 1880-1910.
   a. General tendencies: reaction against doctrinaire liberalism; cult of material growth; foreign investment and trade.
   b. Specific cases: Mexico's Díaz as a new style of dictator; the "Regeneration" in Colombia; gold age of the Argentine oligarchy; the "Old Republic" in Brazil.
4. The tradition order challenged, approximately 1910-1940.
   a. General tendencies: emergence of middle class, peasant and labor unrest; urbanization, industrialization, nationalism.
   b. The Mexican Revolution.
   c. Social and political democratization in the Southern Cone.
5. Contemporary Latin America.
   a. Authoritarian populism in Brazil and Argentina: Vargas and Perón.
   b. Interaction between Latin America and the United States.

        c.   The Cuban Revolution and its antecedents.
        d.   The abortive "Chilean way" of Salvador Allende.
        e.   Other contemporary models: developmen-
        talist dictatorship (Brazil); military re-
        formism (Peru); muddling through (Colombia);
        the democratic potential of petroleum (Vene-
        zuela).

III. Assigned Readings

      Each student is expect to read:
        a.   T. E. Skidmore and P. H. Smith, Modern
        Latin America
        b.   Two sets of xeroxed course readings
        ("The New Commercial Order" and "Andean South
        America") available at University Copycenter.
        c.   F. W. Knight, Slave Society in Cuba
        During the Nineteenth Century.
        d.   J. Reed, Insurgent Mexico.
        e.   S. Schlesinger, Bitter Fruit.
      Except for xeroxed course readings, each of the above can be
found at the reserve desk in Library East. They can also be
purchased in paperback.

IV. Course Requirements

      Map test, on 16 January, for which students should become
familiar with the natural features and territorial division of
Latin America by independent map study, consulting separate list
for details.

      First examination, on 15 February, covering Smith and Skid-
more pp. 3-45, 70-74, 145-149, 225-230, both sets of xeroxed
readings, Knight, and lectures on topics 1 and 2.

      Second examination, on 1 April, covering Skidmore and
Smith, pp. 46-69, 74-80, 149-165, 230-255, 321-330, Reed, and
lectures on topics 3 thru 4b.

      Final Examination, on 30 April, covering the rest of Skid-
more and Smith, Schlesinger, lectures from topic 4c to the end of
course, and at a broad-brush-level only, everything else covered
in the course.

      Written report, due 15 March unless special arrangements are
made beforehand, on a book of travel and description of a Latin
American country in the 19th century, to be chosen from a list of
alternative selections that will be distributed in class; report
should assess the book's value for the study of social history
and should be in length about 3 typed double-spaced pages or
handwritten equivalent.

51

The Latin American nations from independence to the present. Major
themes in the first half of the course are the post-independence
depression which threw power into the hands of crude but colorful
caudillos; the export booms of the late 19th century and the social
and economic diversification which occurred after the 1890s. We will
chart the growth of peasant unrest and labor movements, which con-
tributed to major revolutions in Mexico, Bolivia, and Cuba, and which
destabilized other governments. The last half of the course stresses
20th century politics in the major countries, dealing with populism,
authoritarianism, militarism, and on occasion, foreign intervention.
We will discuss famous Latin American leaders but balance the picture
with such actors as the middle class, organized labor, the peasantry,
big business, foreign interests, and the army. Several slide shows
and a movie.

The grade will be based on a midterm (30%), an essay about a Latin
American novel (30%), and the final (40%).

The essay paper should be from 6 to 10 pages in length and contain
footnote references. More detailed instructions will be handed out
the first week of class.

Required reading: Keen and Wasserman, A Short History of Latin America

Recommended reading: Conniff (ed.), Latin American Populism in Com-
                      parative Perspective

Extra readings (on reserve in Zimmerman, together with the texts):

          Pike, Latin American History
          Tulchin, Problems in Latin American History
          Fagg, Latin America
          Skidmore & Smith, Modern Latin America

You should consult some of the extra readings for use in your essay
and in reviewing for exams. Be sure to take good notes on outside
readings. Mention of outside sources will almost certainly improve
your grade. I also welcome discussion of extra readings in class.

Day   Topic   Readings

Jan. 14 Introduction

     16 Geography, Climate, & the Place of Man

53

Mar.	20	Review session (look over your notes and readings!)	
	22	MIDTERM EXAM	
	25	Backwaters: The Caribbean	
	27	Central America	431-69
	29	Panama: The Canal & Beyond	496-524
Apr.	1	The Modern Era; Mexico since Cárdenas	285-93; Conniff Chapter 5
	3	Perón's Argentina	307-19; Conniff Chapter 3
	5	Chile's Drift Toward Socialism	328-34
	8	Brazil's Search for Greatness	354-75
	10	Middle-Ranked Countries: Venezuela and Oil	Conniff, Ch. 7
	12	Colombia: Elites and Masses	F 638-51
Essay due	15	Ecuador: Land of Contrasts	379-81
	17	Paraguay: Hellhole or Paradise?	F 706-12
	19	The Revolutionary Societies: Bolivia 1952	376-9
	22	Cuba 1959	404-29
	24	Cuba since the Revolution	
	26	Peru 1968	385-403, Conniff chapter 6
	29	Chile 1970	334-41
May	1	Nicaragua 1979	
	3	Review session	470-95
	10	FINAL EXAM (8-10 am in classroom)	

Essay Assignment

Part of the total grade will be based on your essay about a historical novel by a Latin American. You are asked to relate the work to its historical setting, discussing whether or not it faithfully depicts the country and period in which it is cast. Depending on the novel, you should include such subjects as politics, revolution, social life, race relations, religiosity, economic development or backwardness, philosophy, great men, etc. In other words, use the novel to illuminate the important things in life, as perceived by historians. Do not write a simple literary essay. If literature synthesizes life, then it should lend itself to historical discussion.

You will need to consult books and magazines, or perhaps the New York Times, available in the Zimmerman Library. Please see me or the reference librarian for help in finding appropriate materials. References to these books, articles, and newspapers should be made in the following manner:

1st citation [1]James Cargrove, Zapata as seen in the Mexican Novel (New York, 1968), p. 53.

2nd citation [2]Cargrove, Zapata, pp. 103-105.

1st citation [3]Samual Mead, "Will the Real Gaucho Please Stand," Journal of Spanish-American Literature, Vol. 4, No. 2 (June 1974), p. 83.

2nd citation [4]Mead, "The Real Gaucho," p. 78.

[5]Philander C. Knox, "General García Takes Charge," New York Times, 4 June 1962, p. 15.

These footnotes should appear at the end of your essay, followed by a bibliography of all works cited or consulted. You may wish to purchase a manual for writing term papers at the bookstore, or you can see me about style. If at all possible, please typewrite your paper.

The dates in parentheses following the titles refer to the original year of publication, not when the book appeared in English. Some books not available at Zimmerman may be borrowed through inter-library loan. See me if you are not able to locate the book you want.

55

Aguiar, Adonias (Adonias Filho), _Memories of Lazarus_ (1952). These are the recollections of Alexandre--his life, his death-in-life, and his ultimate death as they are played out against the resisting hills and black sky of the badlands of the state of Bahia, Brazil.

Aguilera Malta, Demetrio, _Manuela la Caballeresa del Sol_ (1964). This Ecuadorian writer has composed a story about the campaigns of Independence using Bolívar's famous mistress, Manuela Saenz, as the lead character.

Alegria, Ciro, _Broad and Alien is the World_ (1941). Novel of social protest, encompassing indigenous and mestizo life in different parts of Peru.

Altamirano, Ignacio, _El Zarco the Bandit_ (1901). Emphasizes the equality of the Mexican Mestizo and Indian as compared to those of Anglo-Saxon stock. Set in the 1860s, an unwitting prelude to the great revolution.

Amado, Jorge, _Gabriela, Clove and Connamon_ (1958). A rich and sensual novel about life and development in a small cocoa town in Northeastern Brazil in the 1920s.

Arenal, Humberto, _The Sun Beats Down_ (1958). One of the more intriguing novels available, this depicts the 1950s kidnapping of a Mexican boxer in order to embarrass the corrupt Batista regime in Cuba. Revolutionary tone.

Assis, Machado de, _Don Casmurro_ (1900). One of Machado's masterpieces, which examines the life of its middle class protagonist and society in late 19th century Rio de Janeiro. Latin America's greatest introspective writer, Machado was a poor mulato who through hard work achieved the highest recognition of his country.

Asturias, Miguel Angel, _The Cyclone_ (1950). Examines social and economic exploitation by a U.S. banana company in Guatemala, the author's native land. Asturias is one of the Hemisphere's best contemporary writers and is read throughout the world. Title also appeared as _Strong Wind_.

_____. _The Green Pope_ (1954). Sequel to the above work.

_____. _El Señor Presidente_ (1946). Prize-winning novel which depicts corruption and repression during one of Guatemala's worst dictatorships.

Azevedo, Aluízio de. _A Brazilian Tenement_ (1890). Portrays in sordid detail and dramatic narrative, life in a crowded Rio de Janeiro slum. Regional and ethnic-racial conflict is highlighted.

Azuela, Mariano, _The Flies and the Bosses_ (1917-1918). Two short
novels set in the Mexican Revolution, famous for their depiction
of the roles played by different social classes.

_____. _The Trials of a Respectable Family and the Underdogs_
(1916-1919). More novelistic accounts by this famous Mexican
writer.

Blest Gana, Alberto, _Martín Rivas_ (1862). A classic portrayal of
Chilean society in the middle of the 19th century.

Calderón de la Barca, Frances, _Life in Mexico_ (1843). Fascinating,
witty, perceptive account of travels in Mexico during a stay
from 1839-1842. A journal by the Scottish wife of the Spanish
minister in Mexico.

Callado, Antonio, _Don Juan's Bar_ (1971). Depicts the trials of a
group of Brazilian revolutionaries who wish to join Che Guevara's
ill-fated guerrillas in Bolivia. Fine insights on Middle-class
revolutionaries.

Desnoes, Edmundo, _Inconsolable Memories_ (1965). First person narrative on Cuban life before and after the revolution, featuring
anguished accounts of the personal trials of middle class
individuals.

Donoso, José, _This Sunday_ (1965). Novel about the social relationships between the poor and the rich in Chile, a country long
plagued by status and income disparities.

_____, _The Obscene Bird of Night_ (1971). Social relationships in
Chile.

Fuentes, Carlos, _The Good Conscience_ (1959). Set in Guanajuato in
prerevolutionary Mexico, this excellent novel examines the life
of a well-to-do family and its reaction to the injustices which
would cause the revolution.

_____, _The Death of Artemio Cruz_ (1962). Fine novel about a man
who became rich by selling out the Revolution's ideals and
becoming a capitalist lackey.

_____, _Where the Air is Clear_ (1965). Important novel documenting
Mexico's social stratification. Dense and powerful.

Galindo, Sergio, _The Precipice_ (1960). This is the intimate picture of
the complexity of life for a modern Mexican family, and a novel
of anticipation which shows events of earlier times playing a
role in the present. Memories of revolutionary upheaval and
socialist indoctrination cast long shadows.

Gallegos, Rómulo, Döna Bárbara (1929). Classic about Venezuelan
llaneros (cowboys) and the struggle between civilization and
barbarism. Gallegos later became president of his country.

García Márquez, Gabriel, One Hundred Years of Solitude (1967). The
all-time classic of Latin American literature, this fascinating
novel traces several generations of the Buendia family of the
mythical town of Macondo, Colombia, ending with its feud with a
banana company. Faulknerian but often hilarious style.

Guido, Beatriz, End of a Day (1964). The classic novel of an upper
class family in Argentina, and its gradual decay under the
Perón government.

Guiraldes, Ricardo, Don Segundo Sombra (1926). The acocunt of a
youth in the Argentine pampas (perhaps Huck Finn?) and his relationship with an idealized gaucho.

Guzmán, Martín Luis, Memoirs of Pancho Villa (1938-1940). Semi-
fictionalized account of Villa's exploits during the Mexican
Revolution, written by a man who rode with the Army of the
North.

Hernández, José, El Gaucho Martín Fierro (187?). A famous Argentine
narrative poem, neither nostalgic nor idealistic, about life on
the pampas in the mid-nineteenth century. This work almost
single-handedly created the myth of the gaucho and his exploits.

Icaza, Jorge, Huasipungo (1934). Famous Ecuadorian novel of Indianist
genre depicting the exploitation and subsequent rebellion of
Andean peasants.

Lafourcade, Enrique, King Ahab's Feast (1959). Political novel about
the dictator Trujillo in the Dominican Republic.

Mármol, José, Amalia (1851-1855). Romantic political novel of Buenos
Aires during the regime of Juan Manuel Rosas.

Martínez Bilbao, Oscar, Hacienda (195?). Social protest novel of the
Chilean peasantry, showing the rotos taking over lands which
they till.

Mondragón Aguirre, Magdalena, Someday the Dream (1944). Another
social protest novel, this time set in a Mexico City slum.
Implicit critism of the failure of the revolution.

Octavio Paz, Labyrinth of Solitude (1959). Internationally recog-
nized writer and philosopher contemplates the meaning of being
a Mexican, in part by looking at those who have left and gone to
the United States, Classic.

Prado, Renato, The Breach (1969). One of the few revolutionary novels written by a Bolivian.

Prig, Manuel, Betrayed by Rita Hayworth (1968). Brilliant vision of the provincial middle class society of Argentina, in which the language of the characters is a real achievement.

Rego, José Lins do, Plantation Boy (1932-1934). Outstanding account of the declining style of life in the Northeastern sugar zone of Brazil.

Riera, Pepita, Prodigy (1955). Biographical novel about Beatriz del Real during the political upheavals of Cuba in the 1930s.

Rivera, José Eustasio, The Vortex (1924). A couple flees into the Amazon jungle, only to be transformed and eventually destroyed there. Not a tarzan novel, it portrays the gruesome struggle of man against an incredibly hostile jungle.

Roa Bastos, Augusto, Son of Man (1961). Outstanding novel of popular resistance to dictatorship in Paraguay from Independence to the Chaco War of the 1930s.

Rosa, João Guimaraes, The Devil to Pay in the Backlands (1956). Widely acclaimed story about life in rural Brazil. Exceptional for the author's use of language, probably the most innovative and influential in modern times.

Sarmiento, Domingo F., Life in the Argentine Republic (1845). At once a protest of caudillos and an unsympathetic protrayal of the rude life and politics of provincial Argentina. Sarmiento is one of the most famous Argentines, and he later became president. A must for understanding the gaucho.

Setubal, Paulo de Oliveira, Domitila, the Romance of an Emperor's Mistress (1924). Historical novel based on the life and loves of Pedro I of Brazil. Set in the 1820s.

Uslar, Pietris Arturo, The Red Lances (1931). Depicts adventure and tragedy during the independence struggles of Venezuela, the author's native land.

Vargas, Llosa, Mario, The Green House (1965). Brilliant novel set in the Peruvian jungle and in the northern coastal city of Piura.

_____. Conversations in the Cathedral (1969). Perhaps Vargas's greatest novel, it is an indictment of the corrupt Odría regime in Peru between 1948-1956. The novel covers through 1962, however.

Verissimo, Enrico, His Excellency the Ambassador (1965). The ambassador is from the imaginary Caribbean republic Sacramento, ruled by a Castro-like revolutionary.

Villaverde, Cirilo, The Quatroon, or Cecilia Valdez (1882). Social and racial conflict in 19th century Cuba are found in this novel, which centers on a mulatta woman.

Womack, John, Zapata (1969). Detailed and accurate account of Zapata's rise and fall, by a Harvard Historian. Shows how history can be more fascinating than fiction.

Yanez, Agustín, The Edge of the Storm (1947). His best novel, it deals with the period just before the Mexican Revolution, capturing the cohesiveness and repressive nature of Mexico's political, economic, and religious elites of the time.

_____. The Lean Lands (1962). The theme of this powerful novel is the impact of modern technology on a few isolated, tradition-bound Mexican hamlets in the aftermath of the Revolution.

Amado, Jorge, The Violent Land (1942).

Epic story about the famous "colonels," or powerful planters, in Brazil's northeastern cacao region. Set in the 1930s, the plot depicts bloody rivalries for control of fertile lands. Romance, superb character development by Brazil's best-known novelist.

Amado, Jorge, Dona Flor and Her Two Husbands (196?).

Charming and humorous novel set in Salvador, Bahia, in the 1930s and early 1940s. Explores relationship between several archtypical Brazilian personalities: the mulatta (dona Flor), the malandro or rogue, and the upright citizen (her second husband). An enjoyable film version has appeared in the U.S.

Amado, Jorge, Tereza Batista Home from the wars (196?).

The story of Tereza, who at the age of 12 was sold by her aunt into slavery. She later emerges as leader of poor women and prostitutes and evantually as queen of samba in Bahia's famous carnival.

Assis, Machado, Epitaph of a Small Winner (1880)

First novel by Brazil's greatest writer, this is the story of the life, love, and philosophy of a modern 19th century man as narrated by his ghost. Difficult but rewarding book.

Benítez, Fernando, The Poisoned Water (Mexico, 1961).

Novel based on actual occurrences in a small Indian town in Michoacán. The villagers are brutally exploited by the local boss, whose authority is then challenged by a group of younger villagers. In the ensuing power struggle, the well water is rumored to be poisoned, and the villagers rise up in revolt. Comparable to Ycaza's Huasipungo.

Fernández de Lizardi, José Joaquín, The Itching Parrot (Mexico, 1842).

This is the account of the fictional life of El Periquillo, a free-thinking, rabble-rousing bard extraordinaire. Lizardi, also known as the Mexican Thinker, was a famous propagandist of the cause of independence. One of Latin America's best picaresque novels.

García Márquez, Gabriel, Autumn of the Patriarch (Columbia, 1975).

Portrait in composite of a Latin American despot, his rise from colonial times, and eventual demise. One of the best in recent years, though its structure is somewhat difficult. Colorful.

López y Fuentes, They That Reap (El Indio) (Mexico, 1937)

Novel about rural life in Mexico after the Revolution. Author uses an interesting literary technique to assure the reader's intimacy with characters. Illustrations by Diego Rivera enhance the text.

Souza, Marcio, Emperor of the Amazon (197?).

A raucous tale about an adventurer who parlays a chance meeting into leadership of a revolution in the rubber-rich province of Acre, disputed by Brazil and Bolivia at the turn of this century. Bawdy, hilarious story by the major fiction writer of the Amazon.

HISTORY 332
LATIN AMERICA, NATIONAL PERIOD

Spring, 1982   Dr. J. W. Cooney

GENERAL CLASS INFORMATION

History 332.   M W F, 10:00 - 10:50 a.m., Bingham 117.

Instructor: Dr. J. W. Cooney

Office: Gottschalk 301A.   588-6817.

Office Hours: M W F 9:00-9:50 & 11:00-11:30 a.m.
              T & R 10:00-10:30 a.m.

If you cannot make these office hours, arrange an appointment with the instructor. See him before or after class, or call him at the above number. If an emergency arises and you cannot get in touch with me, call the Secretary of the History Depart ment at the same number, leave your name and phone number, and I will try to get back to you. Please use the office hours if you have problems; that is why they are there.

Texts

    John E. Fagg, Latin America: A General History.
    Benjamin Keen, Latin American Civilization II. The National Era.

The purpose of this class is to acquaint with the history of Latin America since independence. The texts will supplement the lectures, not replace them. Good attendance is recommended as a good proportion of the tests will come from the lectures.

RESPONSIBILITIES OF THE STUDENT

Pop Quizzes. These can and may be given at the discretion of the instructor. Best to have good attendance. No make-ups on Pop Quizzes.

Map Quiz. There will be given to each student in the first week of class a practice map and a list of Latin American geographical locations. Please use the text and maps in the library, etc., to make sure that you know where these locations are. In the second or third week of class there will be a quiz of a selected number of locations from the original list. A blank map, same as the practice map, will be provided. Pencil allowed. No make-ups allowed. The quiz will be announced in advance. 25 points.

Tests. There will be three announced tests (two mid-terms and a Final). They will all be about 50% Essay and the rest Identifications or Multiple Choice. There will be choices on both Essays and Identifications. Make-ups allowed. Grading is on a numerical system. About 87% to 100% is an A, 75% to 86% a B, 65% to 74% a C, 53% to 64% a D, below 52% an F. The same percentage will hold true for your overall numerical total which will determine your semester grade. Each mid-term will count 100 points, the Final 200 points. The Final will be given at the regularly schedule Final time.

Outside Readings. You will be given a bibliography of books dealing with the National History of Latin America in English in the U of L library. By no means is it complete. Students will read two books of their choice and give to the instructor a written review on each of them (see book review sheet). The first review will be due about seven weeks into the semester, the second one due the last class day of the semester. You are not confined to books in the bibliography but you must stay within the time period and the topic. Typewritten reports are appreciated but handwritten ones are O.K. Each book review is worth 25 points. If they are late, you may be penalized for the lateness.

Other Comments. On the mids and the Final, bluebooks and blue or black ink are required. Please use them. If you ever are puzzled in the lectures, please raise your hand and I will try to answer you immediately. Please try to avoid Incompletes as A & S is getting very sticky about giving them. But if you do get an Incomplete then it is your responsibility to remove it within a semester before it turns into an F. If you are on the enrollment sheets for this class, you will receive a grade. This is where the correct withdrawal procedure is necessary since I have to give an F to anyone who is on the final grade sheet even though that student has not attended since the beginning of the semester. You must take the Final and if you do not and do not inform the instructor before the Final that for some reason or another you cannot make it, then I will have to assign you an F for the Final. Please get hold of the Students Bill of Rights and understand your rights and responsibilities. Understand the Grievance procedure. Understand the definitions of cheating and plagiarism and avoid them. If you do not hand in the Book Reviews, then you cannot expect any better than a C for the course. I do not post grades, mail them out, nor do I release them until after the Registrar has given them to you. I cannot discuss personal grades in the class, you must see me in the office.

REMEMBER THAT IN CASE OF ANY PROBLEMS, PLEASE SEE THE INSTRUCTOR AND USE THE OFFICE HOURS. ATTEND THE CLASS, TAKE GOOD NOTES, ASK QUESTIONS IF PUZZLED, STUDY HARD, AND YOU SHOULD DO WELL.

GOOD LUCK

J. W. Cooney

History 332—Latin America, Modern Era--Spring 1982 -- Dr. Cooney

READING TOPICS SHEET.

The following is a general outline of the topics which we will be covering
in this course, and the readings to accompany the topics. You will notice
that the main concentration of the lectures will be upon Mexico, Chile,
Argentina and Brazil. You will also see that the readings from Fagg
deal with those countries, and often other countries' portions of Fagg
are not assigned. THIS IN NO WAY PREVENTS YOU FROM READING ON OTHER
COUNTRIES THAN THOSE ASSIGNED IN FAGG. However, there will be no test
questions on those countries for which you are not held responsible for
reading about in Fagg.

F = Fagg   K = Keen.

I.   The Aftermath of Independence. F 303-372. K 3-10, 40-46.

II. Organizing the Nations. F 400-402.
     A. The Age of Dictators
         1. Mexico and Santa Anna. F 391-395, 402-411. K 69-85.
         2. Rosas and the Río de la Plata. F 375-380, 433-442.
             K 10-18, 91-97, 116-119.
     B. The Conservative Solution of Chile. F 492-498. K 106-111.
     C. A Monarchical Solution in Brazil. F 492-498, 471-472.11.

III. Liberalism Triumphant
     A. Mexico & Juárez. F 506-519. K 21-32, 35-38.
     B. Argentina, Mitre and Sarmieto. F 445-454. K 32-35.
     C. The Liberal Emperor. F 472-482. K 128-160.

IV. The New Oligarchy.
     A. The Porfiriato of Mexico. F 519-530. K 49-53.
     B. Beef & Wheat Barons of Argentina. F 454-464. K 60-68,
         97-105, 283-291.
     C. Chile Triumphant. F 498-504. K 53-60.

V.   Protest, Change, and the Middle Class.
     A. Mexico and the Revolution. F 533-544. K 167-192.
     B. The Rise of the Argentine Middle Class. F 464-470- K 291-294.
     C. Imperial End and the Coffee Republic. F 482-492. K 46-49,
         122-127, 160-165, 308-326.
     D. Chile loses her way. F 504-505, 690-692.

VI. Depression & 20th Century Pressures.
     A. Cárdenas + the Revolution. F 544-556. K 192-218.

     B. Argentina and the Military. F 712-724.
     C. Brazil and Vargas F 747-764- K 326-330.

VII. Industrialization and Maturity?
     A. Mexico and "Progress" F 556-562.
     B. Brazil, leap to power status. F 764-772. K 330-344
     C. Perón and Argentine Disaster. F 724-747. K 294-307.

VIII. The Popular Challenge.
     A. Brazil and the Military. F 772-774. K 344-352.
     B. Argentina--What went wrong?
     C. Mexico and the Party Dictatorship. K 218-227
     D. Cuba and Venezuela--2 different approaches. F 562-584, 624-638.
         K 353-416.

CONTEMPORARY LATIN AMERICA
(History 161)
University of California, Riverside

Spring, 1985
TuTh 11–12:30
Lib.S. 3117

Cárlos E. Cortés
Office: Lib.S. 4153
Office Hours: TuTh 1–3

Scope: History 161 is the second part of a two-quarter survey of Latin American history from pre-Columbian times to the present. The course will focus on five major themes: (1) the formation of nations and national boundaries; (2) the quest for internal stability; (3) the development of societal institutions; (4) the persistence of societal inequities; and (5) Latin America's struggle for survival in the international jungle.

Prerequisites: None. History 160 **is not** a prerequisite for History 161.

Course Requirements: There will be one ten-page term paper or comparative book analysis, an optional midterm examination on Thursday, May 2, and a required final examination covering the entire course on Thursday, June 13, 3–6 p.m. For students who take the optional midterm examination: the term paper/book analysis and midterm examination will each be worth thirty percent of the course grade and the final examination will be worth forty percent. For students who do not take the midterm examination: the term paper/book analysis and final examination will each be worth fifty percent of the course grade.

Term paper/book analysis deadlines will be May 23 (+), May 30 (o), and June 6 (–). Students who turn in their papers by Friday, April 19, will receive their grades by Thursday, April 25, to help in their decisions whether or not to take the optional midterm examination. Papers submitted after Thursday, June 6, will receive reduced grades. Papers submitted after Friday, June 14, will receive severely reduced grades. All term paper topics and books for review must be approved in advance by the instructor.

Required Reading:

Aguilar, Alonso. Pan-Americanism from Monroe to the Present: A View from the Other Side.

Azuela, Mariano. The Underdogs.

Jesús, Carolina María de. Child of the Dark.

Sarmiento, Domingo Faustino. Life in the Argentine Republic in the Days of the Tyrants.

Skidmore, Thomas and Smith, Peter. Modern Latin America.

(Note: The course schedule specifies reading assignments for all books except Modern Latin America. Specific reading assignments in Modern Latin America have been made only for pages 3–69 and 321–385. However, students are expected to read the appropriate chronological sections of the other chapters in accordance with the daily lecture topics and to complete the book by the end of the course.)

Course Schedule

April 2   (Tues.) -- The Struggle for Independence (1808-1825)

April 4   (Thur.) -- Birth Pangs of the New Nations (1825-1845)
                     Modern Latin America, pp. 3-43
                     Pan-Americanism, pp. 9-30

April 9   (Tues.) -- Film: SIMÓN BOLÍVAR: THE GREAT LIBERATOR
                     Life in the Argentine Republic, pp. 1-275

April 11 (Thur.) -- Crisis, Conflict, and Territorial Decapitation (1845-1870) (I)
                     Modern Latin America, pp. 43-45, 321-326
                     Pan-Americanism, pp. 31-35

April 16 (Tues.) -- Crisis, Conflict, and Territorial Decapitation (II)
                     Life in the Argentine Republic, pp. 276-396

April 18 (Thur.) -- Consolidation of Control (1870-1898)
                     Modern Latin America, pp. 46-51, 326-330
                     Pan-Americanism, pp. 36-42

April 23 (Tues.) -- Pan-Americanism and the Quest for New Directions (1898-1910)
                     Modern Latin America, pp. 51-56
                     Pan-Americanism, pp. 43-54

April 25 (Thur.) -- The Mexican Revolution and World War I (1910-1920)
                     Modern Latin America, pp. 330-331
                     Pan-Americanism, pp. 54-60

April 30 (Tues.) -- Film: THE RAGGED REVOLUTION
                     The Underdogs , pp. 14-149

May 2   (Thur.) -- Optional Midterm Examination

May 7   (Tues.) -- The Aftermath of World War I (1920-1929)
                     Pan-Americanism, pp. 61-66

May 9   (Thur.) -- The Great Depression (1929-1939)
                     Modern Latin America, pp.56-60, 331-334
                     Pan-Americanism, pp. 67-75

May 14   (Tues.) -- World War II (1939-1945)
                     Pan-Americanism, 75-79

May 16   (Thur.) -- Films: PERÓN AND EVITA
                            EVITA PERÓN

May 21   (Tues.) -- Latin America in the Early Cold War Era (1945-1959)
                     Child of the Dark, pp. 7-159
                     Pan-Americanism, 80-109

May 23   (Thur.) -- Castro, Kennedy, and Coups (1959-1975)
                 Modern Latin America, 60-69, 334-351
                 Pan-Americanism, pp. 109-154

May 28   (Tues.) -- Film: CUBA: ART AND REVOLUTION

May 30   (Thur.) -- Latin America: The Last Decade (1975-1985)
                 Modern Latin America, pp. 352-358
                 Pan-Americanism, pp. 155-167

June 4   (Tues.) -- Film: AMERICAS IN TRANSITION

June 6   (Thur.) -- Latin America Today
                 Modern Latin America, pp. 359-385

Final Examination: Thursday, June 13, 3-6 p.m.

Prof. Donna Guy

Office: Social Science 129

Office Hours: Tues. 1-2:30 p.m. and by appointment

HISTORY 467-CONTEMPORARY LATIN AMERICA

SPRING 1985, TUES., THURS., 11:00-12:15

ECONOMICS 302

The focus of this course is Latin America since 1930, although it is not intended to cover every country or event. Rather, we will take a look at some of the problems and groups common to all Latin America, as well as some special cases. Central America will receive indepth coverage, as well as the relationship between the United States and Latin America since 1930. The goal of this course is to introduce students to common themes in Latin American history and current events; to teach students how to identify bias in current and historic reporting; and to provide an opportunity to research and write about a controversial current topic in a way that demonstrates the skill of identifying the nature of debate and different opinions about Latin America.

The required books are available at the bookstore in paperback:

> Foundation for the Independent Study of Social Ideas, Democracy and Dictatorship in Latin America
>
> Newfarmer, From Gunboats to Diplomacy. New U.S. Policies for Latin America
>
> Kissinger, Report of the Presidential Committee on Central America
>
> Sweet Ramparts: Women in Revolutionary Nicaragua
>
> Current History: Latin America 1985

In addition, other articles have been assigned. They are listed in individual assignments by an asterisk (*) and will be placed on reserve in the main library reserve reading room.

All students will have two long term assignments. First they will monitor a magazine, newspaper or journal either individually or in groups until May 2. The purpose of this assignment is to see if all of Latin America is given equal, fair coverage in the media. An oral report is due from each student.

The second assignment will be a written term paper on a topic approved by the instructor and related to contemporary Latin America. It will be due on March 26. The paper, a maximum of 10 pages for undergraduates and 20 pages for graduate students, should examing the topic by consulting both scholarly and popular writings on the subject including those that reveal a bias, or point of view. These biases should be identified and discussed in the paper. All work must represent the individual effort of each student, and all material quoted directly or paraphrased must be identified through the use of footnotes. All sources used in the paper should be listed alpha- betically in a bibliography. Otherwise the paper will be considered to have been plagiarized. Footnotes should be standardized according to a handbook of style such as Kate Turabian, 4th ed., A Manual for Writers. Please note that you must decide which topic you wish to write on and inform me by February 12th.

In order to follow the lectures and special assignments, it is vital that you become familiar with the geography of Latin America. You should have a map and be able to identify and spell correctly countries and capitals. You will also be expected to have completed all reading assignments before the corresponding lecture.   A part of each class will be devoted to a discussion of readings.

ASSIGNMENTS

Jan. 17   Introduction

Jan. 22-24   Early history of U.S.-Latin American Relations
                   Go to the library and select any standard textbook on
                   U.S.-Latin American relations to 1945; Newfarmer, Ch. 2

Jan. 29-31   The world depression and the rise of economic nationalism;
                   Urbanization and population pressures since the 1930s
                   Nicolas Sánchez Albornoz, The Population of Latin
                       America, pp. 182-261.*
                   Barbara Erenreich, "Life on the Global Assembly Line,"*

Feb. 5-7   Land and Peasants
                   Gabriel Zaid, "The Promise of Progress," in Democracy
                       and Dictatorship in Latin America
                   Stavenhagen, ed., Agrarian Problems and Peasant Movements
                       in Latin America, Chapters 3 & 4, pp. 101-158.*

Feb. 12-14   The Catholic Church: Classic Stand and the Third World Movement
                   Sweet Ramparts, part 5.
                   Peggy Lernoux, Cry of the People, pp. 28-55*
                   Wolf and Hansen, The Human Condition in Latin America, pp. 101-
                       110.*

Feb. 19-21   The U.S. and Latin America in an era of social change: Bolivia,
                   Guatemala and Cuba, 1952-1970

                   Cole Blasier, The Hovering Giant, pp. 46-54; 128-176.*
                   Paul Sigmund, "Cuba, Nationalization with Soviet Support,"
                       in Multinationals in Latin America*
                   Franqui Chapter, Democracy and Dictatorship in Latin America

Feb. 26   Mid Term

March 5   Film: The CIA Story-The Secret Army

March 7   Cuba in the 1980s
                   Sergio Roca, "Cuba Confronts the 1980s,"*
                   Chapter 9, Newfarmer book

March 12   No Classes

March 14   U.S. Latin American Relations since the Cuban Revolution:
                   A Case Study of Chile, 1973

                   Sigmund, "Three Views of Allende's Chile"*
                   Newfarmer, Ch. 1
                   Richard Fagen, "The U.S. and Chile, Roots and Branches"*

March 26-28	Modern Militarism in Latin America: Guerrilla Warfare in the 1960**s**, 1970s and 1980s
	Werlich, "Peru: The Shadow of the Shining Path"*
	Corradi Article, <u>Democracy and Dictatorship</u>
	Each student should select one example from below and find some information to share with the class:
	Che Guevara, Montoneros, Hugo Blanco, Carlos Marighella, Tupamaros, Squadrons of Death, Argentine Anti-Communist Alliance, Any right or left-wing terrorist group in LA
April 2-4	Background to the Central American Crisis; The Overthrow of Somoza
	Chapters 4-8, Newfarmer
	Chapters 1-3, Kissinger
April 9-11	Video on Guatemala and Central America; Women and Revolution in Central America-Discussion of <u>Sweet Ramparts</u>
	Finish Sweet Ramparts
April 16-18	The Caribbean Basin Initiative; The Refugee Problem in the U.S.
	Finish Kissinger
	Chapters 14-15, Newfarmer
April 23-25	Discussion of current conditions in Central America; The Latin American Dept problem
	Chapter 13, Newfarmer
	Jacqueline Sharkey, "The Tug of War", <u>Common Cause</u>*
April 30-May 2	Grenada: the "popular" little war; U.S. Press Coverage-Class Report
	Reading to be announced
	Regd <u>Democracy and Dictatorship</u>
May 7	The future of democracy in Latin America
	Finish <u>Democracy and Dictatorship</u>
May 13	Final Exam, 10:30-12:30
GRADING POLICY:	Mid-Term 25% Term Paper and Newspaper Assignment 25% Final Exam 50

71

HST 262 (section 2360)
Latin American History
MWF 1:00-2:07
209 ODH
Winter 1985

Prof. M. Karasch
374 ODH
370-3530 or 370-3510
Office hrs: MWF 9:15-10:30 am
                       2:15- 4:00 pm

Latin American History: The National Period

Readings:

Thomas E. Skidmore and Peter H. Smith, **Modern Latin America**
Ernest Rossi and Jack Plano, **The Latin American Political Dictionary**
Jorge Amado, **Tent of Miracles**
Mariano Azuela, **The Underdogs**
Handouts as noted below

Requirements:

Three tests 60%
Class participation (two grades) 20%
Two book reviews 20%

Options

An additional book review, 4-5 pages typewritten (follow required guidelines)
An oral presentation to the class (15-20 min.)

Reading Assignments:

Jan. 4: Introductory session

Jan. 7-11: Geographical review (no map test _if_ class passes the review)
                  Spain in the New World
                  Portugal in Brazil

   Reading: S & S, pp. 3-29
                  R & P, pp. 1-53

Jan. 14-18: Legacies of the wars for independence

   Reading: S & S, pp. 29-45

Jan. 21-25: National consolidation

   Reading: R & P, pp. 55-80, 141-163
                  Handout

Jan. 28-30, Feb. 1: Economic and social transformations

   Reading: S & S, pp. 46-69

Feb. 4: **First Test** (identifications, short answers, 1 out of 3 essays)

Feb. 6-8: The Porfiriato in Mexico, 1876-1911

   Reading: Handout
                  Begin **The Underdogs**

Feb. 11-15: The Mexican Revolution--and After
"The Ragged Revolution" (movie, Feb. 15)

Reading: S & S, pp. 225-255

Feb. 18-22: Argentina: The Failure of Democracy
Due Feb. 22: Review essay of The Underdogs

Reading: S & S, pp. 70-112

Feb. 25-Mar. 1: Spring Recess

Mar. 4-8: "Peron and Evita" (movie, Mar. 4)
The Chilean Way

Reading: S & S, pp. 113-144
R & P, pp. 99-126

Mar. 11: Second Test (ids, short answers, 1 out of 3 essays)

Mar. 13-15: Imperial and Republican Brazil
The Estado Novo

Reading: S & S, pp. 145-172
Begin Tent of Miracles

Mar. 18-22: Kubitschek and the construction of Brasília
The military dictatorship of Brazil, 1964--

Reading: R & P, pp. 127-140
S & S, pp. 172-186

Mar. 25-29: The Cuban Revolution
The "Bay of Pigs" (movie, Mar. 27)

Reading: S & S, pp. 256-285
R & P, pp. 81-98

Apr. 1-5: Introduction to Central America
"Roses in December" (movie, Apr. 3)
El Salvador

Reading: S & S, pp. 286-303, 310-320

Apr. 8-12: Nicaragua: the Somoza dynasty
The Nicaraguan Revolution
The US and Latin America
Due: April 12: Review essay on Tent of Miracles

Reading: S & S, pp. 303-310, 321-358

Apr. 15: What Future for Latin America?

Reading: S & S, pp. 359-385

Apr. 16: Final Test, 3:30-6:30 pm (ids, short answers, 1 out of 3 essays)

II. TOPICAL COURSES IN LATIN AMERICAN HISTORY AND CULTURE

History 100 (section 2280)   Prof. M. Karasch
Winter 1985   Office: 374 ODH
MWF 8:00-9:07 am   Phone: 370-3530 or
207 ODH
Office Hrs. MWF 9:15-10:30 am
            2:15- 4:00 pm

                  LOST EMPIRES: AN INTRODUCTION TO THE
                  INDIAN CIVILIZATION OF LATIN AMERICA
Readings:

      N. Davies, The Ancient Kindoms of Mexico
      C. Gallenkamp, Maya, 2nd rev. edition
      A. Metraux, The History of the Incas
      M. León-Portilla, Broken Spears
      Handouts as noted below

Requirements:

      Three exams (objective and essay...........75%
      Class participation......................25%

Options:

      Bookreview(20 pts)--seeDavies, pp. 2557-264for
        suggested readings
      Oral presentation to the class, 15-20 minutes (20 pts.)
      ReproductionofPre-Colombianart--weaving,painting,
        ceramics, etc. (5-20 pts.)
      All options are due April 12.

Schedule of Classes:

      Jan. 4:   Introductory session

      Jan. 7-11:   Ancient America: The setting (maps)
                   Concepts
                   "Excavation at La Venta" (movie on the Olmec,
                   Jan. 11)

      Readings: Davies, pp. 11-62
                   Gallenkamp, pp. 14-86

      Jan. 14-18: Teotihuacan: "The Rome of Mesoamerica" (slides)
                   Introduction to the Maya
                   Maya Religion

      Readings: Davies, pp. 63-113
                   Gallenkamp, pp. 116-131

      Jan. 21-25: Intellectual, Scientific, and Artistic

                              75

Achievements of the Maya
"Sentinels of Silence" (movie, Jan. 23)

Readings: Gallenkamp, pp. 87-115, 147-154; photos, pp. 86-87

Jan. 28-30, Maya Merchants and Lords
Feb. 1:   The Classic Maya Collapse--why?

Readings: Gallenkamp, pp. 132-146, 155-164

Feb. 4:   First Test (objective, map test, and one essay)

Feb. 6-8:   Tropical Forest Farmers of the Amazon

Readings: Handouts

Feb. 11-15: Peruvian environments
            Desert Kingdoms of Peru: Moche, Chimu, Nazca,
            and Paracas
            Civilizations of theAndes:Chavinand
            Tiahuanaco

Readings: Metraux, pp. 3-37, 199-200
            Handout

Feb. 18-22: The people of El Dorado (slides)
            The origins of the Incas
            Sacred Cuzco

Readings: Metraux, pp. 39-90

Feb. 25-   Spring Break
  Mar. 1:

Mar. 4-8:   "Ancient Peruvians" (movie, Mar. 4)
            Inca religion: Inti and the huacas
            Art, Architecture, and Engineering (slides)

Readings: Metraux, pp. 121-149

Mar. 11-15: The Inca empire

Readings: Metraux, pp. 91-120

Mar. 18:   Second Test (objective and one essay)

Mar. 20-22: Imperial Tula and the Toltecs
            The Aztecs: Origins and Wanderings

Readings: Davies, pp. 114-191

Mar. 25-29: Two cities: Tlatelolco and Tenochtitlan
            Religion
            Art (slides)

Readings: Davies, pp. 219-246

Apr. 1-5:   Aztec society and economy
             The Aztec state and empire

Readings: Davies, pp. 192-218

Apr. 8-12:   The Conquest of the Aztecs
             Discussion: Broken Spears
             "Ten Who Dared"--the conquest of the Incas
             (videotape, Apr. 12)
             Options are due on April 12.

Readings: Davies, pp. 247-253
             León-Portilla, Broken Spears, entire
             Metraux, pp. 151-196

Apr. 15:   The Conquest of the Mayas

Readings: Gallenkamp, pp. 165-214

Apr. 19   Final Test, 8:00-11:00 am (objective and one
             essay)

FIDEL CASTRO

Scope: History 30, Themes and Personalities in Historical Perspective, is a
lower-division course designed for non-majors who have had little or no background
in History. Each section, deals historically with a particular personality
who has made a significant imprint on their times and whose life offers an appropriate means of better understanding the age. One of the most important reasons
for studying history is to come to some realistic understanding of human nature
out of the abstract and apply it to real life situations. This is the objective
of History 30.

Fidel Castro is undoubtedly the best-known Latin American political person-
ality since El Libertador Simón Bolívar, the nineteenth-century hero of Latin
American independence. A man of enormous charisma and talent who spearheaded the
most complete social revolution to occur in Latin American during the 20th Century,
Castro is a fascinating personality whose life history can teach us much about
Cuban and contemporary Latin American History. To treat Castro as merely a calculating strategist is to miss the essential dimensions of his historic role in
Latin American history. This course history and the complex politics of the
island that helped catapult him to political prominence. His career as a revolutionary and statesman will be covered against the backdrop of the Cuban Revolution
of 1959. Post-revolutionary developments, particularly Castro's emergence as a
leader of the Third World bloc and Cuba's international actions under his governance,
will also be studied. Slides and films depicting aspects of Cuban history since
1959 will be shown regularly.

Readings. There is one text for the course: Hugh Thomas, The Cuban Revolution
(1977), a long essay on the meaning of the Revolution and Fidelismo.

Course Requirements: This course is designed as a lecture and discussion course.
The instructor will give general lectures on a variety of topics but the controversial nature of Fidel Castro and his revolution demands that time be given
over to class discussion of this fascinating personality. Students are expected
to attend class with the assignments read and to participate in class discussion
of the assigned readings. Besides the midterm each student will be required to
hand in a term project of 15 pages on a topic chosen in consultation with the
instructor. The papers are to be typed and double-spaced and will be due on the
last day of class.

The course grade will be based on attendance and class participation (20%),
a midterm examination (30%), and a final paper (50%).

Week I (April 1-5)	Introduction Cuba: Island in the Stream	Thomas, XXI-XXV, 311-355
Week II (April 8-12)	Sugar, Tobacco and Underdevelopment Film: The Other Francisco The Spanish-Cuban War	Thomas, 356-409
Week III (April 15-19)	Film: Fidel The Young Fidel	Thomas, 413-521 Thomas, 3-37
Week IV	The Revolution: From Moncada to the Sierra Maestra The Revolution Triumphant	Thomas 38-107 Thomas, 108-237
Week V (April 29-May 3)	Cuba and the New Order, 1959-69 The Bay of Pigs (1961) The Cuban Missile Crisis (1962)	Thomas, 238-308 Thomas, 522-641
Week IV (May 6-10)	"Che" Guevara Films: Che: End of the Revolution? Fidel castro Speaks	
Week VII (May 13-17)	Midterm Examination Postrevolutionary Cuba Since 1970	Thomas, 645-697
Week VIII (May 20-24)	Film: Memories of Underdevelpment Cuba in the International Jungle	Thomas, 698-708
Week IX (May 27-31) ı	Film: Cuba: Art and Revolution Hemispheric Fidelismo: The Caribbean the U.S. and the USSR Film: The Castro Connection	
Week X (June 3-7)	The Cuban Revolution: Retrospect and Prospect Discussion of Term Projects	Thomas, 709-720

History 167
Spring, 1985
Office Hours: Wed. 1-3
   & by appointment

Leon Campbell
LibS. 4138
ext. 5401/5420

PERSONALITY AND POWER IN LATIN AMERICA

Scope of the Course: Political power in Latin America, from pre-Columbian to modern times, has been held by notable and often charismatic
personalities. These caudillos, be they dictators or revolutionaries,
have wielded power in a highly individual fashion, often in open violation
of constitutional norms. This course will deal with the phenomenon of
caudillismo, or the "man on horseback" syndrome to determine if it is
particular to the political culture of Latin America or part of a more
universal phenomenon. Selected political personalities from Cortes to
Castro will be examined in light of psychohistorical, sociological, and
national forces.

Prerequisites: No background in Latin America history is required or
even expected.

Required Readings: E. Bradford Burns, Latin America: A Concise Interpretive History (Third edition, 1982), Hugh M. Hammill, Jr., Dictatorship in
Spanish America (1965) (UCR Library Reserve), and Gregorio Selzer, Sandino
(1982).

Requirements: The first part of the course will be devoted to an
understanding of the nature of Latin America, the relationship between
personality and political power, and the phenomenon of caudillismo.
Students will take a midterm examination on Thursday, May 16, which will
cover the lectures, readings, and films dealing with these phenomena.
The midterm will constitute 40 percent of the course grade. In addition,
students will write a biographical report dealing with a particular Latin
American caudillo, caudilla, or dictator, which will be due on Friday,
June 7. The paper which is to be clearly and cleanly
typed, double-spaced, and with appropriate references, is to be at least
10 pages in length and should incorporate the ideas on personality and
power developed during the first part of the ocurse. The subject of the
paper must be cleared with the instructor beforehand. The paper is worth
60 per cent of the final grade. There is no final examination.

Week	Lecture Topic/Readingss/Films
I	1. Introduction
(April 1-5)	2. Latin America: An Overview
	Burns, Latin America, 1-63.
II	3. The Caudillo Phenomenon
(April 8-12)	Hamill, Dictatorship in Spanish America, 1-24
	R.A. Humphreys, "The Caudillo Tradition," in
	Humphreys, ed., Tradition and Revolt in Latin
	America (Both on reserve)
	4. Film: Aguirre, Wrath of God

Week		Lecture Topic/Readings/Films

III
(April 15-19)

5. Caudillismo and Post-Independence
   Burns, Latin America, 64-119
   Hamill, Dictatorship, 25-68 (Reserve)
   Eric Wolf, "Caudillo Politics: A Structural
   Analysis," Comparative Studies in Society and
   History 9: 2 (1967), 168-179 (Reserve)

   Film:

6. Regional Caudillos: Quiroga and Rosas in Argentina
   Hamill, Dictatorship, 71-103 (Reserve)
   Articles by Safford, Graham, and Love in
   R. Graham and P. Smith, New Approaches to Latin
   American History, 71-155 (Reserve)

IV
(April 22-26)

7. Brazil and Caudillismo
   Burns, Latin America, 64-119 (passim)
   Amaury de Souza, "The Cangação and the Politics
   of Violence in Northeastern Brazil," in Ronald
   Chilcote, ed., Protest and Resistance in Angola
   and Brazil (Reserve)

8. Film: Cangaceiro

V
(April 29-May 3)

9. Theories of Personality and Power

10. Theories of Personality and Power

VI
(May 6-10)

11. The Mexican Revolution and its Caudillos
    Burns, Latin America, 120-171

12. Caribbean Caudillismo
    Hamill, Dictatorship, 125-136, 211-219 (Reserve)

VII
(May 13-17)

13. The Sandino Affair
    Selzer, Sandino (complete)

14. Midterm Examination

VIII
(May 20-24)

15. Twentieth-Century Dictatorship in Latin America
    Hamill, Dictatorship, 137-175 (Reserve)
    Burns, Latin America, 172-189

16. Film: Evita: Queen of Hearts

IX
(May 27-31)

17. The Perons: Caudillos or Dictators?
    Hamill, Dictatorship, 188-210 (Reserve)
    Burns, Latin America, 190-210

X
(June 3-7)

18. Fidel Castro: Caribbean Caudillo
    Burns, Latin America, 210-249

19. Film: Fidel

20. Caudillismo and Dictatorship: Retrospect and Prospect
    Burns, Latin America, 249-268
    Hamill, Dictatorship, 203-234 (Reserve)

Friday, June 7   FINAL PAPERS DUE

ZAPATA AND VILLA
(History 30)
University of California, Riverside

Winter, 1981   Carlos E. Cortés
TuTh 2-3:30   Office: Lib.S. 4153
Hum 1127   Office Hours: Tu 1-2
                                                                Th 1-2, 3:30-4:30

Scope: History 30 (Zapata and Villa) will focus on three major themes.
First, what aspects of Mexican history help account for the appearance of
Emiliano Zapata and Francisco Villa as critical figures on the Mexican
historical scene? Second, what roles did Zapata and Villa play in the Mexican
Revolution and how did they influence the course of Mexican history? Third,
how have the lives of Zapata and Villa been interpreted by their contemporaries,
retrospectively by historians, and in popular culture?

Course Requirements: There will be one ten-page term paper, an optional
midterm examination on Tuesday, February 17, and a required final examination
covering the entire course on Friday, March 27. For students who take the
optional midterm—the term paper and midterm will each be worth thirty percent
of the course grade and the final examination will be worth forty percent.
For students who do not take the midterm examination—the term paper and final
examination will each be worth fifty percent of the course grade.

Term paper deadlines will be March 5, March 12, and March 19. Students
who turn in their papers by Thursday, February 5, will receive their grades by
Thursday, February 12, to help in their decision whether or not to take the
optional midterm examination. Papers submitted after Thursday, March 19,
will receive reduced grades. Papers submitted after Friday, March 27, will
receive severely reduced grades. All term paper topics must be approved in
advance by the instructor.

Required Reading

Bazant, Jan. A CONCISE HISTORY OF MEXICO FROM HIDALGO TO CARDENAS, 1805-1940.

Reed, John. INSURGENT MEXICO.

Womack, John. ZAPATA AND THE MEXICAN REVOLUTION.

Course Schedule

I. Mexican Historical Background

January 13 (Tues.) — Introduction

January 15 (Thur.) — Colonial Mexico
                       CONCISE HISTORY, pp. 1-29

January 20 (Tues.) — Independent Mexico: Iturbide to Juárez
                       CONCISE HISTORY, pp. 30-94

January 22 (Thur.) -- Era of Porfirio Díaz
                     CONCISE HISTORY, pp. 95-124

January 27 (Tues.) -- The Mexican Revolution
                     CONCISE HISTORY, pp. 125-155

January 29 (Thur.) -- Mexico since the Revolution
                     CONCISE HISTORY, pp. 156-189
                     Film: MEXICO: THE FROZEN REVOLUTION

II. Zapata and Villa as Historical Figures

February 3 (Tues.) -- Francisco Villa: A Journalistic Portrait (I)
                     INSURGENT MEXICO, pp. 1-134

February 5 (Thur.) -- Francisco Villa: A Journalistic Portrait (II)
                     INSURGENT MEXICO, pp. 137-252

February 10 (Tues.) -- Emiliano Zapata: A Historical Portrait (I)
                     ZAPATA, pp. 3-190

February 12 (Thur.) -- Emiliano Zapata: A Historical Portrait (II)
                     ZAPATA, pp. 191-387

February 17 (Tues.) -- Optional Midterm Examination (covering lectures and
                     reading assignments through February 12)

III. Zapata and Villa as Figures in U.S. Popular Culture

February 19 (Thur.) -- Mexico in U.S. Films

February 24 (Tues.) -- Film: JUAREZ

February 26 (Thur.) -- Discussion of JUAREZ

March 3   (Tues.) -- Film: VIVA VILLA!

March 5   (Thur.) -- Discussion of VIVA VILLA!

March 10   (Tues.) -- Film: VIVA ZAPATA!

March 12   (Thur.) -- Discussion of VIVA ZAPATA!

IV. Conclusion

March 17   (Tues.) -- Zapata and Villa in Retrospect

March 19   (Thur.) -- The Future of Zapata and Villa

Friday, March 27, 11:30 a.m.-2:30 p.m. -- Final Examination

POPULIST DICTATORS IN LATIN AMERICA

Course Description
This course is designed to acquaint students with the broad currents of social, economic, and political changes in 20th-century Latin America, exmained through the rise and fall of rightwing and leftwing populism as well as the lives and regimes of principal populist dictators. Although the course will concentrate on the three best known cases of Juan Domingo & Evita Perón of Argentina, Getúlio Vargas of Brazil, and Lázaro Cárdenas of Mexico, it will also study lesser known cases as well recent changes in Latin America's populist movements.

Required Book
Michael L. Conniff, ed. Latin American Populism in Comparative Perspective.

Course Requirements
(1) One Mid-Term: Date to be announced
(2) Final Exam: On the regularly assigned date: June 4, 1984
(3) Gradaute Credit: A short paper or a review essay on a theme; undergraduates wishing to do extra credit work can do the same.

A. Juan Domingo Perón and Populism in Argentina, 1943-1976

1. Defining Populism in History: Corporatism to Populism to Corporatism?
2. Pre-Peronist Liberal Populism in Argentina, 1890-1930
3. Peronismo, National Populsim, and "Third War" Options
4. The Military Response to Personismo in the 1960s and 1970s
5. The Faklands War, Alfonsin, and the future of Peronismo

Readings
Conniff, Chaps. 1-3
R.J. Alexander, Juan Domingo Peron: A History. (Sterne Reserve)
R. Gillespie. Soldiers of Peron: Argentina's Montoneros. (Sterne Reserve)

A Select Bibliography
R. J. Alexander. The Peron Era.
C. Dobson, et al. The Falklands Conflict.
M. Goldwert. Democracy, Militarism, and Nationalism in Argentina, 1930-1966.
N. Fraser & M. Navarro. Eva Peron.
R. Fox. Eyewitness Falklands.
J. Lynch. Juan Manuel de Rosas 1829-1852: Argentine Dictator.
M. Main. Evita: The Woman with the Whip.
J. Page. Peron: A Biography.
H.F. Peterson. Argentina and the United States 1810-1960.
R. A. Potash. Army and Politics in Argentina, 1945-1962: Peron to Frondizi.
D. Rock. Politics of Argentina 1890-1930: The Rise and Fall of Radicals.
D. Rock, ed. Twentieth-Century Argentina.
H. A. Spalding, Jr. Organized Labor in Latin America (on Argentina).
The Sunday Times. The Falklands War. The Full Story.
J. W. Taylor. Eva Peron: The Myths of a Woman.
A. P. Whitaker. The United States and Argentina.

B. Getúlio Vargas, Creole Corporatism, and Its Legacy since 1930

1. The Politics of Oligarchy and Populist Movements, ca. 1890-1930
2. Vargas, the Estado Novo, and Creole Corporatism
3. Developmentalism, JK, and ESG Ideology: Reaction to National Populism?
4. Brazilian Populism since 1964

Readings
Conniff, Chap. 4
E.S. Pang, Bahia in the First Brazilian Republic. (Sterne Reserve)
R. Levine. The Vargas Regime. (Sterne Reserve)
J.W.F. Dulles. Vargas of Brazil. (Sterne Reserve)

A Select Bibliography
M.L. Conniff. Urban Politics in Brazil: The Rise of Populism 1925-1945.
K. P. Erickson. The Brazilian Corporative State & Working Class Politics.
J.W.F. Dulles. Anarchists and Communists in Brazil 1900-1935.
J.W.F. Dulles. Brazilian Communism 1935-1945.
P. Flynn. Brazil.
S.A. Hewlett. Brazil and Mexico: Patterns in Late Development.
P. McDonough. Power and Ideology in Brazil.
N. Macдlay. The Prestes Column.
T. E. Skidmore. Politics in Brazil 1930-1964.
A. Stepan. The Military in Politics.
J. Wirth. The Politics of Development in Brazil 1930-1954.

C. Lázaro Cárdenas and the Mexican Revolution, 1936-1984

1. The Populist Aspects of the Mexican Revolution
2. Revolutionary Elite and Populist Ideology
3. Lázaro Cárdenas and Economic Nationalism
4. PRI and Populist Heirs: Is the Mexican Revolution Dead?

Readings
Conniff, Chap. 5
Victor Alba, The Mexicans (Chaps. 9-10) (Sterne Reserve)
Nora Hamilton, The Limits of State Autonomy (Chaps. 1-5) (Sterne Reserve)

A Select Bibliography
J.I. Domínguez, ed. Mexico's Political Economy: Challenges at Home and Abroad.
A.L. Michaels. "The Crisis of Cardenismo." Journal of Latin American Studies
(May 1970), 51-79.
J.L. Reyna & R.S. Weinert, eds. Authoritarianism in Mexico.
N. Weyl & S. Weyl. The Reconquest of Mexico: The Years of Lazaro Cardenas.
J.W. Wilkie & A.L. Michaels, eds. Revolution in Mexico: Years of Upheaval 1910-
1940.
J. W. Wilkie. The Mexican Revolution.

D. Other Latin American Populist Movements

1. Indian Populism: APRA, Haya de la Torre, and Peru's Oligarchy

2. The Peruvian Military Corporatism and APRA
3. Acción Democrática and Rómulo Betancourt in Venezuela
4. Populism in Non-Latin Societies

Readings
　　Conniff, Chaps. 6-10
　　A. Stepan. The State and Society: Peru in Comparative Perspectives.(Sterne
　　　　Reserve)
　　A. Alexander. The Acción Democrática in Venezuela. (Sterne Reserve)

A Select Bibliography
　　G. Hilliker. The Politics of Reform in Peru.
　　D. Collier. Squatters and Oligarchs.
　　H. Blanco. Land or Death: The Peasant Struggle in Peru.
　　D. Chaplin, ed. Peruvian Nationalism: A Corporatist Revolution.
　　A. Lowenthal, ed. The Peruvian Experiment.
　　C. Mc Clintock & A. Lowenthal, eds. The Peruvian Experiment Reconsidered.
　　D. Becker. The New Bourgeoisie and the Limits of Depndency.
　　G. Germani. Authoritarianism, Fascism, and National Populism.

History 442
Ullman #230

Spring Q. 1981
Prof. Pang

The Military in Latin America

Required Texts

David Collier, ed. The New Authoritarianism in Latin America.
Donald C. Hodges. Argentina, 1943-1976: The National Revolution and Resistance.
Ronald M. Schneider. The Political System of Brazil: Emergence of "Modernizing" Authoritarian Regime, 1964-70.
Alfred Stepan. The State and Society: Peru in Comparative Perspective.

Course Requirements

A. Mid-term: May 4, 1981 --details to be announced
B. Final: June 1, 1981: 6-9 pm, Ullman 230
C. Graduate Credit: A short paper or book review

Lecture and Discussion Schedule

A. Introduction

3/26   1. Defining the Course

B. Case Study 1: Argentina since 1930

3/30   2. Argentine Oligarchy, Populism, and GOU (ca. 1880-1945)
4/2   3. Peronimso I and Military Antipopulism (1946-55)
4/6   4. Chaotic Civilian Rule and Return of Generals (1955-66)
4/9   5. Peronismo, Urban Guerrillas, and the military (1966-73)
4/13   6. Failure of Peronismo and Military Hardliners (1973-81)

readings:
        Hodges, Argentina, 1943-1976, whole book
        Collier, The New Authoritarianism, Chaps. 5, 7

C. Case Study 2: Brazil since 1922

4/16   7. Tenentes and the Vargas Revolution (1922-54)
4/20   8. ESG: 'Security and Development' Ideology (1954-61)
4/23   9. The Left, Revolution of 64, and Technocracy (1961-67)
4/27   10. The "Brazilian Miracle" and Authoritarianism (1967-74)
4/30   11. The road to Abertura: From Geisel to Figueiredo (1974-81)

readings:
        Schneider, The Political System of Brazil, whole book
        Collier, The New Authoritarianism, Chap. 4

MID-TERM EXAM: May 7, 1981

D. Case Study 3: Peru since 1948

5/7   12. Oligarchy, APRA, and Odria's Rule, ca. 1920-54
5/11   13. Acion Popular, APRA, and the Military (1954-68)
5/14   14. Military Populism: Phase I (1968-75)
5/18   15. Military Populism: Phase II (1975-80)

readings:
       Stepan, The State and Society, whole book
       Collier, The New Authoritarianism, Chap. 6.

E. The Latin American Militarism: Past, Present, and Future

5/21   16. The Military and New Ideologies: Populism vs. Corporatism
5/25   17. The U.S. and Latin American Military in the 1980s

readings:
       Collier, The New Authoritarianism, Chaps. 3, 9

REVIEW DAY: May 28, 1981

F. A Select Bibliography on the Military in Latin America.

Latin America

J. Johnson. The Military and Society in Latin America.
E. Liewin. Arms and Politics in Latin America.
B. Loveman and T. Davies, Jr. The Politics of Antipolitics. The
      Military in Latin America.
A. Lowenthal. Armies and Politics in Latin America.
J. Malloy, ed. Authoritarianism and Corporatism in Latin America.
F. Nunn. Latin America: The Hegemonic Crisis and the Military Coup.
P. Schmitter, ed. Military Rule in Latin America.

Argentina

R. Alexander. Argentine Upheaval.
C. Corbett. The Latin American Military as a Socio-Political Force.
G. Germani. Authoritarianism, National Populism, and Fascism.
M. Goldwert. Democracy, Militarism, and Nationalism in Argentina,
      1930-1966.
J. Imaz. Los que mandan (Those Who Rule).
H. Peterson. Argentina and the United States, 1810-1960.
R. Potash. The Army and Politics in Argentina, 1928-1945.
D. Rock. Politics in Argentina, 1890-1930.
P. Snow. Political Forces in Argentina.

Brazil

B. Ames. Rhetoric and Reality in a Militarized Regime: Brazil
   since 1964.
J. Dulles. Unrest in Brazil: Political-Military Crisis 1955-1964.
P. Evans. Dependent Development: The Alliance of Multinational,
   State, and Local Capital in Brazil.
N. Macaulay. The Prestes Column: Revolution in Brazil.
R. Roett, ed. Brazil in the Sixties.
R. Roett, ed. Brazil in the Seventies.
T. Skidmore. Politics in Brazil, 1930-1964.
A. Stepan. The Military in Politics: Changing Patterns in Brazil.
A. Stepan, ed. Authoritarian Brazil: Origins, Policies, and Future.

Peru

F. Bourricaud. Power and Society in Contemporary Politics.
D. Collier. Squatters and Oligarchs: Authoritarian Rule and
   Policy Change in Peru.
A. Lowenthal. The Peruvian Experiment: Continuity and Change
   under Military Rule.
R. Webb. Government Policy and the Distribution of Wealth in
   Peru, 1963-1973.

GEORGETOWN UNIVERSITY
HISTORY DEPARTMENT

Women in Latin American History   Professor Dorn
(144-606-01)   Spring 1985

Objectives and format

We will study the changing roles of women in Latin America from the
colonial period to the present, with emphasis on the last hundred
years, and taking into account class and racial stratifications, and
cultural as well as regional differences. Analyses within different
time frames and in a cross-cultural context will give us the opportunity to examine continuity and change in various milieus throughout
Latin American history. There will be references to notable female
personalities and their contributions. Parallels will be drawn with
the history of women in the United States, to integrate the topic
further. The course will consist of lectures and class discussions.

Requirements

The assigned readings include scholarly writings, biographic materials,
and some primary sources written by women. An additional bibliography
will also be provided for further readings. Readings and papers will
be discussed in class. There will be a written mid-term and an oral
final exam. Each student will prepare a research paper.

Schedule of Meetings and Topics

1. Jan. 22. Implanting Old World Patterns in America: The Iberian
   Woman in the New World
   A. Lavrin, "Introduction," Lavrin, ed., Latin American Women,
   pp. 3-22.

2. Jan. 29. Women in the Conquest
   "Hardship and Bravery in the Conquest of the Rio do la Plata,"
   J. Hahner, ed., Women in Latin American History, pp. 17-20.
   "Malinche," "Ines de Suárez," and "The Nun Ensign," Henderson,
   Ten Notable Latin American Women, pp. 1-72.

3. Feb. 5. Marriage, Children, and Family: Evolving Roles
   "Homemakers and Encomenderas," Martin, Daughters of the Con-
   quistadores, pp. 35-57.
   S. Bourque, Women of the Andes, pp. 87-113.

4. Feb. 12. Race and Class: Intermarriage, Politics, and the
   Catholic Church
   V. Martínez-Alier, Marriage, Class and Colour in Nineteenth
   Century Cuba, pp.20-56, 82-99.
   A.J.R. Russell-Wood, "Female and Family in the Economy and
   Society of Colonial Brazil," Lavrin, Women, pp. 60-100.

91

5. Feb. 19. Women and Religion in Latin America: The Convent as a Provider of Female Autonomy (the Case of Sor Juana Inés de la Cruz)
Octavio Paz, "Juana Ramírez (Sor Juana Inés de la Cruz)," 5 Signs; A Journal of Women in Culture and Society (Autumn 1979): 80-97.
Martin, Daughters, pp. 201-242.
Henderson, Ten Notable, pp. 73-98.

6. Feb. 26. Sexual Division of Labor in Rural Areas. Growing Urbanization and Women
Bourque, Women, pp. 114-149.
S. Tanzer, "La Quisqueyana: The Dominican Woman," Pescatello, ed., Female and Male in Latin America, pp. 209-229.

7. Mar. 5. The Education of Women
Martin, Daughters, pp. 73-103.
C. J. Little, "Education, Philanthropy and Feminism; Components of Argentine Womanhood," Lavrin, Women, pp. 235-252.

8. Mar. 19. Changing Roles in the Period of Nation-Building The Empress Leopoldina. María Crajales. In, Henderson, Ten Notable, pp. 121-168.
E. Cherpak, "The Participation of Women in the Independence Movement of Gran Colombia," Lavrin, Women, pp. 219-233.

9. Mar. 26. Issues of Feminism in Latin America
"The U.S. Suffrage Movement and Latin America," Hahner, Women, pp. 78-95.
A. Macias, "Felipe Carrilo and Women's Liberation in Mexico," Lavrin, Women, pp. 286-300.

10. Apr. 2. "Marianismo," the Other Face of "Machismo" in Latin America
E. Stevens, "Marianismo," Pescatello, Female, pp. 89-102.
Bourque, Women, pp. 39-86.

11. Apr. 9. Focus on Women Authors and Their Impact
(Audio-tapes of Grabriela Mistral and Victoria Ocampo will be played for the class)
"Gabriela Mistral," Henderson, Ten Notable, pp. 169-191.
G.M. Dorn, "Four Twentieth Century Latin American Women Authors, 10 SECOLAS Annals (March 1979): 125-133.
F. Dauster, "Success and the Latin American Writers," Mayer, Contemporary Authors, pp. 78-90

12. Apr. 16. Images and Reality of Female Life in Fiction
J.S. Jaquette, "Literary archtypes and Female Role Alternatives," Pescatello, Female, pp. 3-27.
A. Pescatello, "The Brasileira," Ibid., pp. 29-57.
C.B. Flora, "The Passive Female and Social Change," Ibid., pp. 59-83.

13. Apr. 23. Women in Latin American Politics
    "The Most Powerful Woman in Latin America," Hahner, Women,
    pp. 103-111.
    "Eva Peron," Henderson, Ten Notable, pp. 193-212.
    E. Chaney, "Women in Politics: The Case of Peru and Chile,"
    Pescatello, Female, pp. 103-140.

14. Apr. 30. Contemporary Revolutionary Movements: The Changing
    Role of Women
    S.K. Purcell, "Modernizing Women for a Modern Society: The
    Cuban Case," Pescatello, Female, pp. 257-271
    G. Fox, "Honor, Shame, and Women's Liberation in Cuba: Views
    of a Working-Class Emigre," Ibid., pp. 273-289.
    "A Mexican Peasant Woman Remembers," Hahner, Women, pp. 253-165.

15. May 14. Final exam

Required texts (available at the bookstore and the articles on reserve
shelf in the Lauinger library)

Bourque, Susan C. Women of the Andes: Patriarchy and Social Change
    in Two Peruvian Towns (1981)
Dorn, Georgette M. "Four Twentieth Century Latin American Women
    Authors," 10 SECOLAS Annals (1979): 125-133
Hahner, June E., ed. Women in Latin American History. Rev. ed.
    (1980)
Henderson, James D., and Linda R. Henderson. Ten Notable Women of
    Latin America (1978)
Lavrin, Asuncion, ed. Latin American Women: Historical Perspectives
    (1978)
Martin, Luis. Daughters of the Conquistadores: Women of the Viceroyalty
    of Peru (1983)
Martínez-Alier, Verena. Marriage, Class and Colour in Nineteenth
    Century Cuba: A Study of Racial Attitudes and Sexual Values in
    a Slave Society (1974)
McGuinn, Noel F. "Marriage and Family in Middle-Class Mexico, 28
    Journal of Marriage and the Family (August 1966): 305-313
Meyer, Doris, and Marguerite Fernández Olmos, eds. Contemporary
    Women Authors of Latin America (1983)
Pescatello, Ann, ed. Female and Male in Latin America (1973)

Office hours (606 ICC)

Tuesday, 5:00 - 6:00
and by appointment; call Prof. Dorn at 287-5397

Bibliography (Suggested Additional Reading)

Berlinck, Manoel Costa. The Structure of the Brazilian Family in the
    City of São Paulo (1969)
Bermudez, Maria Elvira. La vida familiar del mexicano (1955)

Catt, Carrie Chapman. "Anti-Feminism in South America," Current History (Apr.-Sept. 1923): 1028-1036

Elmendorf, Mary. Nine Maya Women: A Village Faces Change (1976)

Friez, Irene, and others. Women and Sex Roles: Social Psychological Perspectives (1978)

Chaney, Elsa. Supermadre (1979)

Lavrin, Asuncion. "Values and Meaning of Monastic Life for Nuns in Colonial Mexico," Catholic Historical Review 58 (Oct. 1972): 367-387

Macias, Anna. Against All Odds; The Feminist Movement in Mexico to 1940 (1982)

_____. "Women and the Mexican Revolution, 1910-1920," The Americas 27 (Jul. 1980): 53-82

Knaster, Meri. Women in Spanish America: An Annotated Bibliography (1977)

_____. "Women in Latin America: The State of Research," Latin American Research Review 11 (Summer 1976): 3-74

Hahner, June E. "Feminism, Women's Rights, and the Suffrage Movement in Brazil," 15 (1) Latin American Research Review: 65-111

Meyer, Doris. Victoria Ocampo; Against the Wind and the Tide (1979)

Nash, June, and Helen I. Safa, eds. Sex and Class in Latin America (1976)

Navarro, Marysa. Eva Peron (1983)

Ramos, Donald. "Marriage and Family in Colonial Vila Rica," Hispanic American Historical Review 55 (May 1975): 220-225

Rosaldo, Michelle, and Louise Lamphere, eds. Women, Culture, and Society (1974)

Socolow, Susan Migden. "Marriage, Birth, and Inheritance: The Merchants of Eighteenth Century Buenos Aires," Hispanic American Historical Review 60 (Aug. 1980): 387-406

Soeiro, Susan A. "The Social and Economic Role of the Convent; Women and Nuns in Colonial Bahia," Hispanic American Historical Review 54 (May 1974): 209-232

Stevens, Evelyn P. "The Prospects of a Women's Liberation Movement in Latin America," Journal of Marriage and the Family 35 (May 1973): 313-321

Taylor, Julie M. Eva Perón; The Myths of a Woman (1976)

Lbarca Hubertson, Amanda. A donde va la mujer? (1934)

Moreau de justo, Alicia. La mujer en la democracía (1945)

Acosta-Belen, Edna. The Puerto Rican Woman (1979)

94

Prof. Donna J. Guy
Office: Social Science 129, 621-3737
Office Hours: Tues. 1-2:30p.m. and by appointment

HISTORY 469X
WOMEN IN LATIN AMERICA
Social Science 128
7:00-9:30p.m.

The focus of this course is the history of women in Latin America from the
Conquest to the present. Rather than look at each individual country and specific historical event, we will examine a series of concepts, institutions and
factors that have affected Latin American women, and, equally important, women have
reacted to these circumstances. The aim of the course is to introduce new ways
to examine Latin American history through the methodologies employed in womens
history. Classes will be held once a week and will consist of lecture and group
discussion of required readings. In addition, each student will prepare two papers,
one on the colonial period and one on the national period. Each topic must be
approved by the instructor. The first paper will be due on March 26 and the second
on May 2. The papers, a maximum of 10 pages for undergraduates and 20 pages for
graduate students, should examine a topic by consulting secondary, and if possible,
primary sources. All work must represent the individual effort of each student,
and all material quoted directly or paraphrased must be identified through the use
of footnotes. All sources used in the paper should be listed alphabetically in a
bibliography. Otherwise the paper will be considered to have been plagiarized.
Footnotes must be standardized according to a handbook of style such as Kate Turabian,
4th ed., A Manual for Writers. Please note that you must decide which topic you wish
to write on and inform the instructor as soon as possible.

ASSIGNMENTS

Jan. 22   Introduction to Women's History and Latin American History
                  Asunción Lavrin, Latin American Women.   Historical Perspec-
                        tives, Introduction, pp. 1-22.
                  Juliet Mitchell, "Four Structures in a Complex Unity," *
                  Ann D. Gordon, Mari Jo Buhle, etc., "The Problem of Women's
                        History,"*

Jan. 29   Women and the Conquest
                  Clendinnen, Inga, "Yucatec Maya Women and the Spanish Conquest:
                        Role and Ritual in Historical Reconstruction," Journal
                        of Social History, Vol. 15 (1982)*
                  Burkett, Elinor, "Indian Women and White Society: The Case
                        of Sixteenth-Century Peru," in Lavrin, pp. 101-128.

                  Recommended: James Lockhart, Spanish Peru, Ch. 9, 11, pp.
                        150-170; 199-220.*

February 5   The Church in Colonial Latin America
                  Lavrin, "Women and Religion in Spanish America," in Reuther,
                        Women and Religion in America, pp. 42-75.*
                  Karasch, "Damiana da Cunha: Catechist and Sertanista ," in
                        Sweet and Nash, Struggle & Survival in Colonial America#
                  Martín, Luís, Daughters of the Conquistadores, Ch. 8, 10.*

                  Recommended: Susan Soeiro, "The Feminine Orders in Colonial
                        Bahia, Brazil: Economic, Social, and Demographic
                        Implications, 1677-1800," in Lavrin, Latin American
                        Women*

95

Feb. 12   Colonial Institutions: Marriage, Property and the State
Martín, Ch. 5*
Russell Wood, AJR, "Female and Family in the Economy and
Society of Colonial Brazil," in Lavrin, Latin American
Women, pp. 60-100.*
Lavrin and Edith Couturier, "Dowries and Wills: A View of
Women's Socioeconomic Role in Colonial Guadalajara
and Puebla, 1640-1790," Hispanic American Historical
Review, 59:2 (May, 1979), pp. 280-304.*
Sweet and Nash, Ch. 13#

Feb. 19   Non-White Women in Colonial Latin America
Flusche and Korth, Forgotten Females: Women of African and
Indian Descent in Colonial Chile, 1535-1800, pp. 1-68.*
Schwartz, "The Manumission of Slaves in Colonial Brazil:
Bahia, 1684-1745," HAHR 54:4 (Nov. 1974), pp. 603-635.*
Sweet and Nash, Ch. 11, 15.#

Feb. 26   Women and Work in Colonial Latin America
Sweet and Nash, Ch. 14, 20, 21#
Martín, Ch. 3*

March 5   Family and Household Structure-Myth and Reality
Freyre, Gilberto, "The Patriarchal Basis of Brazilian
Society," in Maier and Weatherhead, Politics of Change
in Latin America, pp. 155-173.*
Ramos, Donald, "Marriage and the Family in Colonial Vila
Rica," HAHR 55 (1975), pp. 200-225.*
Kuznesof, Elizabeth, "The Role of the Female-Headed Household
in Brazilian Modernization: Sao Paulo 1765-1826,"
Journal of Social History 13 (Summer 1980), pp. 589-611.*

March 12   MID TERM; The Impact of Independence on Latin American Women

March 26   Women, the State, and Ideology
Guy, "Women, Peonage and Industrialization, Argentina 1810-
1914," Latin American Research Review (1981)*
Nash and Safa, Ch. 2, 3#
Pescatello, Ch. 2, pp. 89-102, 209-229.#

April 2   Women and Work
Pescatello, pp. 159-208#
Safa and Nash, Ch. 6-7#

April 9   Education
Vaughan, Mary K., "Women, Class and Education in Mexico,
1880-1928," Latin American Perspectives," pp. 135-152.*
Saffiotti, Women in Class Society, pp. 140-178.*
Pescatello, pp. 59-85.

April 16   Origins of Latin American Feminism
Safa and Nash, Ch. 11, 14#
Pescatello, 103-159.#
Saffiotti, Women in Class Society, pp. 197-136.

April 23   **Women** and Politics
                     Safa and Nash, Ch. 12, 13, 15, 16

April 30   Fertility and Population Control
                     Latin American and Caribbean Women's Collective, <u>Slaves of Slaves</u>, Ch. 9,10
                     Kinzer, Nora Scott, "Priests Machos and Babies: Or Latin American Women and the Manichaean Heresy," <u>Journal of Marriage and the Family</u> (May, 1973), pp. 300-307.

May 7   **Women** and Revolution in the Twentieth Century
                     Pescatello, pp. 257 to finish
                     Nazarri, Muriel,

Final Exam: May 14, 7:30-9:30p.m.

Anani Dzidzienyo
Office Hours
Tuesday 10:00-11:30
Wednesday 3:30-5:00

This course deals with Afro-Latin Americans in Latin American societies.
Readings for the course are drawn from history, sociology, anthropology,
and literature. It is intended to provide students with a broad enough
background to enable them to better understand this very important but
often neglected group within the 'African Diaspora'. Ultimately it is
hoped that such an understanding will contribute to an appreciation of
the multi-meaning nature of the designation Afro-American which, properly
speaking is applicable to groups from Alaska to Uruguay. The focus is on
Hispanic America though some attention will be devoted to Brazil at the
end of the semester.

STUDENT RESPONSIBILITIES AND GRADING

1) Short, critical review, 4-6 pgs. of The African Experience

2) Mid-Term, Take-Home Examination

3) Map Exercise

4) Final, Take-Home Examination

5) Class Participation

Attention

The importance of reading assigned materials before class meetings cannot be
over-emphasized. It is the best guarantee for meaningful class participation.

Students with a reading knowledge of Spanish should appraise the Instructor
of this fact by the end of the second week of classes.

LECTURE TOPICS

Week

1) "The Concept of Afro-Latin America"

2) "The Trans-Atlantic Slave Trade and Its Consequences for African and
     Latin American History and Society"

3) "Religion, Culture, Nationality, and Comparative Slavery: Afro-American
     Perspectives"

4) "Slavery and Race Relations: Continuities and Discontinuities"

5) "Afro-USA and the Other Afro-Americans: "The 'Myth' of the Negro Past"
     Re-Examined"

6) "The Uses and Misuses of African Culture in Latin America"

7) "Race, Color, and Class and Afro-Latin Americans"

8) "Rescuing the Missing or Relocating the Disappeared"

9) "Race and Literature: Afro-Hispanic and Afro-Brazilian Dimensions"

10) "The Blessings of Liberty and the Anguish of Marginality"
11) "And What About Afro-Latin American Leaders?"
12) "Afro-Latin American Issues: Beyond Religion, Literature, and Folklore"
13) "Prejudice and/or Discrimination: Afros and Latin American Race Relations and Society"
14) "Afro-Brazilian Counterpoints"

CLASS MEETINGS
Week

1) 9/6   No Reading Assignment

   9/8   Rout, The African Experience In Spanish America
        chs. 1-3, pp.3-98, Preface
        NB 1-2 Page assignment, "What I Know About Latin America and How I Came to Know it"

2) 9/13   Rout, chs. 4-6, pp. 99-182

   9/15   Rout, chs. 7-9, pp. 185-260

3) 9/20   Rout, chs. 10-12, pp. 261-330, plus Appendix
   9/22   No Reading Assignment: Critical Review Paper Due (4-6 pgs.)

4) 9/27   Price, Maroon Societies
        Intro., pp. 1-34, pp. 35-103
   9/29   Guest Lecturer, Rhett Jones, "Maroon Societies: The Case of Jamaican Maroons"

5) 10/4   Price, pp. 226-319
   10/6   James, The Black Jacobins
        pp. 3-117, plus Preface

6) 10/11   James, pp. 118-240
   10/13   James, pp. 241-377

7) 10/18   Reid Andrews, The Afro-Argentines of Buenos Aries, 1800-1900
        chs. 1-4, pp. 3-64
        NB TAKE-HOME MID-TERM EXAMINATION QUESTIONS TO BE HANDED OUT
   10/20   Andrews, chs. 5-7, pp. 65-137

8) 10/25   Andrews, chs. 8-12, pp. 138-219
        NB TAKE-HOME WRITTEN ANSWERS DUE

9) 11/1
   11/3   Jackson, The Black Image in Latin American Literature

10) 11/8   García Márquez, The Autumn of the Partiach
        pp. 7-119

   11/10   Márquez, pp. 120-251

11) 11/15   Alejo Carpentier, Reasons of State
        chs. 1-7, pp. 9-107
   11/17   Carpentier, chs. 8-14, pp. 107-202
        NB MAP EXERCISE IN CLASS

12) 11/22 Carpentier, chs. 15-22, pp. 202-311
    11/24 HAPPY THANKSGIVING

13) 11/29 H. Hoetink, <u>Caribbean Race Relations: A Study of the Two Variants</u>
           WHOLE BOOK
    12/1   Jackson, <u>Black Writers in Latin America</u>

14) 12/8   LAST CLASS--TAKE-HOME FINAL EXAMINATION QUESTIONS TO BE HANDED OUT
    12/15 TAKE-HOME FINAL EXAMINATION ANSWERS DUE

RESERVE READING/RECOMMENDED READING

1) Patricia Fagan, "Antonio Maceio: Heroes, History and Historiography"
   <u>Latin American Reserach Review</u>, Vol. XL No. 3 (1979): 69-93

2) H. Sternbery, "A Geographer's View of Race and Class in Latin America"
   in Magnus Morner ed. <u>Race and Class in Latin America</u>, ch. 13

3) M. Morner, "Historical Research on Race Relations in Latin-America During
   the National Period" ibid. ch. 10

4) M. Morner, "The Impact of Regional Variety on the History of Afro-Latin
   Americans" in <u>Secolas Annals</u>, Vol. IX March 1978 (1-13)

5) Antonio Olliz Boyd, "The Black Protagonist in Latin American Literature:
   A Study in Ethnic Identity/Cultural Assimilation" in <u>Secolas Annals</u>,
   Vol. IX, March 1978 (14-33)

6) Betty Tyree Osiek, "Placido: Critic of the Vice-Ridden Masters and of
   the Abuses of the Enslaved Black" in <u>Secolas</u>, Vol. IX (62-67)

7) Marvin Harris, <u>Patterns of Race in the Americas</u>, NY Walker & Co., 1964

8) Miriam DeCosta Ed., <u>Blacks in Hispanic Literature</u>, NY Kennikat Press, 1977

9) Rolando Mellafe, <u>Negro Slavery in Latin America</u>, Berkeley & LA Univ. of
   Calif. Press, 1975

10) Colin A. Palmer, "Religion and Magic in Mexican Slave Society, 1570-1650"
    in S. Engermand and E. Genovese, Eds., <u>Race and Slavery in the Western
    Hemisphere: Quantitative Studies</u>, Princeton Univ. Press, 1975 (311-328)

11) Frederick P. Bowser, "The Free Person of Color in Mexico City and Lima:
    Manumission and Opportunity, 1580-1650", <u>Ibid</u> (331-363)

12) John V. Lombardi, "The Abolition of Slavery in Venezuela: A Nonevent" in
    Robert-Brent Toplin, Ed., <u>Slavery and Race Relations in Latin America</u>,
    Westport, CT, Greenwood Press, 1974 (228-252)

13) Franklin W. Knight, "Slavery, Race, and Social Structure in Cuba During the Nineteenth Century" Ibid (204-227)

14) Robert-Brent Toplin, "Abolition and the Issue of the Black Freedman's Future in Brazil" in Toplin, Ed., Slavery and Race Relations in Latin America, (253-276)

15) Roger Bastide, African Civilizations in the New World

16) Thomas G. Matthews, "The Question of Color in Puerto Rico" in Toplin, op-cit pp. 299-?23

17) Franklin Knight, The African Dimension in Latin American Societies

Anani Dzidzienyo AA 121

"BLACKS IN LATIN AMERICAN HISTORY AND SOCIETY"

Essay: Due 27th September, 1983

     Write a critical essay of no less than 4 pages and no more than
6 pages discussing the following issues.

a. Images and stereotypes about blacks in Latin American
    history and society

b. The contribution of Afros. to the economic, political
    and cultural development of Latin America

c. Some assessment of slavery's impact on Latin America

d. The contribution of Rout's, The African Experience to
    your understanding of Latin American history and society

     Rather than trying to follow the above points as outlined above,
you are urged to attempt to write a cohesive essay with the points
serving as a guideline.
     Where you cite specific dates, names, etc. You must use proper
references.
     Critical, means you should put forth your reactions to the book
and issues rather than merely summarising it.

102

Write a critical essay in which you compare Hoetink, Carvalho-Neto, Girvan and Fierher's positions in terms of the relationship between slavery, race and class as they impact on contemporary Afro-Latin Americans. In your essay you must delineate similarities and differences in their respective approaches as well as stating your considered reactions to these positions.

Minimum 5 pages. Maximum 6 pages. Due March 2, 1984.

TAKE-HOME
FINAL EXAMINATION
(December 6, 1983)

A. Recalling your first 'paper' for this course, "What I Know About Latin America and How I Came To Know It," write an essay of no less than four (4) pages and no more than five (5) pages on what you consider to be the most important contributions to your present knowledge of Afro-Latin Americans in Latin American History and society. You must cite specific works or arguments to support your choice.

B. "Independence ended the caste system on paper, but it did not make every-one white. What has since evolved in many areas is a flexible concept called 'social race', which allows anyone to be whatever he wishes under limited circumstances."

Leslie Rout, THE AFRICAN EXPERIENCE IN SPANISH AMERICA (Page 319)

Using Rout's quote as your point of departure, discuss the position of Afro-Latin Americans in the post-colonial Latin American societies. In your discussion you must deal with the area generally, as well as citing specific national examples.

NOTE: ALL ANSWERS ARE DUE DECEMBER 16th BY 6:00PM IN CHURCHILL HOUSE.

HAVE A GOOD!

HISTORY 446:
STUDIES IN LATIN AMERICAN HISTORY

THE INSTITUTION OF SLAVERY IN LATIN AMERICA: 1502-1888

Winter/1985   Professor Rout

Course meeting: Monday and Wednesday: 7:00-9:00 pm.

Course requirements Mid-term examination, final examination and one short paper. No grade will be given until all work has been accepted. The Professor reserves the right to reject papers which are poorly written.

Course teaching methods: Lecture and discussion. A regular intermission will be held at 8:00 (ten minutes) during each session.

Attendance: No attendance record will be kept, but students who miss four or five sessions during the ten week quarter are to be warned that they may have difficulties, since much of the material to be presented will not be found in any English-language text.

Problems

The Spanish (1502) and the Portuguese (1538) were responsible for the introduction of African slavery in the New World. Indeed, it was to service the labor needs of their New World possessions that the Transatlantic slave trade was introduced. Just as interesting perhaps, is the fact that African slavery persisted in Spanish and Portuguese America longer than it did anywhere else in the Western Hemisphere. The official termination of the institution in Cuba came in 1886, and in Brazil in 1888. Bluntly, African slavery was a pervasive, long-lived institution which was brought to an end usually after a long, bitter, and often violent socio-economic struggle. Seen from the perspective of the twentieth century, a number of questions have been raised concerning the nature, the rationale, and the economic viability of this institution. In this class, a number of issues will be dealt with. Specifically, the following questions will be asked, and hopefully answered:

a) What connection exists between African slavery as it existed in the Iberian Peninsula before 1492, and the abominable system which came to exist in Spanish and Portuguese America? Why was African slavery necessary? (one week)
b) What were the moral justifications provided by the Spanish and Portuguese for African slavery in the New World prior to 1810? (one week)
c) What were the tasks performed by African slaves in the various regions of the Americas? What was the significance of

the economic role played by the African slave in maintaining Spanish and Portuguese prosperity in the Americas? (two weeks) d) Did Africans resist the slavery regimen? How did they do so? What rights, duties, and social prohibitions were granted, required, or enforced against freed slaves and/or their descendants? (two weeks) e) How did the Latin American Wars of Independence affect the institution of slavery? How did the "liberators"--in particular, Bolívar and San Martín--deal with the issues of slavery and abolition? (one week) f) In what ways were the abolition campaigns fought in the various Hispanic American republics similar? How were they different? What role did the British play in the abolition struggles? Why did the British play the role they did in the abolition battle? (one week) g) What was the aftermath of abolition in Latin America? Which republics chose to reimburse the slave owners? Which ones did not? Why? Could these republics have done much to help the slaves adjust to their new status as free citizens? (one week)

Useful texts and written assignments

The short paper to be completed will require the use of several of the texts listed below. In writing the paper, the student will take one of the questions listed above, and then report what other writers have said about it. The student will then present his/her analysis of the issue, and present his/her reasons for the position taken on said issue. The paper is to be no longer than six-seven pages. The books to be used are listed below:

Bibliography of works

1. Andrews, George Reid, The Afro-Argentines in Buenos Aires, 1800-1900 (1980)
2. Bowser, Frederick, The African Slave in Colonial Peru: 1524-1650 (1974)
3. Boxer, C. R., Race Relations in the Portuguese Colonial Empire, 1415-1825 (1963)
4. Conrad, Robert, The Destruction of Brazilian Slavery, 1850-1888 (1972)
5. Curtain, Phillip, The Atlantic Slave Trade: A Census (1969)
6. Jackson, Richard L., The Black Image in Latin American Literature (1976)
7. Klein, Herbert S., The Middle Passage: Comparative Studies in the Atlantic Slave Trade (1978)
8. Knight, Franklin, Slave Society in Cuba during the Nineteenth Century (1970)
9. Lombardi, John V., The Decline and Abolition of Negro Slavery in Venezuela (1971)
10. Moreno Fraginals, Manuel; Moya Pons, Frank; and Engerman, Stanley, eds., Between Slavery and Free Labor: The Spanish-Speaking Caribbean in the Nineteenth Century (1985)
11. Palmer, Colin, Human Cargoes: The British Slave Trade to Spanish America (1981)

12. Prado Júnior, Caio, The Colonial Background of Modern Brazil (1967)
13. Price, Richard, ed., Maroon Societies: Rebel Slave Communities in the Americas (1973)
14. Rout, Leslie B., The African Experience in Spanish America: 1502 to the present (1976)
15. Russel-Wood, A. J. R., The Blackman in Slavery and Freedom in Colonial Brazil (1982)
16. Scott, Rebecca, Slave Emancipation in Cuba: The Transition to Free Labor, 1860-1899 (1985)
17. Sharp, Frederick, Slavery on the Spanish Frontier (1976)
18. Stein, Stanley, Vassouras: A Brazilian Coffee County, 1850-1890 (1957)
19. Toplin, Robert, The Abolition of slavery in Brazil (1971)

LATIN AMERICA: A FILM SURVEY
(History 109L)
University of California, Riverside

Spring, 1982
TuTh 3:30-5
Watkins 1111

Carlos E. Cortés
Office: Lib.S. 4153
Office Hours: TuTh 1-3

Scope: History 109L, "Latin America: A Film Survey," focuses on the analysis of filmic treatments of Latin America, particularly as made by Latin American filmmakers. The course has four goals: (1) to develop in students a better understanding of Latin America as a historical region; (2) to introduce students to techniques for analyzing films as socio-historical documents; (3) to help students learn to integrate filmic and published sources in historical analysis; and (4) to provide students with practical exercises in the interpretation of these documents through the writing of critical analyses of filmic and written source materials.

Prerequisites: None.

Requirements: Students will read three books, two on Latin America and one on film. In addition, in class they will view seven feature films which treat Latin America. Students will write analyses of three of the seven feature films shown during the course. Upon request, a student may select a film on Latin America viewed outside of class for one of the three reviews. Should you wish to use an outside film, please obtain the instructor's approval in advance.

Each of the three papers will be typed, double-spaced, and five pages in length and will be worth 20 percent of the course grade. To be acceptable, papers on a film shown in class Thursday must be turned in by the beginning of the Tuesday class meeting following the screening of that film. Papers on films viewed outside of class will be due by the beginning of class on Tuesday, June 1. Failure to submit one or more papers on time will result in F's on the missing papers. No late papers will be accepted. The remaining 40 percent of the course grade will be based on a final examination (30 percent) and class participation (10 percent).

Substance of Film Analyses: Papers must emphasize your analysis and evaluation of the usefulness of the film for a better understanding of Latin America. Included in each paper should be an analysis of the filmmaker's goals in making the film, a statement of the thesis (message) conveyed, and an evaluation of the techniques which were used to convey and dramatize this message. Papers are to be neither summaries of plots nor esthetic evaluations of the film as art, although you may wish to include a discussion of plot and/or esthetics to strengthen your analysis.

Required Reading:

Burns, E. Bradford. Latin America: A Concise Interpretive History.

Huss, Roy and Silverstein, Norman. The Film Experience: Elements of
Motion Picture Art.

Latin American Perspectives. Culture in the Age of Mass Media.

108

Course Schedule

I. Introduction to Film and History

March 30 (Tues.) -- Introduction

April 1 (Thur.) -- The Film as Historical Document
The Film Experience, pp. 1-156

April 6 (Tues.) -- U.S. Filmic Treatment of Latin America
Culture in the Age of Mass Media, pp. 2-48

April 8 (Thur.) -- European Filmic Treatment of Latin America
Film: AGUIRRE, THE WRATH OF GOD

April 13 (Tues.) -- Latin American Filmic Treatment of Latin America
Culture in the Age of Mass Media, pp. 49-150

II. Filmic Interpretations of Latin America

Brazil

April 15 (Thur.) -- Film: BARREN LIVES

April 20 (Tues.) -- Discussion of BARREN LIVES

April 22 (Thur.) -- Film: THE GIVEN WORD

April 27 (Tues.) -- Discussion of THE GIVEN WORD

The Andean Nations

April 29 (Thur.) -- Film: THE PRINCIPAL ENEMY

May 4 (Tues.) -- No Class

May 6 (Thur.) -- Film: CHUQUIAGO

May 11 (Tues.) -- Discussion of THE PRINCIPAL ENEMY and CHUQUIAGO

Argentina

May 13 (Thur.) -- Film: REBELLION IN PATAGONIA

May 18 (Tues.) -- Discussion of REBELLION IN PATAGONIA

The Cuban Revolution

May 20   (Thur.) — Film: MEMORIES OF UNDERDEVELOPMENT

May 25   (Tues.) — Discussion of MEMORIES OF UNDERDEVELOPMENT

May 27   (Thur.) -- Film: ONE WAY OR ANOTHER

June 1   (Tues.) — Discussion of ONE WAY OR ANOTHER

III. Conclusion

June 3   (Thur.) — Latin American Film: A Critical Reevaluation

Final Examination: Saturday, June 11, 8-11 a.m.

THE OHIO STATE UNIVERSITY

SYLLABUS
History 694
Jews of Latin America

Winter 1986   Dr. Judith Elkin

This is a one quarter course designed to explore the area
where Latin American history and Jewish studies intersect. The
course opens with an overview of fifteenth-century Iberian
society and continues with the history of covert migration of
Jews and conversos ("Marranos") to the Spanish and Portuguese
colonies in the New World. The balance of the quarter is devoted
to Jewish settlement in Latin America in the post-independence
period; the varying accommodations reached between immigrant and
host cultures; and the status of the contemporary Latin American
Jewish communities.

* * *

Required Texts (All books have been ordered through SBX)

Judith Laikin Elkin, Jews of the Latin American Republics
Eugene Sofer, From Pale to Pampa
Jacobo Timerman, Prisoner without a Name, Cell without a Number
Course Pack (CP), see attached table of contents

* * *

Reference Works (To be found in...)

American Jewish Year Book, 1985
Encyclopedia Judaica, 1972
Latin America and Caribbean Contemporary Record, 1982-83
Resources for Latin American Jewish Studies, LAJSA Publication
     No. 1, 1984.
Martin Sable, Latin American Jewry: A Research Guide

* * *

On Reserve (To be found in...)

American Jewish Archives 34 no. 2 (1982)
Burns, E. Bradford, Latin America: A Concise Interpretive History
Judith Elkin, "Latin America's Jews: A Review of Sources," Latin
     American Research Review vol. 20 no. 2 (1985):124-41
Louis Finkelstein, ed. The Jews: Their History, Culture, and
     Religion. 2 vols.

SCHEDULE OF TOPICS

Introductory Session

Week I
Jew, Christian, Moor: The Iberian Matrix
    Elkin, Ch. 1
    Recommended readings (see list attached)

Week II
The Colonial Period: Through a glass darkly...
    Stanley M. Hordes, "Historiographical Problems in the Study
    of the Inquisition and the Mexican Crypto-Jews," in AJA 34
    (Nov 1982):138-52
    Anita Novinsky, "Jewish Roots of Brazil," CP

Week III
Prelude to the National Period
    Burns, ch. 4-6
    Finkelstein, ch. 30 and 35
    Book Reviews due

Week IV
Jewish Immigration to Latin America
    Elkin, ch. 2-4
    Sofer, ch. 2

Week V
Jewish Agricultural Settlement
    Elkin, ch. 6
    Winsberg, "Jewish Agricultural Colonization..." (CP)
    Avni, "Argentine Jewry: Its Socio-Political..." (CP)
    Elkin, "Goodnight, Sweet Gaucho," (CP)

Midterm exam

Week VI
Occupations and Social Status: The Case of Argentina
    Elkin, ch. 5
    Mirelman, "The Semana Trágica of 1919," (CP)
    Segal, "Jews and the Argentine Center," (CP)
    Sofer, ch. 1, 3-6

Week VII
The Jewish Street
    Elkin, ch. 7
    Rattner, "Brazil," (CP)
    Sapir, "Jews in Cuba," (CP)

Week VIII
A Demographic Profile
    Elkin, ch. 8, 9
    U.O. Schmelz and Sergio Della Pergola, "The Demography of
    Latin American Jewry," AJYB 1985:51-102

Week IX
Antisemite and Jew
    Timerman, entire
    articles reproduced in CP under "Antisemitism"

Week X
Latin American Jewish Communities Today
    Elkin, ch. 10
    Levine, "Adaptive Strategies..." (CP)
    Schers & Singer, "External and Internal..." (CP)
    Elkin, "Latin American Jewry Today," American Jewish Year
    Book 1985:3-49.

Requirements of the Course

    All students should read the assignments before coming to
class, and arrive prepared to discuss them. Knowledgeable class
participation will constitute an important element of your grade.

    There will be one midterm exam (at the end of the fifth
week) and one final exam (at the time scheduled by the
University). Exams will combine essay with short-answer
questions. Attendance at these exams is mandatory. Make-ups
will be authorized only in highly unusual cases, where a valid
and persuasive medical or personal emergency can be shown to
exist.

    All students will be asked to read and review a book either
on the Spanish/Portuguese background to the settlement of the New
World as this relates to Jews; or a book on the immigration and
settlement of crypto-Jews (called Marranos, conversos, or New
Christians) in the Spanish and Portuguese colonies. This book
should be selected from the list of Recommended Readings which is
attached; other books may be selected with the permission of the
instructor. Guidelines for reviewing books will be passed out in
class. Students should be prepared by the beginning of the
second week to contribute to class discussion on the basis of
this outside reading; the written assignment is due by the end of
the third week.

    In addition, graduate students will be asked to design a
research project on a topic in the modern period which would take
them beyond the content of this course. The object is to
identify a subject that has not been dealt with satisfactorily in
the literature and to design a research strategy for exploring
it. A specific time period or a specific community may be

113

selected; or the student may wish to explore along functional lines, looking at subjects such as Jewish participation in Argentine labor unions, careers of Jewish individuals in the state governments of Brazil, or the publishing of antisemitic materials in Mexico. The biography of a particular individual whose life as a Jew in Latin America illuminates points of contact between minority and majority society would also be a suitable topic. The paper should:

define the issue that is to be explored
develop a bibliography of secondary sources to be brought under control before focusing on the topic, making use of both "Jewish" and "Latin American" sources
describe the types of primary sources to be sought
present a strategy for pursuing the research.

The project is to be described in a paper no more than 5 pages in length and should be discussed individually with Dr. Elkin before work is begun.

Determination of Final Grade

100 - Book Review
150 - Midterm
200 - Final exam
 50 - Class participation
100 - Research design (graduate students only)

Attendance Policy

Learning is a cooperative enterprise. Both student and instructor are expected to attend all sessions of the class, and to contribute to the development of an atmosphere conducive to learning.

114

The Iberian Matrix

Yitzhak Baer, History of the Jews in Christian Spain
José Rubia Barcia, ed., Américo Castro and the Meaning of Spanish
    Civilization
Américo Castro, The Spaniards: An Introduction to their History
Solomon Katz, Jews in the Visigothic & Frankish Kingdoms of Spain
Benzion Netanyahu, The Marranos of Spain
Abraham Neuman, The Jews in Spain
    Vol. 1 - A Political-Economic Study
    Vol. II - A Social-Cultural Study
Ronald Sanders, Lost Tribes and Promised Lands
Yosef Haim Yerushalmi, The Lisbon Massacre of 1506

The Colonial Period

Martin A. Cohen, The Martyr: Luis de Carvajal. The Story of a
    Secret Jew and the Mexican Inquisition in the Sixteenth
    Century
Isaac S. Emmanuel and Suzanne A. Emmanuel, History of the Jews of
    the Netherlands Antilles
Richard E. Greenleaf, The Mexican Inquisition of the Sixteenth
    Century
Louis D. Hartz, The Founding of New Societies
Henry Charles Lea, The Inquisition in the Spanish Dependencies
Seymour B. Liebman, The Jews in New Spain: Faith, Flame, and the
    Inquisition
Raphael Patai, Tents of Jacob
Arnold Wiznitzer, Jews in Colonial Brazil

* * *

Ethnicity and Assimilation

David Schers and Hadassa Singer, "The Jewish Communities of Latin America: External and Internal Factors in Their Development." _Jewish Social Studies_ 39 (Summer 1977):241-58.

Robert M. Levine, "Adaptive Strategies of Jews in Latin America." Albuquerque.

Judith Laikin Elkin, "Recent Developments in Latin American Jewish Communities: Lessons & Implications." Albuquerque.

COURSEPACK
TABLE OF CONTENTS
History 694
Jews of Latin America

HISTORY 319
LATIN AMERICA IN WORLD AFFAIRS

Michigan State University   Professor Bratzel

1. OBJECTIVES: History 319 is intended to give students a general overview of Latin America as an international entity. After completion, I hope that students will have a better understanding of the role Latin America plays in the world and will be able to interpret future events with greater sophistication.

2. EVALUATION: There will be two hourly exams, (each counting 25% of your grade), a final exam (25% of your grade), and two five page thought papers (12.5% each). Class participation will also be counted in determining final grades.

3. BOOKS AND READINGS:

Howard Wiarda, ed., Rift and Revolution: The Central American Imbroglio
Federico Gil, Latin American-United States Relations
Schlesinger and Kinzer, Bitter Fruit: The Untold Story of the American Coup in Guatemala
Assigned reading in the library will be given throughout the term.

4. ATTENDANCE: I will not be taking attendance, but history suggests that those students missing class do very poorly. I strongly encourage you to attend on a regular basis.

5. OFFICE HOURS: I will be in my office (255 Bessey) on Monday, Wednesday, and Friday from 1:30 to 3:30 and will be glad to see you. If you cannot make these times, I am sure a mutually agreeable time to meet can be arranged. I can be reached by phone in my office at 355-3508 or a message can be left with the History Department at 355-7500 or with the ATL office at 355-2400.

6. SCHEDULE

```
Jan.   4, Introduction
       7, Latin America as client
       8, Spain under siege                          Gil, 2-24
       9, The British are coming                     Gil, 29-51
      10, The British in the Caribbean
      14, The British in South America
      15, The Slave trade I
      16, The Slave trade II
      17, The Monroe Doctrine                        Gil, 56-81
      21, U.S. and Latin America, 19th Century
      22, Texas and Mexican War
      23, Intra-American wars I
      24, Intra-American wars II
      28, First hourly exam                          Bring a blue book
      29, U.S. and the Caribbean I                   Gil, 86-115
      30, U.S. and the Caribbean II
      31, The Inter-American system                  Gil, 120-140
Feb.   4, The Good Neighbor Policy                   Gil, 144-154
       5, Latin America in WWII                      Gil, 155-183
       6, German espionage in Latin America          1st paper due
       7, The Russians are coming                    Gil, 188-220
      11, Guatemala                                  Schlesinger, all
      12, Cuba and Fidel Castro                      Gil, 226-237
      13, Cuba and the Soviets
      14, Cuba since 1963
      18, The Alliance for Progress                  Gil, 238-280
      19, Second hourly exam                         Bring a blue book
      20, Chile and Salvador Allende I
      21, Chile and Salvador Allende II
      25, The U.S. and Mexico I
      26, The U.S. and Mexico II
      27, Carter and Human Rights I                  2nd paper due
      28, Carter and Human Rights II
Mar.   4, Reagan and South America                   Wiarda, 3-26
       5, Reagan and Central America I               Wiarda, 27-196
       6, Cent. Am. in international politics         Wiarda, 197-382
       7, Cent. Am. in international politics
```

Fall, 1983
Wed. 2-5
Lib-S 4211

History 164 or
History 191Z

Leon G. Campbell
Lib-S 4138, Ext.
5420/5401
Office Hrs: W 1-2
and by appointment

Scope: History 164 (Inter-American Relations) reviews the history of relations between the nations of Latin America and the United States. To a lesser degree, it considers the relationships between Latin American nations themselves and their relationship to the rest of the world. Special attention will be paid to U.S. relationships with Cuba, Mexico, and Central America.

Readings: There are five required books for the class, which will be conducted on a lecture-discussion basis. Federico Gil, Latin-American-United States Relations (1971) and Alonso Aguilar, Pan-Americanism From Monroe to the Present: A View from the Other Side (1967) provide U.S. and Latin American perspectives which are quite opposed to one another. Lester Langley, The U.S. in the Caribbean in the Twentieth Century (Rev. Ed., 1982) offers a sound perspective on contemporary events in this troubled region, while Stephen Schlesinger and Stephen Kinzer, Bitter Fruit: The Untold Story of the American Coup in Guatemala (1982) provides a fascinating case study of one aspect of U.S. involvement in a single Central American country. Finally, Robert McBride, Ed., Mexico and the United States: Energy, Trade Investment, Immigration, Tourism (1982) treats several of the issues facing these two countries at the present.

Requirements: The class will be conducted on a lecture-discussion basis on Wednesday afternoon, 2-5 p.m. Each week students will be asked to complete the assigned readings on a particular topic. The necessity of reading and seriously considering the assigned material prior to class cannot be over-emphasized, as all lectures and discussion will be based on the assumption that this has been done.

The class will be conducted along the lines of the National Bipartisan Commission on Central America (you can think of me as "your" Henry Kissinger) in that each week we will approach a particular aspect of U.S.-Latin American relations from a variety of perspectives and write position papers on these topics (see course syllabus, attached). Grades will be based on 1) class attendance and discussion -- 20 per cent, 2) presentation of class reports on a particular topic -- 40 per cent, and 3) a final paper -- 40 per cent. There are no other examinations. Position papers are short statements about the topic under consideration, to be delivered in class (10-15 min.) and are not research papers, but simply based on the assigned readings and your own opinion. They will be assigned occasionally but no student will make more than two reports. The final paper is to be 10-15 pages in length and based on sources which you and I will agree on. The purpose is to give you experience in writing clear and logical, short analyses of contemporary and historical problems such as you will be asked to do in business, government, or academic life.

COURSE SCHEDULE

Sept. 28   I.   Introduction: U.S.-Latin American Relations
                  Gil, 3-27
                  Langley, 3-14

Oct. 5   II.   U.S.-Latin American Relations: Monroe Doctrine to the
                  Mexican War
                  Gil, 29-85
                  Aguilar, 9-30

Oct. 12   III. Intervention and Warfare in Latin America, 1904-1933:
                  The Panama Canal and After
                  Gil, 87-143
                  Aguilar, 31-66
                  Langley, 17-136

Oct. 19   IV.   Panamericanism, The Good Neighbor Policy, and Containment
                  Gil, 145-170
                  Aguilar, 67-79
                  Langley, 137-161

Oct. 26   V.   Latin America, the U.S. and World War II
                  Gil, 170-187
                  Aguilar, 80-86
                  Langley, 162-184

Nov. 2   VI.   Case Study: The U.S. and Guatemala, 1944-present
                  Schlesinger and Kinzer, Complete
                  Langley, 187-210
                  Aguilar, 87-105
                  Gil, 189-225

Nov. 9   VII. Case Study: The U.S., Cuba, and Fidel Castro
                  Gil, 227-238
                  Aguilar, 106-118
                  Langley, 211-233

Nov. 16   VIII. Inter-American Relations in the 1960s: The Alliance
                  for Progress, the Canal Issue, and Wars for National
                  Liberation
                  Langley, 234-267
                  Gil, 238-282
                  Aguilar, 118-154

Nov. 23   IX.   The U.S. and Mexico Since 1970: Problems and Prospects
                  McBride, Complete

Nov. 30   X.   The U.S. and Latin America Since 1970: Central America
                  and the Caribbean
                  Langley, 268-288
                  Aguilar, 155-167
                  Gil, 283-287

Mon. Dec. 5   Final Papers Due

INTER-AMERICAN RELATIONS
Spring 1985

History 384   Prof. Conniff
Mitchell 208   Mesa Vista 1118
MWF 8 am   hours MW 9:00, F 11

This course surveys relations among the Latin American nations
and with the Great Powers during the 19th and 20th centuries. We
first examine the tumultuous years after Independence, which saw
wars and continued imperial rivalry. Panamericanism also emerged
in this era. Then we turn to the period of United States imperialism and gunboat diplomacy, during which this country assumed
the role of protector in Central America and the Caribbean.
since the 1930s relations have become more complex, with the
advent of inter-American defense arrangements, the Cold War,
economic development aspirations, foreign investment and military
intervention. The last half of the course touches on special
Latin American features of diplomacy, such as guerrilla warfare,
common markets, and the Third World politics. The focus is on
ideas, economics, politics, and coercion rather than diplomacy
per se. The post-World War II section brings up economic relationships which shaped inter-American affairs.

The grade will be based on a midterm (worth 30% of the total
grade), a final (40%), and a 12-page term paper (30%).

Required reading:

        Harold E. Davis, et al., Latin American Diplomatic History
        Cole Blasier, The Hovering Giant

Recommended readings, on reserve at Zimmerman:

        Black, Latin America (anthology)
        Baily, United States & the Development of South America
                (economic policy)
        Mecham, United States & Inter-American Security (defense)
        Atkins, Latin America in the International Political System
                (survey)
        Wood, Making of the Good Neighbor Policy (1930s & 1940s)
        Levinson & Onis, Alliance that Lost its Way (1960s)
        Connell-Smith, The United States and Latin America (survey)

              Lectures and Discussion Schedule

Jan. 14   Introduction

     16   Monroe Doctrine   Davis, 1-3

     18   Early Panamericanism

     21   Manifest Destiny & the Mexican War   Davis, 4

                              122

	23	Transition from Nationhood to Internationalism	
	25	Balance of Power Politics	Davis, 5
	28	Paraguayan War	
	30	War of the Pacific	
Feb.	1	Panamericanism Yankee-style	
	4	United States Imperialism and the Spanish War	Davis, 6
	6	The Panama Canal	
	8	Backyard Imperialism	Blasier chs. 1-2
	11	ABC Powers against Imperialism	
	13	The United States and Mexico to 1910	
	15	Diplomacy of the Mexican Revolution	Blasier, 33-45, 71-86, 101-116
	18	Class Discussion	
	20	New Diplomacy in the 1920's	Davis, 7; Blasier 116-121
	22	The Sandino Affair	
	25	Roosevelt's Good Neighbor Policy	Wood, skim
	27	The Chaco War	
Mar.	1	Economic Aspects of the Good Neighbor Policy	Davis, 8; Blasier, 121-128
	4	Defense Aspects of the Good Neighbor Policy	Mecham, skim
	6	Latin America in World War II	Davis, 9
	8	MIDTERM EXAM	
	9	Spring Break	
	18	Transition to Peacetime	
	20	The Cold War and Rio Treaty	Davis, 10
	22	Discussion session: "Death of the Monroe Doctrine"	

	25	Organization of American States (OAS) vs. Peron	
	27	Latin american Development, Yankee-style	
	29	Development Ideas in Latin America	
Apr.	1	Frigid Fifties: Guatemalan Escapade	Blasier 46-68, 86-90
	3	Cuban Revolutionary Diplomacy	Blasier, 177-210
	5	Bay of Pigs and the Missile Crisis	
	8	Kennedy's Alliance for Progress	Davis, 11
	10	Disaffections with the Alliance	Levinson/Onis skim
	12	Economic Integration Attempts	PAPER DUE
	15	Class Discussion on economic programs	
	17	Crisis in the Dominican Republic	
	19	Rise of the Guerrillas	
	22	Inter-American Militarism	Blasier, ch. 7
	24	The Case of Chile	Blasier, ch. 8
	26	New Panama Canal Treaties	Black, ch. 19
	29	Brazil Super-Power	
May	1	Nicaraguan Revolution	
	3	Review Session	

Final Exam: Wed. May 8, 8-10 am   (bring bluebooks)

History 534--The US and Latin America -- Dr. Cooney -- Spring 1984

GENERAL INSTRUCTIONS

Instructor: Dr. J. W. Cooney
Office Hours: To be announced in class. Office Phone 588-6817. If you cannot make the announced office hours, please feel free to arrange an appointment with me. If an emergency arises and you have to phone me and should I not be in my office, please leave your name and phone number with the Secretary of the History Department (same phone number) and I will try to get back to you as rapidly as possible.

Texts: Wm. H. Goetzmann, When the Eagle Screamed: The Romantic Horizon in American Diplomacy, 1800-1860. Arthur P. Whitaker, The Western Hemisphere Idea: Its Rise and Decline. Robt. Freeman Smith, The United States and Latin American Sphere of Influence. Vol. I. The Era of Caribbean Intervention. 1890-1930. & Vol. II. Era of Good Nieghbors, Cold Warriors, and Hairshirts, 1930-1982.

The purpose of this course is to acquaint the student with the history of the United States Diplomatic Relations with Latin America. The Instructor will survey these relations from the late 1700's to the present.

You will be given various handouts. One will be a Topics-Reading Sheet which will inform you as to the various topics I will cover, and the readings from the texts that will accompany the lectures. You will receive a Book Review Instruction Sheet. You will receive a handout which will give you tips on taking my exams. You will receive a Bibliography of books in the University of Louisville Library concerning the USA and Latin America. You will also receive a map list and a practise map in preparation for your map quiz.

Pop Quizes can be given at the discretion of the instructor. Within the first three weeks of the course there will be an announced map quiz. You will be given a list of geographical locations of Latin America along with a practise map. Please use atlases, etc., to discover those locations. About two and a half weeks into the semester you will be quizzed on about twenty five of those locations taken at random. You will be supplied a map for the map quiz.

There will be three announced tests--two midterms and a final. They will be about 60 % essay and the remainder identifications. The midterms will count 100 points each, the final 200 points. I generally run my grading from about 87 to a 100 for an A, 77-86 for a B, 66-76 for a C, 54-65 for a D, and below an F. This holds for the overall grade in the semester as well as for the individual exams. Please use bluebooks and blue or black ink on the exams.

Undergraduate students will read four (4) books in the course of this semester dealing with the USA and Latin America. You will write a book review on all of these. The first two book reviews will be due about 7 weeks into the semester. The last two are due the last class day of the semester. You are given a book review sheet and a Bibliography as part of your handouts. Undergraduates may write a paper in place of the book reviews but must see me quickly about this. Graduate Students will write a 15-20 page, researched paper on some aspect of USA-Latin American relations. Graduate students should see me quickly as to topics.

Please use the office hours if you have problems. Remember that drops are your responsibility. Please feel free to ask questions in the class, and I will try to answer them as rapidly as possible. I don't like to give incompletes, but, if for one reason or another, you get one--remember, it is your responsibility to remove it. Plagiarism and cheating are grounds for dismissal from the class and the school. Get a copy of the Student Bill of Rights so you will know your rights and responsibilities. You can expect no more than a C for the semester if you do not do your book reviews or paper. That is regardless of what you make on the other exams. Please have assignments, etc., in on time. If not, you may be penalized. Makeups are possible for the Map Quiz and the three exams.. If you do not inform me ahead of time that you cannot make the final, then I have, by College Policy, no other choice than to give you an F for the course. I cannot discuss personal grades in class; see me in my office. I do not post or mail grades either.

Please attend regularly as much of the exams will come from the lectures. This is for your own good. I do not grade on attendance, but if you don't know the material from the lectures, you will do badly. If you borrow notes from a fellow student, give that student your name and phone number-- or better yet, just xerox them in the library.

Above all, always feel free to use my office hours and ask questions in class.

J. W. Cooney

History 534 (US and Latin America)--Spring 1984--Dr. Cooney

TOPICS READING SHEET

Below is a list of the topics which will be covered in this course. If there are any changes they will be announced.

TEXTS: Wm. H. Goetzman, When the Eagle Screamed: The Romantic Horizon In American Diplomacy, 1800-1860, Arthur P. Whitaker, The Western Hemisphere Idea: Its Rise and Decline. Robert F. Smith, The United States and Latin American Sphere of Influence. Vol I. The Era of Caribbean Intervention, 1890-1930. & Vol. II. Era of Good Neighbors, Cold Warriors, and Hairshirts, 1930-1982.

G = Goetzmann. W = Whitaker. S I or S II = Smith.

1. Introduction and Orientation. G xiii-xvii & W 1-21.

2. The Spanish Question. G 1-11.

3. Transcontinental Treaty and Latin American Recognition. G 11-16 & W 22-40.

4. Monroe Doctrine. G 16-20.

5. Manifest Destiny and Mexico. G 21-73.

6. Filibusters and Isthmian Problem. G 74-106 & S I 51-55.

7. Civil War and French in Mexico. Lectures only.

8. Grant, the Caribbean & Post Civil War Latin American Policy. S I 1-7 & W 41-60.

9. Pan American Movement. W 61-85 & S I 56-59.

10. Venezuelan Crisis and Redefining the Monroe Doctrine. S I 7-11, 39-40.

11. Cuba and the New Imperialism. S I 11-17, 41-43.

12. Building the Canal. S I 17-18, 75-83.

13. Roosevelt Corollary and Dollar Diplomacy. W 86-107 & S I 18-21, 44-47, 60-65, 83-85.

14. The Brazailian Connection. Lectures only.

15. The USA and the Mexican Revolution. W 108-130.

16. Wilson and Missionary Diplomacy. S I 21-24, 86-91.

17. USA, Latin America, & World War I. S I 24-27.

18. USA & Latin America in the 1920's. S I 27-33, 37-38, 66-68, 69-71, 92-96.

19. Good Neighbor Policy. W 133-153. S II vii-18, 115-117.

20. USA, Latin America and World War II. W 154-177 & S II 18-23.

21. USA, Latin America and the Cold War. S II 24-47, 118-125.

22. Cuba and Alliance for Progress. S II 48-66, 126-129, 130-132.

23. The 1970's. S II 67-86, 133-137, 139-143.

24. The 1980's. S II 87-101, 144-147.

LATIN AMERICAN REVOLUTIONS
Professor Thomas Benjamin
Course Syllabus

Objectives

We will have two objectives this semester. First, we will attempt to better
understand social revolution as a modern historical phenomenon. We will
consider such questions as: What characterizes a social revolution? Under
what conditions do social revolutions succeed in overthrowing the established
social-political order? What kind of social-political order emerges from
social revolutions? Second, we will attempt to better understand three
important revolutions in twentieth century Latin American history, the revolutions
of Mexico, Cuba, and Central America with particular emphasis upon Nicaragua.
We will consider such questions as: Are these revolutions truly social
revolutions? What conditions led to the overthrow of the old order? How
has the United States, the dominant power in the region, influenced the course
of these revolutions? What has changed as a result of revolution and how do
you judge these changes?

Why study Latin American revolutions? Latin revolutions have generally been
aimed as much against the United States as against local tyrannies. As citizens
of a democracy, tax payers, and potential soldiers we have a duty to understand
conflicts that affect our nation and state. As citizens of the most powerful
and influential state in the hemisphere we have a moral responsibility to
understand how the United States has affected Latin American nations and work
to change US policy if we see such a need.

Guidelines

Format: My role as instructor is to guide your learning - to set directions,
to insure some continuity and a forward motion in our study, and in general to
provide a framework that will lead to a useful outcome of the efforts we will
all make. Your role is to assume responsibility for expanding your own knowledge
and improving your ability to think critically and express your judgments clearly.
I do my best in the classroom and I expect my students to do the same. This
can be done only by careful week-by-week preparation and participation, by
being present, and by being prepared to the best extent that your time permits.
Class meetings will be devoted to discussion, debate, and friendly disagreement
over selected readings. Please consider attendance to be obligatory.

Evaluation: In many ways it would be a happier situation if neither you nor I
had to worry about grades. But we do, and the responsibility for giving you a
grade is mine. There are no examinations in this class. Instead, I assign
three review essays. These essays, which are due at the conclusion of each
section, should discuss the most important issues involved in each revolution,
concisely review the literature and conflicting interpretations, and conclude
with your best judgment of that revolution. These essays should be typed,
literate, and no less than 10 or no more than 15 pages in length. These essays
will account for approximately 25% of the final course grade. The remaining
25% of the course grade is based upon attendance and active and informed participation
in class discussions.

Miscellaneous: Plagiarism is not tolerated. Students found plagiarizing each
other or published authors will be expelled from the class, assigned a failing
grade for the class, and reported to the Office of Student Life. Papers turned in
late will not be accepted unless accompanied by documentation of some
catastrophic problem.

History 362

Consultation: My office is 120 Anspach and my telephone number is 3454.
I will announce in class the times in which I will be there on   regular basis
and I am always available by prior appointment. We will hold periodic individual
tutorial sessions, one per section, devoted to discussion of the readings and
the review essays. Feel free to drop in and talk and do not hesitate to bring
to my attention any problems you may have with any aspect of the course.

COURSE OUTLINE

Week 1:
January 15-17

Introduction

Week 2:
January 22/24

What is Revolution?
"Revolution," two short articles from
social science dictionaries.
Krammick, "Reflections on Revolution."
Skocpol, "Explaining Social Revolutions."
Cumberland, "Twentieth-Century Revolutions..."
Lodge, "Revolutions in Latin America."
Lewis, "The Roots of Revolution."

THE MEXICAN REVOLUTION

Week 3:
January 29/31

Origins and Initiation
Benjamin, "Approaching the Porfiriato."
Smith, "Mexico and Revolution."
Goldfrank, "Theories of Revolution."
Ruiz, The Great Rebellion, Chs. 1-3.
Gilly, The Mexican Revolution, Chs. 1-2.

Week 4:
February 5/7

The Violent Decade
Knight, "The Mexican Revolution."
Bazant, "Civil War, 1910-1920."
Ruiz, The Great Rebellion, Chs. 10, 12, 13.
Gilly, The Mexican Revolution, Chs. 3-9.

Week 5:
February 12/14

The Revolution Domesticated
Bazant, "Social Reforms, 1920-1940."
Benjamin, "The Leviathan on the Zocalo."
Riding, "From Revolution to Institution."
"Mexico in Revolution," Fortune (1938).
Cosio Villegas, "Mexico's Crisis."
Cosio Villegas, "The Mexican Revolution Then
and Now."

Week 6:
February 19/21

Significance and Meaning
Benjamin and Ocasio, "Organizing the Memory
of Modern Mexico."
Calvert, "The Mexican Revolution: Theory/Fact?"
Womack, "The Spoils of the Mexican Revolution."
Goldfrank, "Theories of Revolution...."

THE CUBAN REVOLUTION

Week 7:
February 26/28

Origins and Initiation
Thomas, "The Origins of the Cuban Revolution,"
and Castro, "The Problem of Cuba," both in
Goodsell, ed., Fidel Castro's Personal
Revolution in Cuba.
Franqui, Family Portrait with Fidel, Ch. 1.
Halperin, The Rise and Decline of Fidel
Castro, Chs. 1-8.

Week 8:
March 5/7

The Struggling Revolution
Halperin, The Rise and Decline, Chs. 9-31.
Chapman, "The First Ten Years,"
and Thomas, "A Summing Up at 10," in
Goodsell, ed., Fidel Castro's Personal Revolutio

Week 9:
March 12/14

Spring Break

Week 10:
March 19-21

Stabilization and Sovietization
Goytisolo, "20 Years of Castro's Revolution."
Walters, "Interview with Fidel."
Dominguez, "Cuban Foreign Policy."
Radosh, "In the Paws of the Bear."
Mesa-Lago, "Evaluation of Socioeconomic
Performace," in The Economy of Socialist
Cuba, Ch. 8.
LeoGrande, "Cuba," in Marxist Governments.

Week 11:
March 26/28

Significance and Meaning
Steif, "Castro's Quarter Century."
Falcoff, "Thinking About Cuba."
Horowitz, "Cuba and the Caribbean."
Philipson, "'The Smile of Lenin': Inside
Cuba's Revolution."
Thomas, "The Revolution on Balance."
Kirkpatrick, "Cuba and Cubans."
Womack, "The Revolution Tightens its Belt."

CENTRAL AMERICAN REVOLUTIONS

Week 12:
April 2/4

Origins and the United States Role
LaFeber, Inevitable Revolutions: The United
States in Central America, Chs. 1-4.

Week 13:
April 9/11

Nicaragua: The Overthrow of Somoza
Fagen, "Dateline Nicaragua: The End of the Affai
LeoGrande, "The Revolution in Nicaragua:
Another Cuba?"
Shirley Christian, "Covering the Sandinistas."
Relevant sections in LaFeber.

Week 14:
April 16/18

Nicaragua: Los Muchachos in Power
Christian, "Freedom and Unfreedom in Nicaragua."
Cruz, "Nicaragua's Imperiled Revolution."
Radosh, "Nicaragua's Drift."
Gleijeses, "Resist Romanticism."

Week 15:
April 23/25

El Salvador: The Unfinished Revolution
Allman, "Rising to Rebellion: Inside
El Salvador."
Dickey, "The Truth about the Death Squads."
Christian, "El Salvador's Left."
Womack, "El Salvador and the Central
American War."
LeoGrande, "A Splendid Little War: Drawing
the Line in El Salvador."

Week 16:
April 30/May 2

Significance and Meaning
Chace, Endless War.
LeFeber, Inevitable Revolutions, Ch. 5.
Pastor, "Our Real Interests in Central America."
Menges, "Central America and Its Enemies"
Feinburg, "Central America: No Easy Answers."
"Can the U.S. Live with Latin Revolution?"

BIBLIOGRAPHY

Assigned Texts:

Adolfo Gilly, *The Mexican Revolution,* 1971, 1983.
Maurice Halperin, *The Rise and Decline of Fidel Castro,* 1972, 1974.
Walter LaFeber, *Inevitable Revolutions,* 1983, 1984.
James Chace, *Endless War,* 1984.

Assigned Readings:

Many of our reading assignments are on library reserve. The listings are
in the library reserve card catalogue under my name and this course number.
To look up the articles and chapters of books for any particular week,
first find the author's last name and then the title which should be organized
alphabetically by author. For the convenience of your fellow students,
please take only one article at a time from the library reserve. Report any
problems you may have with any assigned reading (missing pages, unreadable
copy, etc.) to me as soon as possible.

The following bibliography is organized according to course section. The
titles appear in the order listed in the syllabus. At times it may be
convenient to look up the journal or magazine article in the stacks.

REVOLUTION:

"Revolution," from Julius Gould and William Kolb, eds., *A Dictionary of the
Social Sciences,* 1964.

"Revolution," from Michael Mann, ed., *The International Encyclopedia of
Sociology,* 1984.

Issac Kramnick, "Reflections on Revolution: Definition and Explanation in
Recent Scholarship," *History and Theory,* Vol. XI (1972): 26-63.

Theda Skocpol, "Explaining Social Revolutions: Alternatives to Existing Theories,"
Chapter 1 of *States and Social Revolutions: A Comparative Analysis of
France, Russia, and China,* 1979.

Charles C. Cumberland, "Twentieth-Century Revolutions in Latin America,"
The Centennial Review, Vol. VI (Summer 1962): 279-296.

George C. Lodge, "Revolution in Latin America," *Foreign Affairs,* Vol. 44,
(January 1966): 173-197.

Flora Lewis, "The Roots of Revolution," *The New York Times Magazine,* November 11,
1984.

Additional Suggestions:

Peter Calvert, *Revolution,* 1970.

Lawrence Stone, "Theories of Revolution," *World Politics,* Vol. XVIII
(January 1966): 159-176.

Michael Walzer, "A Theory of Revolution," *Marxist Perspectives,* Vol. II,
(Spring 1979): 30-44.

THE MEXICAN REVOLUTION:

Thomas Benjamin, "Introduction: Approaching the Porfiriato," in Benjamin and William McNellie, eds. *Other Mexicos: Essays on Regional Mexican History* (1984): 3-25.

Robert Freeman Smith, "Mexico and Revolution," in *The United States and Revolutionary Nationalism in Mexico, 1916-1932* (1972): 1-22.

Walter L. Goldfrank, "Theories of Revolution and Revolution without Theory: The Case of Mexico," *Theory and Society*, Vol. 7 (January-March 1979): 135-165.

Ramon Eduardo Ruiz, *The Great Rebellion: Mexico, 1905-1924* (1980).

Alan Knight, "The Mexican Revolution," *History Today* (May 1980):28-34.

Jan Bazant, Ch. 5 "Civil War, 1910-1920," and Ch. 6 "Social Reforms, 1920-1940," in *A Concise History of Mexico from Hidalgo to Cardenas, 1805-1940* (1977).

Thomas Benjamin, "The Leviathan on the Zocalo: Recent Historiography on the Post-Revolutionary Mexican State," forthcoming in *Latin American Research Review* (1985)

Alan Riding, "From Revolution to Institution," Ch. 3 in *Distant Neighbors: A Portrait of the Mexicans* (1985).

"Mexico in Revolution," *Fortune* (1938).

Daniel Cosio Villegas, "Mexico's Crisis," and "The Mexican Revolution Then and Now," in Stanley R. Ross, ed., *Is The Mexican Revolution Dead?* (1966, 1975).

Thomas Benjamin and Marcial Ocasio-Melendez, "Organizing the Memory of Modern Mexico: Porfirian Historiography in Perspective, 1880s-1980s," *Hispanic American Historical Review*, Vol. 64 (May 1984): 323-364.

Peter Calvert, "The Mexican Revolution: Theory or Fact?" *Journal of Latin American Studies*, Vol. 1 (May 1961): 51-68.

John Womack, Jr., "The Spoils of the Mexican Revolution," *Foreign Affairs* (July 1970): 677-687.

THE CUBAN REVOLUTION:

James Nelson Goodsell, ed., *Fidel Castro's Personal Revolution in Cuba: 1959-1973* (1975).

Carlos Franqui, *Family Portrait with Fidel* (1984).

Juan Goytisolo, "20 Years of Castro's Revolution," *The New York Review of Books*, March 22, 1979, pp. 17-23.

Barbara Walters, "An Interview with Fidel Castro," *Foreign Policy* (1977): 22-51.

Jorge I. Dominguez, "Cuban Foreign Policy," *Foreign Affairs*

Ronald Radosh, "In the Paws of the Bear," *The New Republic*, August 22 & 29, 1981, pp. 36-39.

Carmelo Mesa-Lago, *The Economy of Socialist Cuba: A Two-Decade Appraisal* (1981).

William LeoGrande, "Republic of Cuba," Chapter 9 in Bogdan Szajkowski, ed., *Marxist Governments: A World Survey. Volume 2: Cuba-Mongolia* (1981): 237-259.

William Steif, "Castro's Quarter Century," *The Progressive,* Vol. 47 (December 1983): 32-35.

Mark Falcoff, "Thinking about Cuba: Unscrambling Cuban Messages," *Washington Quarterly,* Vol. 6 (Spring, 1983).

Irving Louis Horowitz, "Cuba and the Caribbean," *Worldview,* Vol. 26 (December 1983): 19-21.

Lorrin Philipson, "'The Smile of Lenin': Inside Cuba's Revolution," *Of Human Rights,* Vol. 4 (Winter 1981): 17-20.

Hugh Thomas, "The Revolution on Balance," Reprint of the Cuban American National Foundation, 1983.

Jean Kirkpatrick, "Cuba and Cubans," Reprint of the Cuban American National Foundation, 1983.

John Womack, Jr., "The Revolution Tightens Its Belt," *The New Republic,* May 31, 1980, pp. 19-23.

CENTRAL AMERICAN REVOLUTIONS:

Richard R. Fagen, "Dateline Nicaragua: The End of the Affair," *Foreign Policy,* (Fall 1979): 178-191.

William M. LeoGrande, "The Revolution in Nicaragua: Another Cuba?" *Foreign Affairs,* (Fall 1979): 28-50.

Shirley Christian, "Covering the Sandinistas," *Washington Journalism Review,* (March 1982):33-38.

Shirley Christian, "Freedom and Unfreedom in Nicaragua," in Marvin Gettleman, et. al., eds., *El Salvador: Central America in the New Cold War* (1981).

Arturo J. Cruz, "Nicaragua's Imperiled Revolution," *Foreign Affairs,* (Summer 1983): 1031-1047.

Ronald Radosh, "Nicaragua's Drift," *The New Republic,* October 24, 1983, pp. 7-12.

Piero Gleijeses, "Resist Romanticism," *Foreign Policy,* 54 (Spring 1984): 122-138.

T.D. Allman, "Rising to Rebellion," *Harper's* (March 1981): 31-50.

Christopher Dicky, "Behind the Death Squads," *The New Republic,* December 26, 1983, pp. 16-21.

John Womack, Jr., "El Salvador and the Central American War: Interview with John Womack, Jr." *Socialist Review,*

William LeoGrande, "A Splendid Little War: Drawing the Line in El Salvador," in Marvin Gettleman, et. al., eds., *El Salvador: Central America in the New Cold War* (1981).

Robert A. Pastor, "Our Real Interests in Central America," *The Atlantic Monthly,* (July 1982): 27-39.

Richard E. Feinberg, "Central America: No Easy Answers," *Foreign Affairs,* (Summer 1981): 1121-1146.

"Can the U.S. Live with Latin Revolution?" *Harper's* (June 1984): 35-48.

LATIN AMERICA: REFORM AND REVOLUTION

History 8A   Fall 1984
Prof. E. Bradford Burns

The lectures, movies and discussions in this introductory course will provide
you with a general view of the historical development of Latin America.
Through an emphasis on the major forces that shaped and now are reshaping Latin
America, the course will attempt to present the basic materials to help you to
better understand contemporary Latin America, to gain a deeper insight into the
historcial reasons for the present problems which trouble the area. The
implantation of Iberian institutions, the challenges to those institutions, the
efforts at modernization, and the struggles for and against change will be
among the themes covered during the quarter.

LECTURE TOPICS AND READING ASSIGNMENTS

Dates: October 1-3-5
Topic: Introducing contemporary Latin America. The enigma of mass poverty
         within potential wealth. The concept of dependency and its use as an
         interpretive tool.
Read: Burns, 1-23; Davis, 1-111

Dates: October 8-10-12
Topic: Introducing the Latin American past. The ingredients for a new
         civilization, Indians, Europeans. and Africans, mix together in a vast
         and varied hemisphere.
Read: Burns, 23-62;Davis, 111-169

Dates: October 15-17
Topic: The Presence of the Past. The inheritance in modern times of
         fundamental institutions from the Iberian past.
Read: Burns, 62-119

FIRST PAPER DUE ON OCTOBER 15

Dates: October 19-22
Topic: The consolidation of the past. Independence brought minimal changes to
         Latin America in the 19th century.
Read: Burns, 119-153

Dates: October 24-26
Topic: Cultural conflict. The drive for modernization and its consequences:
         folk versus elite cultures.
Read: Lopez y Fuentes, entire book

Dates: October 29-31; November 2
Topic: Revolutionary change: Mexico. The Mexican Revolution is a landmark in
         its efforts to break with the past and create a new series of
         institutions.
Read: Burns, 153-199

SECOND PAPER DUE ON NOVEMBER 5

Dates: November 5-7-9-12-14
Topic: Revolutionary Change: Guatemala, Bolivia, Cuba, & Nicaragua. Their
         efforts to change, their accomplishments and their failures.
Read: Burns, 199-263; Collins, entire book.

Dates: November 16-18
Topic: Populism. Guiding society and including the masses in government,
         populism tries to maintain order while introducing change.
Read: Lernoux, 3-134

Dates: November 21-26-28
Topic: Change by reform. Latin Americans also tried to reform inherited
         institutions. The Chilean and Uruguayan examples have not been
         successful.
Read: Burns, 263-278; lernoux, 137-310

Dates: December 2-5
Topic: The Unites States and Latin America. The Unites States has played a
         critical role in the affairs of Latin America during the past century.
         It eschews revolution but fails to support reform.
Read: Burns, 281-287; Lernoux, 313-461

Dates: December 7
Topic: The challenge of change. Has the response to the challenge of change
         been adequate?
Read: Burns, 287-292

FINAL EXAM ON THURSDAY, DECEMBER 13, 8:00 am - 11:00 am

_____

The following books are available from the Student Store:

1. E. Bradford Burns, Latin America. A Concise, Interpretive History
2. Shelton H. Davis, Victims of the Miracle. Development and the Indians of
                       Brazil
3. Gregorio López y Fuentes, El Indio
4. Joseph Collins, What Difference Could a Revolution Make?
5. Penny Lernoux, Cry of the People

Copies of these texts will be on reserve in the College Library Reserve Section.

If you wish to consult conventional and traditional Latin American History
texts, you should check out of the library one of these two:

Herbert Herring, A History of Latin America
John Fagg, Latin America: A General History

If you find that you are having any difficulty following the continuity of Latin American history, I recommend that you supplement your assigned reading with the appropriate sections from Herring or Fagg. These two texts also present a different perspective of Latin American history from that to which the student is exposed in the lectures and assigned reading. Suggestions for other paperback books you might find interesting may be found on pp. 300-303 of the Burns' text.

To achieve maximum benefit from the lectures and to be able to enter into discussion, you are urged to read the assignments prior to the first date listed for that assignment.

FILM SCHEDULE

October   5   Americas in Transition (29 min.) Note: this film will be screened
              a second time on October 10 at 4:00 pm, room to be announced.
October   31 The Ragged Revolution (37 min.)
November 2   The Frozen Revolution (55 min.)
November 12 Cuba: Bay of Pigs (25 min.)
November 18 Peron and Evita (25 min.)
December 5   El Salvador. Another Vietnam (50 min.)

THE DISCUSSION SECTIONS: SOME ADVICE AND SUGGESTIONS

Each student has enrolled in a discussion section and should attend that section regularly. Participation in the discussions can constitute one part of the final grade for the course. The following remarks are made with the hope of making the discussions an important and meaningful experience for each student.

Classroom discussions are not the same as casual conversations, bull sessions or therapy sessions. Discussions often fail because students expect too much to come out of discussions too easily. Discussions also fail when students have not read the assignments and thus have nothing to contribute. Students should be aware that discussion is more demanding and frustrating than copying down lecture notes. The purpose of a discussion meeting is to interpret, analyze, organize, integrate and question the lectures and readings. Questioning is fundamental to participating in a discussion. Since the ability to ask the right question is an important part of education, the student should learn to ask them him/herself.

The discussion should not be the place to present new material. However, it is the place for students to present their varying views on the subject under discussion. In fact, the success of a discussion session depends to a large extent on the students' willingness to contribute their views and discuss those of others.

137

OTHER SUGGESTIONS

Learn the name of your teaching assistant, his/her office hours, and the location of the office. Sometime during the first two weeks visit your teaching assistant in his/her office for a few minutes to become acquainted. Your TA is an extremely valuable resource person.

Further, "A Glossary of Concepts and Terms," pp.297-299 of Burns, provides definitions of the most difficult concepts and terms used not only in the text but in the lectures. Acquaint yourself with these concepts and terms as they are used in History 8A. More importantly, you should begin to pepper your own discussions and essays with them.

The book Store will also sell a very brief History 8A: A Student Guide. It provides a reading guide for several of the assigned texts. It also discusses the two writing assignments and will be useful -- nay, essential -- in preparing the type of papers this course requires.

PAPERS AND FINAL EXAM

Students will write two papers of five pages each, typed and double-spaced. They are due on October 15 and November 5. Two points will be subtracted from the grade for each day the paper is late. See History 8A: A Student Guide for details on these writing assignments.

There will be a final exam on Thursday, December 13, 8:00 - 11:00 am. Bring bluebooks with you. Note: There will be no make-up exam. No INCOMPLETE will be given in this course.

GRADE

The final grade for History 8A will be computed as follows:

Each paper	20%	(total 40%)
Final Exam	50%	
Discusson participation	10%	

OFFICE HOURS

I will hold my office hours in Bunche 5361 on Monday, 11:00 - 11:45 am, and Wednesday, 2:00 - 3:00 pm, and Friday, 10:30 - 11:45 am or by appointment.

E. Bradford Burns

History 6361x, Revolution in Latin America
M-F, 9-12, Soc. Sci. 312

The focus of this intensive course in revolution and reaction in Latin America in the twentieth century. It is not intended to cover every event or country. Rather, we will take a look at some of the problems and groups common to all Latin America, as well as special cases. Cuba and Central America will receive indepth coverage, as will the relationship between the U.S. and Latin America. The goal of this course is to introduce students to common themes in Latin American history and current events; to teach students how to understand different historical interpretations of the same incident and to provide the opportunity to write book reviews on topics relative to revolutionary Latin America. The required reading is available at the bookstore in paperback:

De Jesús, Child of the Dark; The Diary of Carolina de Jesus
Guevara, Guerrilla Warfare
LaFeber, Inevitable Revolutions

In addition all students will have to write a short book review to be handed in by June 3. No late papers will be accepted.

In order to follow the lectures, it is vital that you become familiar with the geography of Latin America. You should have a map of Latin America and be able to identify and spell correctly countries and capitals.

There will be a midterm on May 30 and a takehome exam that will be handed out on June 6 and due at 11 a.m. on June 8 in my office, Soc. Sci. 129. Exams will be typewritten or carefully handwritten and will not exceed 15 pages, double-spaced.

ASSIGNMENTS

May 30   Introduction to Latin American revolutions: Film, The Frozen
          Revolution

May 21   Early U.S.-Latin American Relations
          LaFeber, Intro. and Ch. 1

May 22   Important factors in Latin America: Population pressures
          Film: Los Olividados. Begin Child of the Dark

May 24   Social Revolution in the 1950s: Bolivia and Guatemala
          Films: Cuba, Bay of Pigs; Frontline: Cuba

May 27   No Class

May 28   Cuba since the Revolution Film: The CIA's Secret Army

May 29   The Exportation of Guerrilla War from Cuba: Discussion,
          Guerilla Warfare; Film: Report from Cuba

May 30   Response to Guerrilla Warfare: the rise of military
          dictatorship Film: Brazil, the Rude Awakening- 1 hour midterm

139

May 31   Revolution and Reaction in Uruguay Film: State of Siege

June 3   Revolution and reaction in Chile Film: Missing

June 4   Revolution and reaction in Central America- historical origins
            Film: frontline-Central America

June 5   Nicaragua in Revolution Film: Central America in Revolution

June 6   El Salvador in Revolution--La Feber book should be read by
            this time. Take home final will be handed out.

June 8   Take home final due, Soc. Sci. 129, 11 a.m.

The University of Alabama in Birmingham

MARXIST REVOLUTIONS IN LATIN AMERICA

Professor Pang

Textbooks

Cole Blasier. The Giant's Rival: The USSR•and Latin America.
C. Blasier & C. Mesa-Lago, eds. Cuba in the World.
Marvin E. Gettleman, et al. El Salvador: Central America in the New Cold War.
Paul Sigmund. The Overthrow of Allende and the Politics of Chile.

Course Requirements
   (a) Two Exams: Mid-Term and Final
   (b) Graduate Credit: A short paper or review essay

Lectures and Discussions

Part I: The U.S. and Latin America's Early Marxist Movements

   1.   Appeals of Marxism to Latin America
   2.   Guatemala, 1944-1954: A National Revolution vs. Sovietization
   3.   The U,S., Cold War, and Domino Doctrine

Readings:
   Required: Gettleman, Part I-Chaps 1-2

   Recommended:
   Robert J. Alexader. Communism in Latin America.
   Robert J. Alexander. Trotskyism in Latin America.
   Ronald Schneider. Communism in Guatemala.
   Susanne Jonas & David Tobis, eds. Guatemala.

Part II: Cuba: From the American Legacy to the Sovietization of the Island

   4.   The Americanization of Cuban Economy
   5.   The Making of the Revolution
   6.   Fidel's Cuba, Cuba's Castro: the caudillos and ideology
   7.   The Sovietization of Cuba: Marxism, Stalinism, or state capitalism
   8.   Cuba Challenges the U.S. in Africa and Latin America

Readings:
   Required: Blasier & Mesa-Lago, Chaps. 1-6, 9-11, 13, 15

   Recommended:
   Elie Abel. The Missile Crisis.
   Edward Boorstein. The Economic Transformation of Cuba.
   Jorge Domínguez. Cuba: Order and Prevolution.
   Theodore Draper. Castroism: Theory and Practice.
   René Dumont. Cuba: Socialism and Development.
   Richard R. Fagen. The Transformation of Political Culture in Cuba.
   Maurice Halpern. The Rise and Decline of Fidel Castro.
   Neill Macaulay. A Rebel in Cuba.
   Hugh Thomas. The Cuban Revolution.

Part III: Chile: From Christian Democracy to Marxism-Socialism

9. The Road to Allende's Revolution: The Frei Years
10. The Unidad Popular Government: Failure of the Left
11. Social and Economic Revolution: From Marxism to Confusion
12. Nixon, CIA, and the September 1973 Coup

Readings:
Required: Sigmund, whole book

Recommended:
Salvador Allende Gossens. Chile's Road to Socialism.
Edward Boorstein. An Inside View--Allende's Chile.
Stefan de Vylder. Allende's Chile.
Richard E. Feinberg. The Triumph of Allende: Chile's Legal Revolution.
Jay Kinsbruner. Chile: A Historical Interpretation.
Brian Loveman. Struggle in the Countryside: Politics and Rural Labor in Chile.
Brian Loveman. Chile: The Legacy of Hispanic Capitalism.
Robert Moss. Chile's Marxist Experiment.
James Petras. The United States and Chile: Imperialism and the Overthrow of the Allende Regime.
Barbara Stalling. Class Conflict and Economic Development in Chile, 1958-1973.
Kyle Steenland. Agrarian Reform under Allende.

Part IV: The United States, Soviet Union, and Revolutions in Central America

13. The Reagan Administration and New Cold War
14. Many Faces of the Revolution: The Case of Nicaragua
15. Two Faces of the Revolution: The Case of El Salvador
16. Human Rights vs. Cold War in Latin America: Future Options?
17. The Soviet Union, Cuba, and Third Worldism in Latin America
18. Review

Readings:
Required: Balsier, whole book; Gettleman, Parts III & IV

Recommended:
Thomas P. Anderson. Politics in Central America: Guatemala, El Salvador, Honduras, and Nicaragua.
Cole Blasier. The Hovering Giant: U. S. Response to Revolutionary Change in Latin America.
Zbigniew Brzezinski. Between Two Ages: America's Role in the Technetronic Era.
Zbigniew Brzezinski. Power and Principle: Memoirs of the National Security Adviser 1977-1981.
Richard Fagen & Olga Pellicer, eds. The Future of Central America: Policy Choices for the United States and Mexico.
Jeane J. Kirkpatrick. Dictatorships and Double Standards: Rationalism & Reason in Politics.
Walter LaFeber. Inevitable Revolutions: The United States in Central America.
Walter LaFeber, ed. America in the Cold War: Twenty-Years of Revolution and Response.

History 441   Thomas E. Skidmore
"Revolution and Conflict in Twentieth-Century Latin America"

This semester History 441 will focus entirely on the Cuban Revolution: its origins and its development.

I. Colonial and Nineteenth-Century Background

Aug 29: Introductory
Aug 31: The Early Centuries: Spanish Settlement and European Rivalries
Sep 2: Spanish Colonial Institutions in Cuba.

Sep 5: Labor Day
Sep 7: The Nineteenth Century: The Rise of Sugar
Sep 9: The African Presence.

Sep 12: 1860-1895: Agonies of a Rebellious Colony.

Required Reading:

Rius, Cuba for Beginners, entire.

Thomas E. Skidmore and Peter H. Smith, "Cuba: Late Colony, First
   Socialist State," a chapter from Modern Latin America (to be
   published by Oxford University Press in December 1983).

Of Human Rights: A Report on the Human Condition in Cuba, vol. 4, No.
   1 (Winter 1981), published by Georgetown University.

Fidel Castro, Main Report: Second Congress of the Communist Party of
   Cuba (Cuba Update, Vol. II, No. 1, March 1981)--publication of the
   Center for Cuban Studies in New York City.

II. The Cuban Republics

Sep 14: José Martí: Apostle of Nationalism.

Sep 19: 1895-1902: From Spanish Colony to U.S. Protectorate (Title of book for
Sep 21: 1902-1933: A Sugar Republic in the Shadow of   book report due)
                     Uncle Sam.

Sep 26: The Revolution that Failed: 1933-34.

Required Reading:

Ramon Ruiz, Cuba: The Making of a Revolution, entire.

Sep 28: Batista and U.S. Hegemony: 1934-52
Sep 30: "Cuban Encounter" (videotape).

Oct 3: The Cuban Economy of the 1950's
Oct 5: 1952-59: The Dictatorship and the Insurrection
Oct 7: Review.

Oct 10: Six Weeks Exam.

Required Reading:

Hugh Thomas, The Cuban Revolution, 3-252; 311-409.

III. The Cuban Revolution: The Heroic Years

    Oct 12: Guest Lecture
    Oct 14: A Nationalist Revolution Takes Shape: 1959.

    Oct 17: The Turn to Socialism and the East: 1960
    Oct 19: The Bay of Pigs: Graveyard of the Exiles.

    Required Reading:

        Thomas, The Cuban Revolution, 255-308; 413-593.

        Oscar Lewis, Ruth M. Lewis, and Susan Rigdon, Four Women: Living the
           Revolution, ix-xxxviii; 3-125; 129-219.

    Oct 24: Consolidating the Social Revolution: 1961-63 (Book report due).
    Oct 26: Applying the Soviet Model, 1961-63 (Topic for paper due).

    Oct 31: Guest Lecture
    Nov 2: Pragmatic Interlude, 1963-66
    Nov 4: The "New Man": Moral Incentives Under Socialism.

    Nov 7: Exporting the Revolution
    Nov 9: Ché Guevara: Death in the Altiplano.

    Required Reading:

        Lee Lockwood, Castro's Cuba, Cuba's Fidel, entire.
        Max Azicri, "Women's Development Through Revolutionary Mobilization: A
           Study of the Federation of Cuban Women," in Horowitz, ed., Cuban
           Communism, 276-308.
        Robert M. Bernardo, "Moral Stimulation and Labor Allocation in Cuba,"
           in Horowitz, ed., Cuban Communism, 185-218.

IV. The Cuban Revolution: Facing Realities

    Nov 14: 1970: Back to Orthodoxy (Paper due).
    Nov 16: The Arts and the Revolution: Creativity and Conformity.

    Nov 21: "People's Power" and the Military: Key Institutions
    Nov 23: Cuba's African Ventures.

    Nov 28: The Cubans Who Flee
    Nov 30: What Future for the Revolution?

    Dec 5: Guest Lecture
    Dec 7: The U.S. and Cuba
    Dec 9: Review and Overview.

    Required Reading:

        Thomas, The Cuban Revolution, 594-720.
        Fidel Castro Speeches vol. II: Our Power is that of the Working People:
           Building Socialism in Cuba (New York: Pathfinder Press, 1983), 7-24;
           91-136; 154-214; 280-298; 316-358.
        Carmelo Mesa-Lago, "The Economy: Caution, Frugality and Resilient Ideology,"
           Jorge J. Dominguez, ed., Cuba: Internal and International Affairs, 113-166
        William M. Leogrande, "Foreign Policy: The Limits of Success," in Dominguez,
           ed., Cuba: Internal and International Affairs, 167-192.
        Irving L. Horowitz, ed., Cuban Communism, 355-365; 469-504; 603-658; 674-681.
        Howard and Nancy Handelman, "Cuba Today: Impressions of the Revolution in
           its Twentieth Year," American Universities Field Staff: Reports (1979).

        Jeane J. Kirkpatrick, Cuba and the Cubans (speech given October 22, 1982).

History 441 - Sem 1, 1983

Lectures and Discussions:

This course meets three times a week, Monday, Wednesday, and Friday at 11:00. Normally
there will be two lectures and one discussion per week, with the discussions usually during
the class hour on Friday. Some variations are noted on the syllabus and others will be
announced in advance. Students can expect to have ample opportunity to discuss the lecture
and reading material.

Course Requirements:

Undergraduates:

There will be a six-weeks examination and a final examination. (The format of the
exam--take-home or classroom--will be discussed in class.) Undergraduates will also
be required to write a book report and a short paper.

The book report should be a critical analysis of the author's assumptions, line of
argument, evidence used, and conclusions. The book is to be chosen by the student
and should be a significant work not included among the required reading for the
course. Many appropriate titles may be found in the footnotes and bibliographies
which will be distributed. The choice of book must be approved by the instructor,
who will be happy to make suggestions of books that correspond to areas of special
interest. The book report should be approximately 4-6 pages long.

The paper is to be on a topic of student's choosing, and should be approximately 10
pages long. The paper should draw on several secondary sources and present an
original interpretation of the topic discussed, i.e., it should not simply summarize
the sources. Again, the topic must be approved by the instructor. Early choice of
a topic is advisable in order to insure availability of books. Students may wish,
in the paper, to expand upon a topic discussed in their book report. Or they may
prefer to work on a completely different topic.

Title of book for Book Report due on September 19.

Book Report due on October 24.

Topic for paper due on October 26.

Paper due on November 14.

Graduate Students:

Graduate students are required to take the six-weeks examination and the final
examination. They will also be required to write a term paper (of approximately 20
pages) on a topic of the student's choosing. Students should feel free to pursue
any special interests (political sociology, economic history, the military, relations
with the USSR, literary history, the Church, land systems, student politics, etc.)
in choosing their paper topic. The instructor will be happy to suggest bibliography,
of which there is a rapidly growing quantity. Graduate students are expected to use
Spanish language sources, where such sources are relevant and available (the Memorial
Library collection is excellent).

If enrollment justifies, there will be a separate discussion section for graduate
students, at an hour to be arranged. Attendance at these sections is required, since
each graduate student will be asked to present an oral report to the section, which
will then discuss the report. The topic will usually be in the area of the term paper
and is to be agreed upon with the instructor at the beginning of the semester.

Graduate student term papers due on November 28.

Professor Skidmore's History Department is Humanities 5223 (telephone 263-1863 or 263-1800),
and his Ibero-American Studies office is Van Hise 1470 (telephone 262-2811).

History 168
Fall Quarter 1985
T-Th 11:10-12:30
Lib-S 3117

REVOLUTION IN LATIN AMERICA

Thom Whigham
Lib-S 4138
Ext. 5420/5401
Office Hours: W 2-3
and by appointment

Scope: The term "revolution" has come to mean different things to
different people: a rallying cry, a threat, hope for a better world,
the destruction of tradition. Violent social and political upheaval
has characterized the Twentieth Century, and perhaps nowhere more
strongly than in Latin America. Our daily lives now seem to be shaped
by the intensity and global dimension of the changes taking place in
such areas as Mexico, Guatemala, Bolivia, Cuba, and presently in
Central America.

One of the earliest revolutions of the present century took place
in Mexico, amid circumstances not unlike those in other Latin American
nations. What caused the Mexican Revolution? Was it successful? How
does this revolutionary movement differ from those which subsequently
have broken out in Chile, Cuba, Bolivia, Guatemala, Nicaragua, and El
Salvador? What lessons do they hold for students of history? During
this quarter we shall briefly examine Latin American revolutions and
through them attempt to address large questions about change in the contemporary world, and how the U.S. government has seen it.

Readings: There are four required texts for the course: Stanley Ross,
Is the Mexican Revolution Dead?, an excellent edited account that discusses the institutionalization of revolutionary objectives in Mexico;
Mariano Azuela, The Underdogs, a classic novel of the Mexican Revolution
which asks whether or nor those objectives are illusory; Richard Fagen,
The Transformation of Political Culture in Cuba, a fine study of the
social and political changes undergone by the Cuban people as part of
the revolutionary process; and Walter LaFeber, Inevitable Revolutions,
a recent analysis of events in Central America, their historical background, and the general role of the United States in regional affairs.
All readings will be placed on Library Reserve.

Requirements: The class will be conducted on a lecture-discussion basis.
Each week we will concentrate on a particular Latin American revolution
through assigned readings and lectures. I hope to obtain films to help
further illustrate the historical context. Grades will be based on: (A)
An in-class midterm, 30 per cent; (B) A final examination--in class--
30 per cent; and (C) class participation, 30 per cent. The latter requirement is crucial, in my opinion, to an adequate understanding of
the events and processes under study.

T Oct. 1	Introduction: the Concept of Revolution
Th Oct. 3	Crisis in the Ancien Régime
	Ross, 37-69
T Oct. 8	The Revolutionary Process: Mexico
	Azuela, all
Th Oct. 10	The Institutionalization of the Mexican Revolution
	Ross, 73-325
T Oct. 15	Film: "Mexico: the Frozen Revolution"
Th Oct. 17	The Revolutionary Process: Cuba
	Fagen, 1-32
T Oct. 22	The Institutionalization of the Cuban Revolution
	Fagen, 33-261
Th Oct. 24	Discussion: Was the Cuban Revolution Successful?
T Oct. 29	A Failed Revolution? The Case of Chile
Th Oct. 31	Midterm Examination
T Nov. 5	Guerrilla Strategies
Th Nov. 7	Liberation Theology: Religion as a Revolutionary Activity
T Nov. 12	Counterrevolution: the case of Guatemala
	LaFeber, 111-126, 164-172, 256-261
Th Nov. 14	A Revolution Forestalled? El Salvador
	LaFeber, 172-176, 242-256, 284-293
T Nov. 19	The Victory of the Sandinistas: Nicaragua
	LaFeber, 19-83, 98-106, 160-164, 226-242, 293-299
Th Nov. 21	Film
T Nov. 26	The Varieties of U.S. Response
	LaFeber, 146-160, 192-213, 271-284
Th Nov. 28	Thanksgiving vacation
T Dec 3	Discussion: What is the Proper Role of the U.S.?
Th Dec. 5	Speculations on the Future
W Dec. 11	Final Examanition, 11:30-2:30

III. COUNTRY AND REGIONAL COURSES IN LATIN AMERICAN HISTORY

THE EVOLUTION OF MEXICAN HISTORY

I. Lecture One. Mexico before Cortes

   A. Aztec beginnings

   B. The mature Aztec empire, 1427-1520
       1. Political organization
       2. Socio-economic structure
       3. Aztec culture
       4. Aztec religion and the problem of human sacrifice

   C. The civilization of the Aztecs: an assessment

II. Lecture Two. Cortes and the Conquest

   A. An oft-told tale repeated

   B. The conquest as an intellectual and psychological
       legacy.

III. Lecture Three. The Consolidation of Conquest: its
   material aspects

   A. The apparatus of colonial government

   B. Rewarding the conquerors
       1. Indian tribute and labor: the early
           encomienda (1521-1540)
       2. The reformed encomienda (1541-1600)
           a. The conquistador class loses power
           b. The restructuring of Indian economic and
               social life

IV. Lecture Four. The Consolidation of Conquest: its
   spiritual aspects

   A. The rationale and structure of the missionary
       program

   B. Missionary techniques

   C. Missionary accomplishments and failures
       1. Hispanization
       2. Christianization

D. The Indian and the mature colonial church
   1. Forms and quality of religious life
   2. The survivial of pre-Hispanic beliefs and
      practices

V. Lecture Five. The colony matures

   A. The silver boom in the Gran Chichimeca

   B. The institution of the forced labor system
      (repartimiento) (1570's)

   C. Economic development in northern Mexico: The mine
      and the hacienda

   D. Economic development in central and southern
      Mexico
      1. Effects of Indian population decline
      2. Growth of the livestock industry
      3. The repartimiento falters (1580-1610)
      4. The rise of the hacienda and debt peonage,
         1610-1640

   E. Mexico under the late Hapsburgs

VI. Lecture Six. Bourbon Mexico and the seeds of
    Independence

    A. The accession of the Bourbon dynasty and the
       Spanish Enlightenment
       1. Enlightenment ideas and imperial policy, 1713-
          1763
       2. Charles III, José de Gálvez, and the Bourbon
          Reforms, 1763-1789

    B. The Bourbon Reforms in Mexico
       1. The mining industry
       2. Agriculture
       3. Manufacturing and commerce

    C. Mexico in the late eighteenth century
       1. Socio-economic structure
       2. Props to power
          a. The monarchy and militarization
          b. The Church and anti-clericalism
          c. The upper classes and Creole-Spanish
             antagonism

VII. Nationhood and chaos: Mexico from Hidalgo to La
     Reforma, 1808-1855

     A. Dynastic crisis and the Hidalgo Revolt

150

151

COLONIAL MEXICO
(History 163A)

Fall, 1983
T-Th 11-12:30
Lib-S

Leon G. Campbell
Lib-S 4138, Ext. 5420,
5401
Office Hours: T, 2-3
and by appointment

Scope: History 163A-B is a two-quarter survey of Mexico from Aztec to modern times. History 163A, Colonial Mexico, focuses on the native civilizations of early Mexico, the rise of the Aztec Empire, and the establishment of Spanish colonialism after 1519. The course will emphasize the social, cultural, and economic changes imposed by Spanish government and the legacy of colonialism on the modern nation. The course treats the period from about the thirteenth century to independence in 1821.

Readings: The core text for both History 163A-B is Michael C. Meyer and William L. Sherman, The Course of Mexican History (2nd. ed., Oxford, 1983). In addition, I have assigned two books which illuminate particular and important aspects of the colonial experience, Robert Padden, The Hummingbird and the Hawk, a superb and dramatic account of the encounter of Cortes and Montezuma which replaced one civilization with another, different one and forever changed the course of Mexican history, and Doris Ladd, Mexican Women in Anahuac and New Spain, a study guide which offers case studies of the changing roles and status of women in this region. These are meant as much as anything to introduce you to the rich diversity of topics on Mexico and Mexican history.

Requirements: The class will be conducted on a lecture-discussion basis, that is to say, lectures may be interrupted for a discussion on any aspect of the topic at hand. Daily reading assignments from the required texts are listed below the lecture topics. The necessity of reading and seriously considering the assigned material cannot be overemphasized because lectures will not duplicate the materials covered in the books but will build on selected aspects of these readings. Films and slide presentations will supplement the lectures.

Grades will be based on 1) class attendance and participation -- 20 per cent, 2) a midterm examination or paper -- 40 per cent, and 3) a final examination -- 40 per cent. The midterm examination will be given on Tuesday, Nov. 1 and will cover all material to that date, that is reading assignments and lectures through Oct. 27. The final examination, which will emphasize material covered after Nov. 1, will be held on Friday, Dec. 9. Students who prefer to write a midterm paper on a topic of their choosing must notify me well in advance in order that a topic can be agreed upon. The paper is to be a minimum of 10 pages in length with appropriate references and is due on Nov. 1. Incidentally, I do not grade on any "curve," but assign marks by my own discretion and judgement, taking account of a number of factors. In general, this favors the student working to the full extent of his/her abilities.

Course Schedule

I.	T Sept. 27	Introduction
II.	Th Sept. 29	Views of Mexico: Illustrations of Culture and Geography Sherman and Meyer, 3-35
III.	T Oct. 4	Ancient and Aztec Mexico Sherman and Meyer, 36-92 Padden, vii-99
IV.	Th Oct. 6	The Hummingbird and the Hawk Sherman and Meyer, 95-114 Padden, 100-165
V.	T Oct. 9	The Conquest of Tenochtitlan Sherman and Meyer, 115-129 Padden, 166-222
VI.	Th Oct. 11	The Birth of New Spain, 1519-1530 Sherman and Meyer, 130-150 Padden, 224-274
VII.	T Oct. 18	The Viceroyalty of New Spain Sherman and Meyer, 153-167
VIII.	Th Oct. 20	The Economy of New Spain Sherman and Meyer, 168-183
IX.	T Oct. 25	Religion and Culture Sherman and Meyer, 184-202
X.	Th Oct. 27	Race and Race Mixture: La Raza Cósmica Sherman and Meyer, 203-220
XI.	T Nov. 1	Midterm Examination/ Paper Due
XII.	Th Nov. 3	Colonial Mexico: The Quality of Life Sherman and Meyer, 221-247
XIII.	Th Nov. 8	Women and the Family in New Spain Ladd, 3-82 (Bring for Discussion)
XIV.	T Nov. 15	Rationalization and Reform: Mexico in 1700 Sherman and Meyer, 251-263
XV.	Th Nov. 17	Reaction to Reform: The Army, Elites, and Popular Protest Sherman and Meyer, 264-284
XVI.	T Nov. 22	The Wars for Independence in New Spain Sherman and Meyer, 285-298

XVII.   Th Nov. 24   Thanksgiving Holiday

XVIII. T Nov. 29   The First Mexican Empire
                            Sherman and Meyer, 299-309

XIX.   Th Dec. 1   Mexico: The Legacy of Colonialism

Final Examination: Friday, December 9, 11:30-2:30 p.m.

GENERAL INFORMATION SHEET

Dr. Cooney: Office, Gottschalk Hall 301A. 588-6817.
Office Hours: MWF 7:30-7:50 & 9:00-9:50 a.m.
If you cannot make these office hours, see me before or after class and we will
try to arrange a special appointment; or get in touch with me by telephone. If
you still cannot find me, leave your phone number and name with the History
Department Secretary, and I will then try to get back to you.

TEXTS:
Michael C. Meyer & William L. Sherman. The Course of Mexican History.
James W. Wilkie and Albert L. Michaels. Revolution in Mexico: Years of
Upheaval. 1910-1940.

The purpose of this course is to give the student an overview of the history
of Mexico since Independence. As one of the two countries with which the
United States shares a common boundary, it behooves an educated American to
have some understanding of Mexico, one of the largest and most important Latin
American nations and today the largest Spanish-speaking nation in the world.
For better or worse, our history has been intimately intertwined with that of
Mexico and there appears to be no change to this situation for the foreseeable
future.

RESPONSIBILITIES OF THE STUDENT:

Map Quiz: During the first week of class a list of geographical locations of
Mexico will be distributed to you, along with a practice map. From maps in the
texts, atlases in the library, etc., you will learn these locations. In the
second or third week of the course you will be given a map quiz on these locations, with a map similar to the practice one earlier distributed. No makeups
on the map quiz. It will be announced in advance.

Outside Reading or Paper Assignment: Students have a choice of reading two
books on Mexican history and writing a review of each, or writing a research
paper on some aspect of Mexican history. If the student opts for the book
reviews, then the first review will be due some seven weeks into the semester
(date to be announced) and the last one due the last class day of the semester.
If that student desires to write a research paper then he or she must see me
to clear the topic, and to be informed as to research sources, etc. The
research paper will be about fifteen pages (typewritten double-spaced) of
text, with endnotes. Style will follow Turabian. You must clear the topic
of that research paper with the instructor if you take this option. You will
receive a bibliography of books on Mexico also, plus the fact that at the
ends of the chapters in The Course of Mexican History are good bibliographies.
Book Reviews or Papers will be about 20% of your grade. The student must do
this assignment (Book Reviews or Papers) if he/she expects better than a C.

Tests: There will be two midterms and a final. On each midterm you will do
one essay question out of a choice of two or three. You will also do about
six identifications out of a choice of twelve to fifteen. You will use
bluebook and blue or black ink. The final will consist of at least two
essay questions--again a choice on each one; and about ten identifications--
again a choice. On my tests I ask about sixty percent from the lectures,
the other forty percent from the texts.

Please use my office hours if you have difficulties. All credit comes from the assigned work and tests--no extra credit work.

The Map Quiz is worth 25 points. Each midterm is worth 100 points. And the final is worth 200 points--all for a total in this course of 425 points. I grade on a numerical basis. For the semester grade, your grade will be determined as follows: 88%-100% is an A, 78%-87% a B, 67%-77% a C, 57%-66% a D, 0-56% an F. No rounding off. Book reviews are given a letter grade.

1. A & S is hard to get incompletes from. If one is necessary, then it is the student's responsibility to remove it, not the instructor's.

2. Don't miss the Final. If you do and have not notified the instructor, I will have to flunk you automatically.

3. Plagiarism and cheating are grounds for immediate dismissal. Read the relevant catalogs on these matters--also the Student's Bill of Rights.

4. Drops, etc., are your responsibility. Carry through with any paperwork necessary. It is not the instructor's responsibility.

5. I don't post grades. You will get them in the normal way. No exceptions.

6. Makeups allowed on quizzes and tests. See the instructor. Late reviews and papers may be penalized for lateness.

7. You are responsible for knowing how you stand in this class. Pick up your tests and papers. I give out your grade to no one but you. Only with a dated signed request will I give your grade to someone else.

8. The instructor has an office and a phone. Use them if you need to. One way or the other I can be found.

9. You will receive other handouts such as a guide to book reviews, map list, etc.; know them.

Read the texts, study, keep up with the lectures, take good notes and you will do well.

Good Luck

J. W. Cooney

J. W. Cooney

READINGS AND TOPICS

We may not always be able to keep on schedule. If so, the Instructor will inform you in advance what you will be held responsible on tests, etc.

Texts:

Michael C. Meyer and William L. Sherman. The Course of Mexican History.
James W. Wilkie and Albert L. Michaels. Revolution in Mexico: Years of Upheaval, 1910-1940.
                    M equals Meyer.   W equals Wilkie.

SOME OF THE BELOW TOPICS WILL NOT BE PRESENTED IN LECTURES. THEY WILL ONLY BE DEALT WITH IN THIS CLASS THROUGH THE READINGS. IF THE TOPIC WILL NOT BE PRESENTED IN THE LECTURES, THE SYMBOL NL (NO LECTURES) NEXT TO THE TOPIC DENOTES READINGS ONLY.

(While not required, I urgently recommend that you browse through Chapters 1-14 in The Course of Mexican History for the Colonial Background of Mexico).

1. Introduction and the Independence of Mexico. M 264-294. (NL)

2. Iturbide, the Mexican Empire and the Republic. M 294-323.

3. The Age of Santa Anna. M 324-334.

4. Santa Anna and the Texas Rebellion M 335-342 (NL).

5. The Mexican American War and the Return of Santa Anna. M 342-354. (NL)

6. The Reform and Benito Juárez. M 355-384. MIDTERM

7. The French Intervention and Aftermath. M 385-415.

8. Porfirio Díaz and his Mexico. M 416-465.

9. The Porfiriato at its Zenith. M 466-479.

10. The Coming of the Revolution. W 3-32. M 483-510.

11. The Mexican Revolution. W 33-120. M 511-566. MIDTERM

12. Obregón, Calles, and the new Mexico. W 121-204. M 569-595.

13. The Age of Cárdenas. W 205-278. M 596-623.

14. World War II and Modernization. W 279-384. M 627-662.

15. Modern Mexico, Promise and Turmoil. M 663-696.

FINAL.

Bibliography for History of Modern Mexico

List of works in English that are present in the Library of the University of Louisville. This is by no means the entire collection of that library but a fair sampling for Mexico since Independence.

Geography and General Foreign Affairs

Arciniegas, German. Caribbean: Sea of the New World.
Bemis, Samuel Flagg. The Latin American Policy of the United States.
Cline, Howard F. The United States and Mexico.
James, Preston E. Latin America (geography)
Mecham, John L. Church and State in Latin America.
Perkins, Dexter. The United States and the Caribbean.
Rippy, James F. The United States and Mexico.
Stein, Stanley and Barbara. The Colonial Heritage of Latin America: Essays on Economic Dependence in Perspective.
Wilgus, A. Curtis. Historical Atlas of Latin America.

Background to Independence

Fisher, Lillian. The Background of the Revolution for Mexican Independence.
Humphreys, R. A. and John Lynch. The Origins of the Latin American Revolutions, 1808-1826.
Madariaga, Salvador de. The Fall of the Spanish American Empire.
Robertson, William Spence. The Rise of the Spanish American Republics as Told in the Lives of Their Liberators.
Whitaker, Arthur. The United States and the Independence of Latin America.

Independence

Benson, Nettie L. Mexico and the Spanish Cortes, 1810-1822.
Hamill, Hugh. The Hidalgo Revolt: Prelude to Mexican Independence.
Robertson, William S. Iturbide of Mexico.

Post Independence and the Age of Santa Anna

Calderón de la Barca, Francis. Life in Mexico.
Callcott, Wilfred. Church and State in Mexico, 1822-1857.
Callcott, Wilfred. Santa Anna: The Story of an Enigma Who Once was Mexico.
Hale, C. A. Mexican Liberalism in the Age of Mora.

Texas, The United States and Mexico

Barker, E. C. Mexico and Texas, 1821-1835.
Mark, Frederick. The Monroe Doctrine and American Expansion, 1843-1849.

The Reform

Garber, P. N. The Gadsden Treaty.
Knapp, Frank. The Life of Sebastian Lerdo de Tejada.
Roeder, Ralph. Juarez and His Mexico.
Smart, Charles A. Juarez: A Biography.

The French Intervention

Blasio, J. L. Maximilian, Emperor of Mexico: Memoirs of his Private Secretary.
Bock, Karl H. Prelude to Tragedy.
Corti, Egon. Maximilian and Charlotte of Mexico. 2 vols.
Dabbs, Jack Autrey. The French Army in Mexico, 1861-1867.

The Age of Porfirio Diaz

Beals, Carelton. Porfirio Diaz: Dictator of Mexico.
Callcott, Wilfred. Liberalism in Mexico, 1857-1929.
Cosio Villegas, Daniel. The United States versus Porfirio Diaz.
Flandrau, C. M. Viva Mexico!
Fletcher, David M. Rails, Mines and Progress: Seven American Promoters in Mexico, 1867-1911.
Tischendorf, A. P. Great Britian and Mexico in the Era of Porfirio Diaz.

Prelude to the Revolution

Cockcroft, J. D. Intellectual Precursors of the Mexican Revolution, 1900-1913.
Turner, J. K. Barbarous Mexico.

The Revolution

Atkin, R. Revolution: Mexico, 1910-1920.
Blaisdell, L. L. The Desert Revolution, Baja California, 1911.
Braddy, H. Pershing's Mission in Mexico.
Brenner, Anita. The Wind that Swept Mexico.
Calvert, Peter. The Mexican Revolution, 1910-1914. The Diplomacy of the Anglo-American Conflict.
Clendenen, C. C. The United States and Pancho Villa.
Greib, K. J. The United States and Huerta.
Haley, P. E. Revolution and Intervention: The Diplomacy of Taft and Wilson with Mexico, 1910-1917.
Quirk, Robert E. An Affair of Honor: Woodrow Wilson and the Occupation of Veracruz.
_____. The Mexican Revolution, 1914-1915: The Convention of Aquascalientes.
Ross, S. R. Francisco I. Madero, Apostle of Democracy.
Womack, John. Zapata and the Mexican Revolution.

The Post Revolution

Beals, Carelton. Mexican Maze.
Cronon, E. D. Josephus Daniels in Mexico.
Dulles, J. W. F. Yesterday in Mexico. A Chronicle of the Revolution, 1919-1936.
Gruening, E. H. Mexico and its Heritage.
Lieuwin, Edwin. Mexican Militarism: the Political Rise and Fall of the Revolutionary Army, 1910-1942.
Tannenbaum, F. The Mexican Agrarian Revolution.
_____. Mexico, the Struggle for Peace and Bread.
Wilkie, James W. The Mexican Revolution: Federal Expenditures and Social Change since 1910.

Modern Mexico

Brandenburg, F. The Making of Modern Mexico.
Cline, Howard. Mexico, Revolution to Evolution.
Cumberland, C. C. Mexican Revolution, Genesis Under Madero.
_____. Mexico: The Struggle for Modernity.
González Casanova, P. Democracy in Mexico.
Lewis, Oscar. The Children of Sanchez.
Needler, M. C. Politics and Society in Mexico.
Padgett, Leon. The Mexican Political System.
Ramos, S. Profile of Man and Culture in Mexico.
Romanell, P. Making of the Mexican Mind.
Simpson, Lesly. Many Mexicos.

MODERN MEXICO
History 163B
University of California, Riverside

Winter, 1984
TuTh 12:30-2
Sproul 2351

Carlos E. Cortés
Office: LibS. 4153
Office Hours: TuTh 2-4

Scope: History 163 (Modern Mexico) focuses on the history of Mexico from 1810 to the present. The first half of the course will be devoted to Mexico's struggle for independence (1810-1821), the turbulent fifty-five years of post-independence instability (1821-1876), and the thirty-five years of Porfirian peace (1876-1910). The second half of the course will concentrate on the epic Mexican Revolution and its aftermath.

Course Requirements: There will be two five-week examinations (on Thursday, February 9, and Thursday, March 15) and one ten-page research paper. The term paper and each of the examinations will be worth 30% of the course grade, while class participation will be worth 10% of the course grade. There will be no final examination. The research paper deadlines are February 28 (+), March 6 (o), and March 13 (-). Papers submitted after March 13 will receive reduced grades. Papers submitted after Tuesday, March 20, will receive severely reduced grades.

Required Reading

Carlos Fuentes. THE DEATH OF ARTEMIO CRUZ.

Michael C. Meyer and William L. Sherman. THE COURSE OF MEXICAN HISTORY.

W. Dirk Raat (ed.). MEXICO: FROM INDEPENDENCE TO REVOLUTION, 1810-1910.

Course Schedule

January 10   (Tues.) -- Introduction

I. The Nineteenth Century

January 12   (Thur.) -- Mexican Independence (1810-1821)
                        --MEXICAN HISTORY, pp. 264-298
                        --MEXICO, pp. 1-48

January 17   (Tues.) -- From Empire to Republic (1821-1832)
                        --MEXICAN HISTORY, pp. 299-323
                        --MEXICO, pp. 49-54, 122-134

161

January 19   (Thur.) -- The Age of Santa Anna (1832-1855)
                         --MEXICAN HISTORY, pp. 324-334, 355-370
                         --MEXICO, pp. 55-83

January 24   (Tues.) -- Texas and the Rise of Mexican Regionalism (1832-1845)
                         --MEXICAN HISTORY, pp. 335-342
                         --MEXICO, pp. 84-90

January 26   (Thur.) -- The U.S.-Mexican War and Its Aftermath (1846-1855)
                         --MEXICAN HISTORY, pp. 342-354
                         --MEXICO, pp. 91-121

January 31   (Tues.) -- The Age of Benito Juárez (1855-1877)
                         --MEXICAN HISTORY, pp. 371-428
                         --MEXICO, pp. 135-186

February 2   (Thur.) -- The Age of Porfirio Díaz (1877-1910)
                         --MEXICAN HISTORY, pp. 429-480
                         --MEXICO, pp. 187-272

II. The Twentieth Century

February 7   (Tues.) -- The Mexican Revolution Begins (1910-1913)
                         --MEXICAN HISTORY, 481-522
                         --MEXICO, pp. 273-299

February 9   (Thur.) -- First Examination (covering lectures and reading
                         assignments through February 2)

February 14   (Tues.) -- The Constitutionalists Triumph (1913-1920)
                         --MEXICAN HISTORY, pp. 523-566

February 16   (Thur.) -- The Mexican Revolution in Retrospect
                         Film: The Ragged Revolution: The Romance and the
                                Reality of the Mexican Revolution, 1910-1920

February 21   (Tues.) -- The Implementation of the Constitution (1920-1934)
                         --MEXICAN HISTORY, pp. 567-595

February 23   (Thur.) -- The Conflict between Church and State
                         Film: The Fugitive

February 28   (Tues.) -- The Era of Lázaro Cárdenas (1934-1940)
                         --MEXICAN HISTORY, pp. 596-624

March 1   (Thur.) -- No Class

March 6   (Tues.) -- The Revolution Slows (1940-1970)
                         --MEXICAN HISTORY, pp. 625-671

March 8   (Thur.) -- Is the Mexican Revolution Dead?
                        Film: Mexico: The Frozen Revolution
                        --ARTEMIO CRUZ, pp. 1-306

March 13   (Tues.) -- Mexico Today and Tomorrow (1970-)
                        --MEXICAN HISTORY, pp. 671-704

March 15   (Thur.) -- Second Examination (covering lectures, reading
                        assignments, and films from February 7 through
                        March 13)

Modern Mexico

A study of the major developments in Mexican national life since 1821. The first half of the course will deal with the nineteenth century: the era of Santa Anna, the war with the United States, the Reform the French intervention, the age of Porfirio Díaz. The second half will investigate the 1910 Revolution and the resulting transformation of Mexico's political, social and economic institutions.

Common Readings:

    Charles C. Cumberland, Mexico: The Struggle for Modernity
    James Wilkie and Albert Michaels, Revolution in Mexico: Years of Upheaval
    Ricardo Pozas, Juan the Chamula
    Octavio Paz, The Other Mexico: A Critique of the Pyramid

COURSE MECHANICS:

Exams: There will be three essay exams, one of which will be the final. The two term
    exams are tentatively scheduled for the weeks of: February 20 and April 17.

Individual Readings: You will be asked to read widely; beyond the scope of common readings
    for the course. This reading will be from materials placed on reserve in the
    Library and from books and articles perused for your term project.

Term Project: Students will have two options for a term project: A bibliographical essay
    (to be explained later) and a research paper (topic to be selected from a list
    supplied during the first two weeks of class).

Class Format: I will employ a lecture-discussion format. A significant portion of your
    grade is linked to class participation and attendance. So come to class and get
    involved.

Office Hours: My office is 110 Mahar - phone 341-2717. Tentative office hours will be
    11:00-12:15. Do not hesitate to make other arrangements if these hours are not
    convenient. My home phone is 342-4193.

Mexico: Reform and Revolution
Spring 1978

Date	Topics	Readings
Week of: Jan. 16	An overview Mexico before 1821: a brief preface Map exercise	Cumberland chs. 1-6
Jan. 23	The era of Santa Anna, 1821-1854 Two visions: the liberal-conservative struggle The loss of Texas and the war with the United States	Cumberland ch. 7
Jan. 30	The Reform, 1854-1876 The Ayulta Revolution The Liberals in power The Constitution of 1857 The French intervention and Maximilian, 1862-67 The restored Republic The decay of Liberal dreams	

Date	Topics	Readings
Feb. 6	The Porfiriato, 1876-1911 The politics of despotism The científicos The beginnings of industrialization People, land and life	Cumberland ch. 8
Feb. 13	The coming of the Revolution The precursors Francisco I. Madero 1910: "election" and revolt 1911: the fall of dictatorship	Cumberland ch. 9
Feb. 20	The Madero interval, 1911-1913	Wilkie pp. 37-60
Feb. 27- March 6	The Epic Revolution 1913-1920 The War of the Winners Social change during the violent decade	Wilkie pp. 60-123
March 20	Juan the Chamula: The "average Mexican" and the Revolution	Pozas all
March 27- April 3	Politicians and soldiers: the quest for stability, 1920-1934 Land and Labor The Revolution and the Church The Revolution and the U.S.	Cumberland ch. 10 Wilkie pp. 123-205
April 10	The era of Lázaro Cárdenas, 1934-1940	Wilkie pp. 205-293
April 17-24	The "Institutional Revolution" 1940-1978	Paz all
	Opposition and dissent in Modern Mexico	
May 1	A matter of interpretation: How historians see it all	Bailey
May 8	Review: Term project due	

LAH 4433   MODERN MEXICO   FALL 1983

Instructor: Neill Macaulay

Time & Place: 6th period (1:25-2:15 p.m.), Monday, Wednesday, &
               Friday; GPA 1101

Course objective: To familiarize students with the major developments
in Mexico since 1821. Emphasis will be on reformist and revolutionary
movements and their effect on Mexico's political structure, economy,
and, especially, on the everyday lives of Mexican people.

Course Outline

   I. Lecture topics prior to the midterm examination

       A. The Age of Santa Anna, 1821-1855
       B. La Reforma: The Revolution of Ayutla and the Constitution
           of 1857
       C. The War of the Reform and the French Intervention, 1858-1867
       D. The Last Years of Juárez and the Rise of Porfirio Díaz,
           1867-1876
       E. The Porfiriato: Dictatorship and Economic Development,
           1876-1910
       F. The Fall of the Dictatorship, 1910-11

  II. Reading assignments to be completed before the midterm
       examination

       A. M. C. Meyer & W. L. Sherman, The Course of Mexican History,
           pp. 299-505

       B. F. Calderón de la Barca, Life in Mexico

 III. Film to be shown prior to midterm examination: Juárez

  IV. Midterm examination (to be given within a week of October 12,
       the term's midpoint)

   V. Lecture topics after the midterm examination

       A. The Revolution: A "Fiesta of Bullets," 1911-1917
       B. The Constitution of 1917
       C. The Decline of Carranza and the Rise of Obregón, 1917-1920
       D. The Obregón-Calles Era, 1920-1934
       E. The Cárdenas Era, 1934-1940
       F. The "Institutionalized Revolution," 1940-1983

166

VI.   Reading assignments to be completed before the final examination

    A.   Meyer & Sherman, The Course of Mexican History, pp. 506-695

    B.   Octavio Paz, The Labyrinth of Solitude

VII. Film to be shown prior to the final examination: Mexico: The
    Frozen Revolution

VIII. Final examination: 3-5:00 p.m., Wednesday, December 14, 1983

Course requirements:

    1) A two-hour final examination, composed of essay and short-
answer questions, which will account for 50% of the course grade,
unless, for any reason, the student fails to take the midterm examination, in which case the value of the final exam will be 80%. While
the final exam will be cumulative, material covered after the midterm will receive the greater emphasis.

    2) A one-hour midterm examination, composed of essay and short-
answer questions, which will account for 30% of the course grade.
This requirement is flexible to the extent noted in 1) above. The
exact date of the midterm will be announced at least two weeks in
advance.

    3) Two typewritten reports on books read in addition to the
assigned readings (see accompanying "Guide"). Students may report
on any worthy and relevant work, but books not listed in the accompanying bibliography must be cleared with the instructor for worthiness and relevancy. One book report is due at the last class meeting
prior to the midterm exam, and the other at the last class meeting
prior to the final exam. Late book reports will be accepted at any
time before the final exam at a discount of one letter grade.

Additional requirements for graduate students (LAH 5934)

    Although the course is designed for undergraduates, graduate
students are welcome. However, book reports by graduate students
will be judged against higher standards of scholarly criticism than
those applied to undergraduate work. Also, graduate students will
be required to submit four one-page, single-spaced abstracts, each
of a relevant scholarly article, at the last meeting of the class
(see the accompanying sample abstract for guidance). Acceptable
articles are those found in scholarly journals like the Hispanic
American Historical Review, The Americas, or Historia mexicana, and
that deal primarily with Mexican history since 1821; for annotated
listings of titles, graduate students are referred to the appropriate
sections of Charles C. Griffin, ed., Latin America: A Guide to the
Historical Literature, and the Handbook of Latin American Studies.

Each article abstract will count 2½% toward the graduate student's final grade; each book report, 10%; the midterm exam, 30%; and the final exam 40%--or 70% in case the graduate student misses the midterm.

Attachments: 1) Bibliography of books in English
              2) Guide for Writers of Book Reviews

Alba, Victor. The Mexicans: The Making of a Nation

Ashby, Joe C. Organized Labor and the Mexican Revolution under
Lázaro Cárdenas

Bailey, D. C. Viva Cristo Rey: The Cristero Rebellion and the
Church-State Conflict

Barker, Nancy Nichols. The French Experience in Mexico, 1821-1861

Bazant, J. Alienation of Church Wealth in Mexico . . . 1856-1875

Beezley, W. H. Insurgent Governor: Abraham González and the Mexican
Revolution

Beals, Carleton. Porfirio Díaz: Dictator of Mexico

Bernstein, Marvin. The Mexican Mining Industry, 1890-1950

Blaisdell, Lowell. The Desert Revolution: Baja California, 1911

Cadenhead, Ivie E. Benito Juárez

_____. Jesus González Ortega and the Mexican National Politics

Calvert, Peter. The Mexican Revolution, 1910-14: Diplomacy of
Anglo-American Conflict

_____. Mexico

Clendenen, Clarence. Blood on the Border: The U.S. Army and the
Mexican Irregulars

_____. The United States and Pancho Villa: A Study in Unconventional
Diplomacy

Cline, Howard F. Mexico: Revolution to Evolution, 1940-1960

_____. The United States and Mexico

Coatsworth, John H. Growth against Development: Economic Impact of
Railroads in . . . Mexico

Cockcroft, James D. Intellectual Precursors of the Mexican Revolution

Coerver, D. M. Porfirism Interrognum: The Presidency of Manuel
González of Mexico, 1880-84

169

Corti, Egon Caesar. _Maximilian and Charlotte of Mexico_

Cosio Villegas, Daniel. _The United States versus Porfirio Díaz_

Gosteloe, Michael P. _Church and State in Independent Mexico: The Patronage Debate, 1821-57_

_____. _Church Wealth in Mexico_

Cronon, E. David. _Josephus Daniels in Mexico_

Cumberland, Charles C. _Mexican Revolution: The Constitutionalist Years_

_____. _Mexican Revolution: Genesis under Madero_

Dabbs, Jack A. _The French Army in Mexico, 1861-1867_

De Beer, G. _José Vasconcelos and his World_

Dulles, J. W. F. _Yesterday in Mexico: A Chronicle of the Revolution, 1919-1936_

Garber, Paul Neff. _The Gadsden Treaty_

Gilderhus, M. T. _Diplomacy & Revolution: U.S.-Mexican Relations under Wilson & Carranza_

González Cassnova, Pablo. _Democracy in Mexico_

Grieb, Kenneth J. _The United States and Huerta_

Haddox, John H. _Vasconcelos of Mexico: Philospher and Prophet_

Hale, Charles A. _Mexican Liberalism in the Age of Mora, 1821-1853_

Haley, P. E. _Revolution & Intervention: The Diplomacy of Taft & Wilson with Mexico_

Hamilton, Nora. _The Limits of State Autonomy: Post-Revolutionary Mexico_

Hanna, A. J. & K. A. _Napoleon III and Mexico: American Triumph over Monarchy_

Harris, Charles H. _The Sánchez Navarros: A Coshuilan Latifundio_

Haslip, Joan. _The Crown of Mexico: Maximilian & His Empress Carlota_

Helm, Mackinley. _Man of Fire: J. C. Orozco, an Interpretive Memoir_

Hill, Larry D. Emissaries to a Revolution: Woodrow Wilson's Executive Agents to Mexico

Johnson, Richard A. The Mexican Revolution of Ayutla, 1854-1855

Johnson, William Weber. Heroic Mexico: The Violent Emergence of a Modern Nation

Joseph, Gilbert M. Revolution from Without: Yucatan, Mexico, & the U.S., 1880-1924

Katz, Fredrich. The Secret War in Mexico

Knapp, Frank A. The Life of Sebastián Lerdo de Tejadn

Knowlton, Robert J. Church Property and the Mexican Reform, 1856-1910

Lieuwen, E. Mexican Militarism: The Political Rise & Fall of the Revolutionary Army

Meyer, Jean A. The Cristero Rebellion

Meyer, Michael C. Huerta: A Political Portrait

_____. Mexican Rebel: Pascual Orozco & the Mexican Revolution, 1910-1915

Millon, Robert P. Mexican Marxist: Vicente Lombardo Toledano

_____. Zapata: The Ideology of a Peasant Revolutionary

Niemeyer, E. V. Revolution at Queretaro: The Mexican Constitutional Convention of 1916-17

O'Connor, Richard. The Cactus Throne

Olliff, Donathon C. Reforma Mexico and the United States

Paz, Octavio, The Labyrinth of Solitude

Perry, Laurens Ballard. Juárez and Díaz: Machine Politics in Mexico

Pletcher, D. M. Rails, Mines & Progress: Seven American Promoters in Mexico, 1867-1911

Powell, T. G. Mexico and the Spanish Civil War

Quirk, Robert E. An Affair of Honor: Woodrow Wilson & the Occupation of Veracruz

_____. The Mexican Revolution and the Catholic Church, 1910-1929

_____. The Mexican Revolution, 1914-1915: The Convention of Aguascalientes

Ramos, Samuel. Profile of Man and Culture in Mexico

Randall, Robert W. Real del Monte: A British Mining Venture in Mexico

Reed, Nelson. The Caste War of Yucatan

Roeder, Ralph. Juárez and his Mexico

Ross, Stanley R. Francisco I. Madero: Apostle of Mexican Democracy

Ruiz, Ramón Eduardo. The Great Rebellion: Mexico, 1905-1924

Salamini, Heather Fowler. Agrarian Radicalism in Veracruz, 1920-1938

Schmidt, H. C. & W. D. Raat. The Roots of Lo Mexicano: Self & Society in Mexican Thought 1900-1934

Schmitt, Karl M. Communism in Mexico

Scholes, Walter V. Mexican Politics during the Juarez Regime, 1855-1872

Schooner, T. D. Dollars over Dominion: The Triumph of Liberalism in Mexican-U.S. Relations

Smith, Robert F. The United States & Revolutionary Nationalism in Mexico, 1916-1932

Tannenbaum, Frank. The Mexican Agrarian Revolution

_____. Mexico: The Struggle for Peace and Bread

_____. Peace by Revolution: Mexico after 1910

Tischendorf, Alfred. Great Britain and Mexico in the Era of Porfirio Díaz

Townsend, William C. Lázaro Cárdenas, Mexican Democrat

Tuck, Jim. The Holy War in Los Altos: A Regional Analysis of Mexico's Cristero Rebellion

Turner, Frederick C. The Dynamic of Mexican Nationalism

Tyler, Ronnie C. Santiago Vidaurri and the Southern Confederacy

172

Voss, Stuart F. *On the Periphery of 19th Century Mexico: Sonora & Sinaloa, 1810-1877*

Wilkie, James W. *The Mexican Revolution: Federal Expenditures & Social Change since 1910*

Wilkie, Raymond. *San Miguel: A Mexican Collective Ejido*

Wolfe, Bertram D. *The Fabulous Life of Diego Rivera*

Womack, John. *Zapata and the Mexican Revolution*

Course Description

This is a one-quarter course on Modern Mexico taught in a special summer session, June 11-July 14. Latin America's third largest country (only Brazil and Argentina are bigger), Mexico is the most populous Spanish-speaking nation south of the Rio Grande. This course will analyze the principal social, economic, and political development since 1810, with special emphasis on the Liberal Reforms, the Revolution of 1910, and its consequences on the emergence of contemporary Mexico.

Books

Victor Alba. The Mexicans: The Making of a Nation.
Richard N. Sinkin. The Mexican Reform, 1855-1876.
James W. Wilkie, et al. Contemporary Mexico.

Course Requirements

(1) one mid-term: to be given on June 29.
(2) final exam: to be given on the last day of the course, July 14.
(3) graduate credit--a short paper or book report (consult the instructor)

Lectures and Discussions

(I) Independent Mexico, 1810-1855

6/11	1.	Introduction: Colonial Legacy
6/12	2.	Independence Movements: from Hidalgo to Iturbide
6/15	3.	Ideological Confusion: Liberals versus Conservatives
6/16	4.	Santana's Folloy: The Caudillo and his Misrule
6/18	5.	the Mexican War: Whose Manifesty Destiny?

readings:
Alba, Chaps. 1, 2; Wilkie/Meyer, 4

(II) The Mexico of Benito Juárez and Porfirio Díaz, 1855-1910

6/19	6.	The War of the Reformas (I): A Divided Nation
6/22	7.	The War of the Reformas (II): The State versus Fuero Interests
6/23	8.	Imperial Mexico: Maximilian and Carlota of the Hapsburg House
6/25	9.	Científicos and the Pax Porfiriana: The Age of Material Progress?
6/26	10.	Díaz, Mexican Oligarchies, and Foreign Capitalists
6/29	11.	MID-TERM

readings:
Alba, 4, 6; Sinkin, whole book

(III) The Mexican Revolution and Its Aftermath, 1910-1981

6/30	12.	The Intellectual Basis for the Revolution
7/2	13.	Madero, Zapata, and Villa
7/3	14.	The Constitution of 1917 and Northern Presidencies
7/6	15.	Lázaro Cárdenas and Corporatist Revolution

7/7   16. Institutionalizing the Revolution
7/9   17. 'Is the Mexican Revolution Dead?'

readings:
   Alba, 6 through 9; Wilkie/Meyer, 6, 10, 11, 14, 15, 18, 19, 21

(IV)   Mexico and the United States in the 1970s and 1980s

7/10 18. The Mexican-U.S. Relations: Past, Present, and Future
7/13 19. Review
7/14 20. Final Exam

readings:
   Wilkie/Meyer, 25, 43

A Short Bibliography in English for Your Reading Pleasure!

I. Independent Mexico

T. R. Fhrenbach. Fire and Blood: A History of Mexico.
Charles A. Hale. Mexican Liberalism in the Age of Mora, 1821-1855.
Hugh M. Hamill, Jr. The Hidalgo Revolt: Prelude to the Mexican Independence.
Karl M. Schmitt. Mexico and the United States, 1821-1973.
Lesley Byrd Simpson. Many Mexicos.

II. Mexico under Juárez and Díaz

William M. Anderson. An American in Maximilian's Mexico 1865-1866.
Jan Bazant. Alienation of Church Wealth in Mexico: Social and Economic Aspects
         of the Liberal Revolution, 1856-1875.
Daniel Cosio Villegas. The United States versus Porfirio Diaz.
James Creelman. Díaz, Master of Mexico.
Bertita Harding. Phantom Crown: The Story of Maximilian and Carlota of Mexico.
David M. Pletcher. Rails, Mines, and Progress: Seven American Promoters in
         Mexico, 1867-1911.
Ralph Roeder. Juárez and His Mexico, 2 vols.
Walter V. Scholes. Mexican Politics during the Juárez Regime, 1855-1872.
Alfred P. Tischendorf. Great Britain and Mexico in the Era of Porfirio Díaz.

III. The Mexican Revolution and Its Aftermath

C. C. Clendenen. The United States and Pancho Villa.
Howard Cline. Mexico: From Revolution to Evolution, 1940-1960.
Charles C. Cumberland. Mexican Revolution: Genesis under Madero.
William P. Glade and Charles Anderson. The Political Economy of Mexico.
Pablo González Casanova. Democracy in Mexico.
Oscar Lewis. Children of Sánchez.
_____. Pedro Martínez: A Mexican Peasant and His Family.
Jean A. Meyer. The Critero Rebellion: The Mexican People between Church and
         State, 1926-1929.
Martin C. Needler. Politics and Society in Mexico.

Robert Quirk. The Mexican Revolution and the Catholic Church 1910-1929.
_____. An Affair of Honor: Woodrow Wilson and the Occupation of Vera Cruz.
Clark W. Reynolds. The Mexican Economy: Twentieth Century Structure and Growth.
Stanley R. Ross. Francisco I. Madero, Apostle of Mexican Democracy.
_____. Is the Mexican Revolution Dead?
Eyler N. Simpson. The Ejido: Mexico's Way Out.
Evelyn P. Stevens. Protest and Response in Mexico.
Raymond Vernon. The Dilemma of Mexico's Development.
Franz A. von Sauer. The Alienated "Loyal" Opposition: Mexico's Partido
                    Accion Nacional.
James W. Wilkie. The Mexican Revolution: Federal Expenditure and Social
                 Change since 1910.
John Womack. Zapata and the Mexican Revolution.

Periodicals in English

Hispanic American Historical Review
Journal of Inter-American Studies and World Affairs
Journal of Latin American Studies
Latin American Research Review

History 173   Professor E. Bradford Burns
                                                     Fall Quarter, 1984

THE HISTORY OF MODERN BRAZIL, 1850-1980

This general survey course covers Brazil from the advent of modernization,
approximately 1850, until the present. Following a general chronological
sequence, the lectures and discussion treat various selected topics of importance in the political, economic, social, intellectual, and cultural development of Brazil. The principal objective is to chart historically conflict,
change, and continuity within Brazilian society.

The weekly lecture topics and appropriate reading assignments appear
below. These assignments are intended to complement the lectures as well as
provide material for discussion. Therefore, they should be completed prior to the
the first lecture of each week.

Week	Lecture Topic	Reading
Oct. 1-3	Introduction: The Colonial Background	Burns, 1-114
Oct. 8-10	The Challenge of Establishing a Nation	Burns, 115-186
Oct. 15-17	Modernization: The Promise, the Threat and the Reality	Burns, 187-319
Oct. 22-24	Assessing the Empire	Amado
Oct. 29-31	Heyday of the Old Republic	Burns, 320-434
Nov. 5-7	Nationalism and Vargas	Shirley
Nov. 12-14	Race and Culture	Fernandez
Nov. 14	Paper Due	
Nov 19-21	The Urbanization of Brazil	Fernandez
Nov 26-28	Reform and Reaction	Burns, 435-504; De Jesus
Dec. 3-5	The Military in Politics	Burns, 505-538

Final Exam on Wednesday, December 12, 3:00-6:00 p.m.

The Student Bookstore has been asked to stock the following books assigned as
required reading:

    E. Bradford Burns, A History of Brazil
    Florestan Fernandez, The Negro in Brazilian Society
    Robert W. Shirley, The End of a Tradition
    Jorge Amado, The Violent Land
    Carolina María de Jesús, Child of the Dark
    Powell Library has these books on reserve.

177

Film Schedule

Oct. 3   The Tribe that Hides from Man, 62 min.

Nov. 5   Brazil, the Gathering Millions, 30 min.

Nov. 12   Brazil, the Vanishing Negro, 30 min.

Nov. 19   The Land Burns, 12 min.

Nov. 21   Barravento, 75 min.

Nov. 28   Who Is Oscar Niemeyer?, 30 min.

Essay

On November 14, an essay is due. This essay will be based primarily on the books by Jorge Amado and Robert V. Shirley but secondarily on any of the material read, seen, or heard prior to November 12 that complements those two books. Students will select their own theme, so long as the theme derives from the two books and relates to our concerns in modern Brazilian history. Papers will be typewritten, double spaced, and approximately 5-7 pages in length. Two points will be subtracted for each day the paper is late.

Grades

The grades will be computed on the following basis:

a) essay   40 points
b) final exam   60 points

Please note that the final exam will be given on December 12, at 3:00 p.m. The course provides neither a make-up exam nor an incomplete.

Office Hours

I will hold office hours in Bunche 5361 on Monday, 11:00-11:45 a.m.; Wednesday, 2:00-3:00 p.m.; and Friday, 10:30-11:45 a.m.

E. Bradford Burns

HISTORY OF MODERN BRAZIL

The Colonial Background

1. The student should be prepared to write a short essay on each of the following topics and the relationship of that topic to the broader sweep of Brazilian history. In sum, what is the significance of the topic for a fuller understanding of Brazil?
   Social amalgamation,
   Territorial expansion,
   Economic fluctuation, or
   Political evolution.

2. How did non-Europeans fare at the hands of the Portuguese during the conquest and settlement of Brazil?

3. The complex relations between Europeans and Indians which began in this hemisphere in 1492 still characterize much of the Americas. The contemporary thrust to "open" the Amazon is the most recent chapter in those relations. By studying these relations today, we can see an historical continuity which has characterized White-Indian relations or you might phrase the relationship as that of Westernization and the native peoples of this hemisphere.

   Consider these two quotations in light of the film The Tribe that Hides From Man:

   "These Indians are holding back the inevitable development of Brazil. They produce absolutely nothing and are creating conflicts with pioneers who want to integrate our country and make it the major exporter of meat in the world." A rancher in Mato Grosso, quoted in O Estado de Sao Paulo (Sept. 14, 1937).

   "I am of the opinion that an area as rich as this cannot afford the luxury of conserving a half dozen Indian tribes who are holding back the development of Brazil." General Fernando Ramos Pereira, Governor of Roraima, March, 1975.

4. The Indian.
   a) Perhaps as many as 2 million Indians in Brazil when the Portuguese arrived in 1500.
   b) Comment upon: 1. The Crown's attitude toward the Indians; 2. The Church's attitude toward the Indians; 3. The planter's attitude toward the Indians.
   c) Nineteenth century romantization of the Noble Indian: José de Alencar, O Guarani (1857).
   d) 1910 - Indian Protection Service. Cândido Rondon

HISTORY OF MODERN BRAZIL

The Challenge of Establishing a Nation

1. What are the key events in 1808, 1810, and 1827 which determine the economic patterns of the nineteenth century?

2. What are the key events in 1808, 1815, 1821, 1822, and 1824 which determine the political patterns of much of the century?

3. Discuss the causation for independence.

4. What are the broadest implications of Evaristo da Veiga's remark: "Let us have no excesses. We want a constitution, not a revolution."

5. Define the role of Great Britain in Brazil both before and after independence.

6. Be able to connect these dates: 1808, 1815, 1822, 1831, and 1840. You should be able to write a meaningful and significant essay just using those dates.

7. Most texts on Latin American history emphasize the peaceful transition of Brazil from colony to empire as well as its political evolution, contrasting the Brazilian experience with that of Spanish America. What arguments can you make against that generalization?

8. Identify and give the significance of each:

Braganza
Enlightenment
João VI
Pedro I
José Bonifacio
Constitution of 1824
Poder Moderador (Moderating Power)
The Regency
Pedro II
Dependency
Development
Growth

Modernization: The Promise, the Threat, and the Reality

1. The literature on modernization in general and as a concept is vast. Even the bibliography on modernization in Latin America is impressive.

a. General Literature

Marion J. Levy, Modernization and the Structure of Societies: A Setting for International Affairs, 2 Vols. (Princeton Univ. Press, 1966).

Cyril Black, The Dynamics of Modernization: A Study in Comparative History (NY: Harper, 1967).

S. N. Einsenstadt, Modernization: Protest and Change (Englewood Cliffs, Praeger, 1966).

I. R. Sinai, In Search of the Modern World (NY: American Library, 1967).

David E. Apter, The Politics of Modernization (University of Chicago Press, 1967).

b. 19th Century Latin American Modernization

Roberto Cortes Conde, The First Stages of Modernization in Spanish America (NY: Harper, 1974).

Edward D. Hernández, "Modernization and Dependency in Costa Rica during the Decade of the 1880's" (PhD Dissertation, UCLA, 1975).

c. Brazilian Modernization

Richard Graham, Britain and the Onset of Modernization in Brazil, 1850-1914 (Cambridge University Press, 1968).

Joseph A. Kahl, The Measurement of Modernization: A Study of Values in Brazil and Mexico (University of Texas Press, 1968).

d. A Critical View of Modernism

Peter Berger, Brigitte Berger, and Hansfried Kellner, The Homeless Mind: Modernizaton and Consciousness (NY: vintage, 1974). For the Third World, the authors equate modernization with Westernizaion. They conclude that modernization de-cultures the Third World, creating "a spreading condition of homelessness."

Dean C. Tipps, "Modernization Theory and the Comparative Study of Societies: A Critical Perspective," Comparative Studies in Society and History, 15, No. 2 (March, 1973), pp. 119-226. The author notes that the concept of modernization is popular because it obscures rather than clarifies (p. 199) and that ethnocentric criteria becloud modernization theories (p. 226).

2. Be prepared to comment on the evolutionary nature of Brazilian independence as well as the evolutionary nature by which Brazilians took control of their own government.

3. Discuss the anomaly of coffee culture with its many characteristics of the colonial past helping to modernize Brazil.

4. What were the multiple roles Great Britain played in Brazil during the first half of the nineteenth century?

5. What happened during the decade of the 1840's to help accelerate Brazilian modernization after 1850?

6. How are each of these groups affected by and/or contribute to Brazil's drive to modernize: urban middle groups, the military, the slaves, and the immigrants?

7. How would you speculate about the "coincidence" of the almost simultaneous occurrence of rising economic prosperity due to coffee culture and increasing political stability?

8. Quotations from Irma Adelman & Cynthia Taft Morris, Economic Growth and Social Equity in Developing Countries (Stanford University Press 1973).
   "When economic growth begins in a subsistence agrarian economy through the expansion of a narrow modern sector, inequality in the distribution of income typically increases greatly, particularly where expatriate exploitation of rich natural resources provides the motivating force for growth. The income share of the poorest 60 percent declines significantly as does that of the middle 20 percent, and the income share of the top 5 percent increases strikingly." (p. 178)

   "Development policies that ought in principle to have made for a more equitable distribution of income have served merely as additional instruments for increasing the wealth and power of existing elites. Even more serious, new elites, many of whom owe their power to development programs, have become adept at manipulating economic and political institutions to serve their private ends." (p. 201)

9. Identify and give the significance of:

Alves Branco Tariff
Modernization / Progress
Mazombo
Irineu Evangelista de Sousa, Viscount Maua
Tavares Bastos

10. Frequently in the social sciences one encounters schema such as the following one to explain or to help give an understanding for modernization. This one suggested by Joseph A. Kahl in his Measurement of Modernism contrasts the extremes of a model traditional society and a model modern society using seven broad characteristics:

182

HISTORY OF MODERN BRAZIL

Assessing the Empire

1. Characterize the Liberal and Conservative parties. Compare and contrast their views.

2. Explain the fall of the Second Empire.

3. Evaluate the reign of Emperor Pedro II.

4. What are some of the major ideas being discussed in Brazil after 1870? How do you explain the emergence of those ideas at that time? Did the ideas have any consequences?

5. What caused and what are the consequences of the War of the Triple Alliance?

6. Discuss the interplay of the abolition of slavery and immigration.

7. Characterize the relationship of Church and State during the Second Empire.

8. Explain the significance of Positivism.

9. Can you place these areas on your mental map of Brazil? Northeast, Southeast, Rio de Janeiro, Minas Gerais, São Paulo, Rio Grande do Sul, Pernambuco, and Bahia.

10. Identify and give the significance of each:

1850 - Queiroz Law
1871 - Law of the Free Womb (Rio-Branco Law)
1885 - Saraiva-Cotegipe Law
Joaquim Nabuco
José do Patrocinio
André Rebouças
Castro Alves
Princess Isabel
Council of State
Conservatives
Liberals
Second Empire
War of the Triple Alliance
Francisco Solano López
Carlos Gomes

HISTORY OF MODERN BRAZIL

Heyday of the Old Republic

1. Explain how the middle groups lost power by 1894 and conversely how the coffee interests were able to gain national political ascendancy in 1894.

2. Fit the triumph of federalist sentiment after 1889 into the broader centralist/federalist conflict of the nineteenth century.

3. Compare and contrast---in **very general** terms---the constitutions of 1824 and 1891.

4. Why was control of the presidency so important?

5. After 1889, in what states did national political life center? Why?

6. Why did Rio Grande do Sul and the military enjoy such close relations?

7. Characterize voter participation in the Old Republic.

8. Why is Rio-Branco so significant in Brazilian diplomatic history?

9. In general terms, what were the political and economic goals of the coffee interests? How were those goals represented in their national politics?

10. Identify and give the significance of:

coronel, coroneis (colonel)
Deodoro da Fonseca
Constitution of 1891
Floriano Peixoto
Encilhamento
Federal Republican Party
Ruy Barbosa
Prudente de Morais
Machado de Assis
Euclydes da Cunha
Baron of Rio-Branco
Convention of Taubaté

HISTORY OF MODERN BRAZIL

I. Popular Protests
  A. Rebellion
     Example: Quebra-Quilo Revolt, 1874-75
  B. Millenarian Movements
     Examples:
     Pedra Bonita (Pernambuco, 1836-39)
     Canudos (Bahia, 1893-97)
     Jocabina Maurer (Extreme South, 1872-98)
     Padre Cicero (Ceara, 1891-present)
  C. Banditry
     Example: Limpião, 1930's, Northeast, María Bonita
               cangaco, cangaceiros

II. State alinements in 3 contested elections of Old Republic

1910 - Hermes da Fonseca (MG, RG do S, & military)
       Ruy Barbosa (SP & Bahia)

1922 - Artur Bernardes (MG & SP)
       Nilo Peçanha (RG do S, RJ, Pernambuco, Bahia & military)

1930 - Julio Prestes (SP)
       Getúlio Vargas (RG do S, MG & Paraiba)

III. What makes the years 1922-1930 cohesive for purposes of study?

IV. What makes 1922 such a memorable year in Brazilian history?

V. Define nationalism? What is cultural nationalism? What is the
significance of the Modern Art Week?

VI. Discuss the causes for the collapse of the Old Republic? What does the
end of the Old Republic mean for São Paulo? For the urban middle class? For
the nationalists?

VII. Who were the tenentes, what did they stand for, what role do they play in
the 1922-1930 period? Compare and contrast the role of the military in the
1880-89 period with their role in the 1922-30 period.

VIII. How do national and international events coincide to influence the
collapse of the Old Republic?

IX. There is a recent study in English of Brazil's best known bandit: Billy
Jaynes Chandler, The Bandit King. Lampiao of Brazil (Texas A&M University
Press, 1978).

185

HISTORY OF MODERN BRAZIL

Nationalism and Vargas

1. Dependency - Export Economy - Type of Urbanization

One can chart a flow in which a dependent status shapes Brazil's export economy which in turn shapes the type of urbanization Brazil has experienced. An understanding of the mutual interaction relies to some extent on the acceptance of D. C. North's thesis discussed in "Agriculture in Economic Growth," Journal of Farm Economics (1959, pp. 943-51): Agrarian production for external markets has been on occasion "the prime influence inducing economic growth, the development of external economies, urbanization, and eventually industrial development." He discusses the homestead-plantation dichotomy. Those polar models determine the character of urban systems. The homestead model assumes the wide difussion of land ownership which creates the need for more intermediary services and supports small trading, processing, and servicing towns. The plantation model assumes a high concentration of land ownership which weakens urban networks since the plantation is an agrarian-industrial plant organized for export and able to dispense with many of the intermediary services and supports towns provide.

The plantation model shaped much of Brazil's urbanization. What strong cities there are usually service the export economy and hence both depend on exports and further deepen national dependency.

2. Who supported Getúlio Vargas? What new groups did Vargas particularly appeal to in order to enhance his support? Who opposed Vargas in the 1930's?

3. In the larger view of Brazilian history, what do the Vargas years represent?

4. Characterize the economic goals of Brazil under the leadership of Vargas?

5. Explain the idea that faltering economic growth sparks a political crisis. When growth falters what options are open to the Brazilian government?

6. How would you assess the Vargas years, 1930-1945?

7. Identify:

Getúlio Vargas
Ministry of Labor
Ministry of Education
Integralistas

Corporative State Structure
Volta Redonda

HISTORY OF MODERN BRAZIL

Reform and Reaction   —   The Military in Politics

1. Identification

Juscelino Kubitschek
Jânio Quadros
João Goulart
Humberto Castelo Branco
Petrobras
Electrobras

Profit Remittance Law
Brasília
Lucio Costa
Oscar Niemeyer
Social Democratic Party (PSD)
Brazilian Labor Party (PTB)
National Democratic Party (UDN)

2. Try to come to an understanding, satisfactory to yourself, of why the democratic experiment, 1945-1964, failed. True, we have many and complex immediate causes for the military coup d'etat in 1964, but you will want a broader explanation.

3. Nationalism, particularly economic nationalism, has been a powerful force in Brazil. Do you understand it? What are some of the specific goals of economic nationalism? They are very complicated, so don't oversimplify them.

4. Discuss the symbolism and meaning of Brasília.

5. Any study of the Brazilian "miracle," 1968-74, must differentiate between "growth" and "development." In a broader sense, any analysis of the military governments, 1964 to the present, must do the same thing. In terms of the growth/development dichotomy, do you perceive much difference between the periods 1945-64 and 1964 to the present? Be prepared to substantiate your conclusions.

6. Discuss the interplay of the urban proletariat and the urban middle class, 1930-84.

7. Consider this quotation of the relations between a dominant and a subordinate group in society: "The relationship between these groups is exploitative, with the dominat group taking all or most of society's valuables for itself. The dominant group also imposes its own view on its subordinates. The subordinates are, however, a constant threat to the stability of the system, and the dominate group must always be on guard." (A. P. Parelius and R. F. Parelius, The Sociology of Education). Apply their idea to Brazilian history, 1950 to the present.

187

Reading Guide

The Violent Land

by Jorge Amado

Literature---in this case, the novel---provides a splendid document for the historian. It is concerned with a people's social world, their adaptation and rebellion. It treats people's relations with each other, with their institutions, and with their environment. But it transcends simple description and objective analysis to reveal feeling. On one level literature reflects the writer's point of view (world view) on a topic. On another level, it is a document of, a mirror to, a period. Leo Lowenthal points out, "It is the task of the sociologist of literature to relate the experience of the writer's imaginary characters and situations to the historical climate from which they derive. He has to transform the private equation of themes and stylistic means to social equations." (Literature and the Image of Man, p.x). That is exactly what we want to accomplish through the reading of The Violent Land.

The Violent Land, published in 1942, will introduce you to Brazil's premier novelist, Jorge Amado, a master storyteller, whose novels rank among Latin America's best. He was born in 1912 on a cacao plantation not far from Ilheus in southern Bahia---in fact, both Ilheus and cacao plantations are the scenes for The Violent Land. He wrote his first novel at age 18; it was published in 1932. Today, Amado lives in Salvador da Bahia, writing a novel almost every year. These novels are set in the Bahia he knows well. The author can be counted on to introduce his readers to a rich variety of Brazilian types and characters.

The Violent Land is one of the novels of Amado's "cacao cycle." It relates the struggle of Horacio Silveira and Juca and Sinho Badaro over land whose rich soil will produce the cacao tree, a source of chocolate. In this novel, we are interested primarily in the acquisition of land and all the institutions related to the struggle and possession. While this novel concerns only cacao lands, it could just as accurately depict sugar or coffee estates. So, primarily, one wants to get an understanding of how land is acquired, expanded, maintained, and exploited and the political, economic, and social institutions involved in all these processes.

Of course, this novel tells us much more, and I can only suggest a few of the other or corollary themes that should attract your attention.

1. Like most Latin American novelists, Amado uses the grandeur of nature as a counterforce to people, as a chief character of the plot. Witness for example, Amado's statement on the coastal rain forest of Bahia: "The forest! It is not a danger, a menace. It is a god!" (p.35) Be aware of how the novelist uses nature and for what purposes.
2. What does Amado have to say about the rural worker? Note his description of debt peonage and the company store, pp. 103-104. What is the nature and meaning of the contrast of the passengers in first and third class aboard the steamer in Section I?
3. Amado provides some worthwhile insight into conflicting cultures. The Badaros read their Bible, interpreting the scriptures to suit their goals of conquering the forest. Jeremias, the black shaman, calls in his African gods to protect the forest. What is the symbolism here and its broadest significance?
4. The novel relates one story of the frontiers, obviously, then, the essence of the conquest of the New World. The conquest of the cacao lands is the search for quick wealth. It repeats the old incentive that propelled many to the New World in discovery, exploration, conquest, and exploitation. Thus the novel should provide some insight into the violence connected with the settlement of the New World.

Reading Guide

THE END OF A TRADITION
By Robert W. Shirley

Dr. Robert W. Shirley, an, anthropologist, wrote a study of a small
Brazilian community, Cunha, Sao Paulo, in the mid-1960's. We are reading this
book because it offers us a useful perspective on Brazil. On a local level it
provides a study of the institutions, dynamics, themes, and trends we study on
the broader national scale. In short, this book particularizes the general
with which we usually deal. For example, the useful section on land control
(pp. 114-142) describes in detail what has happened in Cunha but also
illustrates the broader Brazilian rural realities. Likewise, Chapter II on
local history presents a microcosm of Brazilian history. We see a very
particular part of Brazil, and yet, we recognize trends and themes
characteristic of the larger Brazil. Cunha and its surroundings provide
individual examples to illuminate more clearly broader Brazilian history.
As you read the book, try to answer these questions:

1. Could you interpret the history of Cunha as the study of "dependency?"
Explain your answer.
2. Do you understand what is the _caipira_ culture (a folk culture)? You will
understand better if you compare and contrast it with the dominant "democratic"
and "capitalistic" ideas of the national elite. Compare and contrast, for
example, education in the folk society with education in the modernizing
society. In this respect, study carefully the final paragraph of Chapter X,
pp. 232-233. What the author relates in that paragraph has far reaching
significance for Brazil, dependency, development, and, of course, for folk
culture.
3. Are you able to explain the changes in Cunha since 1940? Change has been
accelerated by what economic factors? What is the significance of the
statement on p.89; "It is the legalization as well as the commercialization of
land which led to the present changes in Cunha society." Consider carefully
the author's conclusion, "Change must come from the cities. The old
patriarchal agrarian structure is very stable and changes only in response to
external stimuli." (p.254) What is the broadest significance of this
conclusion? What are the implications for the future? Weigh carefully various
interpretations (or arguments) this statement might raise.
4. Describe the evolution of the political system of Cunha through time and be
able to compare and contrast the specific Cunha examples with the broader
national trends. Who held power and who benefited? (p. 79 ff)
5. The book suggests some significant economic topics. For example, we read
on p. 67 the following statement: "The point can justifiably be made,
therefore, that Cunha no longer has a true subsistence economy. It no longer
feeds itself, but is becoming a specialized ranching and dairy district for Sao
Paulo." How did this situation come about and what does it mean for the people
of Cunha? Is this situation unique or can you transpose it to a broader
Brazilian context?
6. Finally, consider the optimistic conclusions Professor Shirley posits on
p. 255 about the benefits of industrialization. Remember that he made those
statements in the mid-1960's. Do those conclusions seem accurate, desirable,
and/or defensible in the early 1980's.

Barravento (1962)

Cast of characters

Firminio - a villager who has gone to the city and returns in his white suit.
He tells the fishermen, "Life never changes here." He preaches against
superstition and the way of life in the fishing village.

Aruan - black son of Iemanja. He is a village leader. He represents folk
values; he is opposed to the exploitation by the bosses.

Cota - black woman who seduces Aruan

Naima - the white woman who becomes the daughter of Iemanja.

1. Series of folkloric tableaux used as the background to the story.
   candomble
   Iemanja
   capoeira
   African dances
   jangada
   berimbau

2. The plot seems to focus on the incursion of the city (represented by
Firminio) into the folk village.
Firminio is determined to free the village of superstition. He persuades Cota
to seduce Aruan, which has the effect of breaking his special relationship with
Iemanja. At the end we see him leaving the village headed for the city.
Meanwhile the wife of Chico whom Iemanja has claimed at sea gives birth to a
new child, whom we can assume will take the place of Aruan as the village
leader and protector (through Iemanja).

The fisherfolk are distant from the city and also opposed to the exploitation
of the bosses. Their return to fishing from the jangada is their reaffirmation
of their independence and folk values.

Glauber Rocha. Barravento is his first film and one of the first of the Cinema
Novo movement.

190

History 489
Fall 1984

Professor M. Conniff
Mesa Vista 1118

BRAZIL: 1500 TO THE PRESENT

The class meets MWF from 11:00 to 11:50 in Mesa Vista 2068
My office hours are M,F 10:00-10:50, and Tu 2-3.

This course provides a broad survey of Brazil's history, with much attention to social, cultural, and economic themes. Race relations and colonization patterns peculiar to Brazil dominate the first half of the course, while political and economic development are major topics of the modern half. Brazil's current quest for international leadership is seen to have deep roots, because the Brazilians have aspired since the 17th century to make the country equal to her territorial and natural resource potential. Many slides, 19th century drawings, movies, and informal discussion take place.

REQUIRED TEXTS:

> Burns, A HISTORY OF BRAZIL
> Conrad, CHILDREN OF GOD'S FIRE

Additional readings and bibliography will be available during the first week of classes. The course grade will be the weighted average of the midterm (30%), the final (35%), and the paper (35%). The paper should be about 12-15 pages long, not counting notes and bibliography. Graduate students should do a long paper (18-22 pp.) utilizing Portuguese and/or primary sources. The paper will be due Nov. 23.

Aug.	20	Major Features of the course	
	22	Portuguese Expansion to 1500	Burns, Ch. 1
	24	Geography, Climate, Amerindians	
	27	Exploration and First Settlements	
	29	Royal Government in Salvador	Burns, Ch. 2
	31	Spanish Annexation of Portugal	
Sep.	5	Mauritz and the Dutch Colony	
	7	Slave Trade and Slave Labor	Conrad, Part 1
	10	Colonial Cities of Brazil	
	12	Plantation Life and Society	Conrad, Part 2
	14	Slides of Colonial Towns	
	17	Vaquerios and Bandeirantes	
	19	First Gold Rush in History	Boxer, Ch. 2
	21	Claim Jumping Wars	Conrad, Part 3
	24	Diamonds and Westward Expansion	Boxer, Ch. 8
	26	Pombaline Reforms	
	28	Rio Comes of Age	

Oct.	1	Conspiracy in the Mines	Maxwell, "Gen. of
	3	Late Colonial Economic Booms	1790's
	8	Revolts Provoke Portuguese Reforms	
	10	Rio, Capital of the Empire	Conrad, Parts 6-8
	12	Independence or Death	Haring, Ch. 1 &
	15	Debret Drawings in Zimmerman	Burns, Ch. 3
	17	MIDTERM EXAMINATION	
	19	The First Empire	Haring, Ch. 2
	22	Pedro II Takes Over	Burns, Ch. 4
	24	Coffee is King in the Paraíba Valley	
	26	Paraguayan War	
	29	The Empire Totters	
	31	Emancipation	Conrad, Parts, 9-10
Nov.	2	Republican Coup	Burns, Ch. 5
	5	Government by Army	
	7	Politics of the Governors and Regionalism	
	9	Rio de Janeiro Remodeled	
	12	The Uneasy 1920s	Burns, Ch. 6
	14	Vargas and the 1930 Revolution	
	16	Years of Populism and Repression	Conniff, Ch. 4 (LATIN AMERICAN POPULISM)
	19	Estado Novo and FEB	
	21	Slides of Modern Brazil THANKSGIVING BREAK	
	26	The Democratic Experiment	Burns, Ch. 7
	28	The Crisis of 1964	Flynn, Chs. 6-8
	30	Military Technocracy	Flynn, Chs. 9-12
Dec.	3	The Amazon and the Economy Under The Military	Sanders
	5	The Quest for International Power	Young, Chs. 6, 9
	7	Abertura: A Return to Democracy?	

Afro-American Studies 121   Anani Dzidzienyo
Afro-Brazilians and the Brazilian Polity.

The participation of Afro-Brazilians in Brazilian Society and Politics of the 20th century is explored. It is not a chronologically oriented course but rather a thematic examination of political movements and organizations with specified reference to Brazilian Blacks. Topics include: The uses and exploitation of "African Heritage," a comparison of race and politics in Brazil and the USA and the Afro-Brazilian role in Brazil's contemporary relations with Africa. While a reading knowledge of Portuguese is not required, students with such a background should immediately appraise the instructor of the fact.

Office Hours:
Tue. 11:30 - 1:00 pm
Thu. 10:00 - 11:30 am
or by appointment ext. 3137 or 3042

Texts at the Brown Bookstore:

Robert Conrad, **Children of God's Fire: A Documentary History of Slavery in Brazil**

J.P. Dickenson, **Brazil**

Jorge Amado, **Tent of Miracles**

Florestan Fernandes, **The Negro in Brazilian Society**

Abdias do Nascimento, Mixture or Massacre

Week

1) Sept. 5: First class, no reading assignment

2) Sept. 2: J.P. Dickenson, **Brazil**

3) Sept. 19: S. Ann Hewlett, **The Cruel Dilemmas**

        Ch. 1, "Tragic Trade-offs" pp. 3-15

        Ch. 2, "Historical Perspective" pp. 16-27

        Ch. 3, "The Brazilian Growth Experience" pp. 31-58

        Ch. 4, "Political and Ideo-Frameworks" pp. 59-85

        Ch. 8, "Social and Political Results Poverty and Inequality" pp.

163-184

4) Sept. 26: Robert Conrad, **Children of God's Fire**

        I "Men of Stone and Iron: The African Slave Trade" pp. 1-52

        II "A Hell for Blacks: Slavery in Rural Brazil" pp. 53-107

        III "Slave Life in the Cities and At the Mines" pp. 109-149

5) Oct. 3: Parts 4,5,6, and 7

        IV "From Babylon to Jerusalem Slavery and the Catholic Church"

pp151-199

        V "Relations Between the Races" pp. 201-233

        VI "Peculiar Legislation: Slavery and the Law" pp. 235-286

        VII "Shamefully Torn Before Thy Eyes: Corporal Punishment" pp.

287-316

6) Oct. 10: VIII "The Perils of Being Black" pp. 317-357

        IX "A State of Domestic War: How Slaves Responded"

        X "The Noblest and Most Sacred Cause: The Abolition Struggle" pp.

415-498

7) Oct. 17: Thomas Skidmore, **Black Into White: Race and Nationality in Brazilian Thought**

194

8) Oct. 24: NO CLASS MEETING: Papers due Oct. 31

For the above paper, each student is required to write a critical review of Florestan Fernandes' **The Negro in Brazilian Society** and Lima Barreto's **Clara dos Anjos.** In your review, you must discuss how the two authors in their respective ways deal with the black condition in Brazil and its relation to the rest of the society. You can also integrate earlier readings in the course to aid your argument (length: 8-10 pgs.).

9) Oct. 31: Guest Speaker - to be announced

10) Nov. 7: Octavio Ianni, **Race and Social Classes in Brazil**

11) Nov. 14: Abdias do Nascimento, **"Racial Democracy" in Brazil: Myth or Reality**

12) Nov. 21: Jorge Amado, **The Tent of Miracles**

Nov. 21, 28, Dec. 5: Individual Class Presentations

Note: 1. During the last three classes there will be individual class presentations. Each student is required to consult with the instructor by the end of the fifth week with a view to selecting the theme for this presentation.

2. *Log Book*

Each student is required to keep a log book to be based on the reading of contemporary newspaper, magazine and journal articles on Afro-Brazilian Society today. Xerox copies of these articles will be available at Jo-Art. The aim of this excercise is to enable students to analyze a range of articles from Brazilian and foreign sources which have dealt with Afro-Brazilian themes. A detailed instruction sheet will be passed out.

195

Course Grade:

The course grade will be based on the following:

    a) mid-term paper

    b) the log-book

    c) class presentation

    d) class participation

    e) final paper

The log-book is due on Friday Dec. 8

The final paper is due Dec. 15

"Afro-Brazilians and the Brazilian Polity"

Fall 1984

Individual Presentations

1) Donald Pierson, Negros in Brazil

2) Gilberto Freyre, The Masters and the Slaves

3) Charles Wagley ed., Race and Class in Rural Brazil

4) Melville J. Herskovits, New World Negro

5) Florestan Fernandes, O Negro no Mundo dos Brancos

6) 80 Anos de Abolição

7) Roger Bastide, The African Religions of Brazil

8) Roger Bastide, Estudos Afro-Brasileiros

9) Peter McDonough, Power and Ideology in Brazil

10) Carlos Hassenbalg, Disigualidades Raciais no Brasil

Log Book Exercise - Reading

1) Gilberto Freyre,

"The Afro-Brazilian Experiment"
Unesco Courier, Sept. 1977 (13-18)

2) Jorge Amado,

"Where Gods and Men Have Mingled",
Ibid. (18-19)

3) Era Bell Thompson,

"Does Race Amalgamation Work in Brazil?"
Ebony Magazine July, Sept. 1965

4) Robert Brent Toplin,

"Exploding the Myths: Brazil
Racial Polarization in the Developing
Giant." *Black World*, Nov. 1972 (15-22)

5) Cleveland Donald Jr.,

"Equality in Brazil: Confronting Reality"
Ibid. (23-24)

6) Hoyt Fuller,

"Brazil: The Struggle for Equality" *First World*
vol. 2 no. 2 1979 (17-20)

7) Jane Coles,

"Brazil: The Beginnings of Black Protest"
us. Africa, no. 101, Jan. 1980 (71-72)

8) Karen Lowe,

Racial Equality in Brazil: a Reality or Myth?"
The Miami Herald Jan. 1, 1980

9)

"Blacks Hit 'Racist' Brazilian Census"
The New Bedford Standard Times Dec. 2,
1979

10) Henry Jackson,

"A New Black Conciousness is Bursting in
Brazil," *Encore: American and World News*
March 5, 1979 (24-26)

11)

"Blacks in Brazil: An Interview with Lelia

Gonzalez," *First World* vol. 2, no. 4 1980
(24-25,62)

12) Joan Dassin,   "Tent of Miracles: Myth of Racial Democracy"
Jumpcut Feb. 1980 (20-22)

13) Jane M. McDivitt,   "Contemporary Afro-Brazilian Protest Poetry"
Caribe, April 1980 (6-10)

14) Jane M. McDivitt,   "Modern Afro-Brazilian Poetry" *Callaloo*,
vol. 3 no. 1-3 Feb-Oct. 1980 (43-61)

15) David Brookshaw,   "Black Writers in Brazil" *Index on Censorship*,
vol, 6, no. 4 July/August 1977, (37-44)

16) Doris Turner,   "Teatro Experimental do Negro and its First
'Black Drama'," *Caribe*, April 1980 (12-15)

17) Antonio Olinto,   "The Negro Writer and the Negro Influence in
. Brazilian Literature" *African Forum* vol. 2
no. 4 Spring 1967 (5-19)

18) J. Michael Turner,   "African Religious Traditions in Brazil" *Caribe*
Sept. 1979 (3,6-7)

19) Robert Stam,   "Slow Fade to Afro: The Black Presence in
Brazilian Cinema," *Film Quarterly*, vol.
xxxvi, no.2 Winter 1983 (16-32)

20) Florestan Fernandes,   "The Negro in Brazilian Society: 25 years Later,"
in M. Margolis and W. Carter, eds. *Brazil:
Anthropological Perspectives* (270-304)

21) Robert M. Levine,   "Brazil's Urban Classes and the Legacy of the
1930's," *South Eastern Latin Americanist*,
vol. xxvi, no.2, Sept. 1982 (1-24)

22) Tom Murphy,   "Millor Fernandes", *Latin America News*,
Nov. 1980

23) Abdias do Nascimento,   Contemporary Ritual Symbols
Caribe Catalogue (1980)

24) Pierre-Michel Fontaine, "Transnational Relations and Racial
Mobilization: Emerging Black
Movements in Brazil" in J. Stack Jr.
Ethnic Identities in a Transnational World

25) Octavio Ianni, "Research on Race Relations in Brazil"
in Magnus Morner, ed. Race and Class in
Latin America

26) Michael Mitchell, "Race, Legitimacy and the State in Brazil"
LASA, Mexico City October 1983.

27) Anani Dzidzienyo, The Position of Blacks in Brazilian Society
and (1979)

28) J. Michael Turner, "African-Brazilian Relations: A Reconsideration"
in Wayne Selcher, ed. Brazil in the
International System (1981)

29) Anani Dzidzienyo, "The African Connection and Afro-Brazilian
Mobility Structures," UCLA (1980)

30) M. Mejia, "Brazil: Blacks Seek Identity" *Mary Knoll
Magazine* vol. xv no.9, Sept. 1981 (25-27)

31) Leslie B. Rout, Jr. "The 'Black Bishops' Mystery" *Luso-Brazilian
Review* vol. ix, no 1, June 1972 (80-92)

32) Manuel Querino, The African Contribution to Brazilian
Civilization (Tr. E. Bradford Burns)

33) June Hahner, "Women's Place in Politics and Economics in
Brazil Since 1964," *Luso-Brazilian Review*,
vol. ix, no. 1 Summer 1982 (84-93)

200

LAH 4620/5934   COLONIAL BRAZIL   FALL 1982

Instructor: Neill Macaulay

Time & place: 8th period (3:35-4:25 pm), Monday, Wednesday, Friday,
               GPA 2322

Course objective: To familiarize students with the development of Portuguese society in South America from the sixteenth century until
1822, when Portugal's colony became independent Brazil, Latin America's
largest and most powerful nation; i.e., to impart a basic understanding of the patterns of settlement, economic exploitation, and race
relations, of the religious and political institutions, and of the
cultural traditions that formed the colonial background of modern
Brazil.

Course outline:

I.   Lecture topics prior to the midterm examination (where possible,
     lectures will be illustrated with slides)

     A. Introduction: the land
     B. Iberian background
     C. The brazilwood era
     D. The donatarios
     E. International rivalry and the captaincy-general
     F. The rise of sugar
     G. The Spanish captivity and the Dutch invasion
     H. Colonial administration, 16 & 17th centuries
     I. Padre Vieira and the Brazil Company
     J. Race and class in colonial Brazil

II. Reading assignments to be completed before the midterm examination

     A. James Lang, Portuguese Brazil: The King's Plantation, pp. 1-114.

     B. One book chosen by the student from list "A", attached; the
         student's choice must be declared to the instructor by Sep-
         tember 29.

III. Midterm examination (to be given within a week of October 13, the
     term's midpoint)

IV. Lecture topics after the midterm examination

     A. The bandeirantes
     B. The golden age of Brazil
     C. Education, literature, art
     D. The Church
     E. Portuguese commercial policy in the 18th century
     F. Colonial administration in the 18th century

G. Wars and the military
H. Colonial conspiracies
I. Dom João VI in Brazil
J. Independence

V. Reading assignments to be completed before the final examination

    A. Lang, Portuguese Brazil, pp. 115-231

    B. One book chosen by the student from list "B", attached; the
       student's choice must be declared to the instructor by
       December 3.

VI. Final examination: 10:30-12:30, Friday, December 17, 1982.

Course requirements (undergraduates)

1) A two-hour final examination, composed of essay and short-answer questions, which will account for 50% of the course grade, unless, for any reason, the student fails to take the midterm examination, in which case the value of the final exam will be 80%. While the final exam will be cumulative, material covered after the midterm will receive the greater emphasis.

2) A one-hour midterm examination, composed of essay and short-answer questions, which will account for 30% of the course grade. This requirement is flexible to the extent noted in 1) above. The exact date of the midterm exam will be announced at least two weeks in advance.

3) Two typewritten reports on books read in addition to the textbook (Lang) and the books declared in IIB and VB (see accompanying "Guide"). Students may report on any worthy and relevant work, but books not on list "A" or "B" must be cleared with the instructor for worthiness and relevancy. One book report is due at the last class meeting prior to the midterm exam, and the other at the last class meeting prior to the final exam. Late book reports will be accepted at any time before the final exam at a discount of one letter grade.

Additional requirements for graduate students

Although the course is designed for undergraduates, graduate students are welcome. However, book reports by graduate students will be judged against higher standards of scholarly criticism than those applied to undergraduate work. Also, graduate students will be required to submit four one-page, single-spaced abstracts, each of a relevant scholarly article, at the last meeting of the class (see the accompanying sample abstract for guidance). Titles may be chosen from the bibliography of Lang, Portuguese Brazil. Each abstract will count 2½% toward the graduate student's final grade; each book report,

10%; the midterm exam, 30%; and the final exam, 40%--or 70% in case the graduate student misses the midterm.

Attachments: 1) List "A" (bibliography)
             2) List "B" (bibliography)
             3) Guide for the Writers of Book Reviews

BIBLIOGRAPHY: LIST "A"

Boxer, Charles R. The Dutch in Brazil

_____. Salvador de Sá: The Struggle for Brazil and Angola

Diffie, Bailey W. Prelude to Empire: Portugal Overseas before Henry the Navigator

Diffie, Bailey W. & George D. Winius, The Foundation of the Portuguese Empire

Dominian, Helen G. Apostle of Brazil: The Biography of Padre José de Anchieta, S.J.

Freyre, Gilberto. The Masters and the Slaves

Hemming, John. Red Gold: The Conquest of the Brazilian Indians, 1500-1760

Kieman, Mathias C. The Indian Policy of Portugal in the Amazon Region, 1614-1693

Lopes Sierra, Juan. A Governor and his Image in Baroque Brazil

Marchant, Alexander. From Barter to Slavery

Prestage, Edgar. The Portuguese Pioneers

Sanceau, Elaine. Captains of Brazil

_____. The Perfect Prince: A Biography of Dom João II

Wiznitzer, Arnold. Jews in Colonial Brazil

BIBLIOGRAPHY: LIST "B"

Alden, Dauril. Royal Government in Colonial Bral

Boxer, Charles R. The Golden Age of Brazil

Cheke, Marcus. Dictator of Portugal: The Life of the Marquis of Pombal, 1699-1782

Costa, Luíz Edmundo da. Rio in the Time of the Viceroys

Francis, Alan D. The Methuens and Portugal, 1691-1708

Koster, Henry. Travels in Brazil

Maxwell, Kenneth R. Conflicts and Conspiracies: Brazil & Portugal, 1750-1808

Moog, Clodomir Vianna. Bandeirantes and Pèoneers

Prado Júnior, Caio. The Colonial Background of Modern Brazil

Russell-Wood, A. J. R. Fidalgos and Philanthropists

Schwartz, Stuart B. Sovereignty and Society in Colonial Brazil

Vellinho, Moysés. Brazil South: Its Conquest and Settlement

205

GUIDES FOR WRITERS OF BOOK REVIEWS

"What is written without effort is read without pleasure."
Dr. Johnson to Boswell

1. Book reviews should consist of three to five double-spaced type-written pages.

2. A four-page review, allowing for ample margins, would have about 1000 words. These 1000 words might be distributed as follows:

    a) Introduction of the author (about 100 words)

    Sketch the author's background: his occupation, professional experience, education, other books, etc. This information usually can be found in <u>Who's Who, Contemporary Authors, Directory of American Scholars, Historians of Latin America in the United States</u>, or in one of the other national, regional, or professional biographical directories. Do not simply copy from your source; use your own words, avoiding abbreviations and omitting such trivia as date of marriage, number of children and literary agent.

    b) Short summary of the contents (about 200 words)

    This should be a brief, bird-eye view, rather than a chapter-by-chapter description. State the theme of the book - or the author's thesis. (Read carefully the preface or foreward.)

    c) Body of the review (about 650 words)

    Here you should give your criticism of the book. Comment on its style, emphasis, and organization. What sources did the author consult? Did he do what he set out to do? Did he prove his point? Does the book conflict with any of the other books you have read on the subject? What error, if any, did you note?

    d) Conclusion (about 50 words)

    Give a concise evaluation of the book. Is it of any use? Who, if anyone, might profit from reading it?

    Each review should have all the above elements (a,b,c, and d), although they may vary proportionately from this model. If you cannot find information on the author, see the instructor for further guidance.

3. All reviews must be proofread. Misspelled words, typing errors, and grammatical errors are to be corrected before the review is handed in; carelessness and misspelling will "count-off."

LAH 4630   MODERN BRAZIL   SPRING 1984

Instructor: Neill Macaulay

Time & place: Tue., 2-3 periods, Thur., 3 period; GPA 1105

Course objective: To familiarize students with the major developments
in Brazil since 1822. The uniqueness of Brazil and its internal
diversity will be emphasized.

Course outline

I.   Lecture topics prior to the midterm examination

     A. The stormy reign of Dom Pedro I, 1822-31

     B. Stopping the carriage of revolution: The Regency, 1831-40

     C. The reign of Dom Pedro II: Internal revolts & foreign wars,
         1840-70

     D. The reign of Dom Pedro II: Social & political ferment,
         1870-89

     E. The Republican Revolution of 1889

II. Reading assignments to be completed before the midterm examination

     A. E. B. Burns, A History of Brazil, pp. 151-285

     B. Robert Conrad, The Destruction of Brazilian Slavery

III. Midterm examination: 3rd period, Tuesday, February 14

IV. Lecture topics after the midterm examination

     A. Order and progress? Vicissitudes of the Republic, 1889-97

     B. Economic foundations of the "Old Republic," 1889-1930

     C. The long fuse: Background of the Revolution of 1930

     D. Getúlio Vargas in power, 1930-45

     E. Experimenting with industrial democracy, 1945-64

     F. From golpe to abertura, 1964-84

V.   Reading assignments to be completed before the final examination

    A.   Burns, A History of Brazil, pp. 285-538

    B.   R. Wesson & D. V. Fleischer, Brazil in Transition

VI. Final examination: 3:00 - 5:00 p.m., Thursday, April 26

Course requirements

1) A two-hour final examination, composed of essay and short-answer questions, which will account for 50% of the course grade, unless, for any reason, the student fails to take the midterm examination, in which case the value of the final exam will be 80%. While the final exam will be cumulative, material covered after the midterm will receive the greater emphasis.

2) A one-hour midterm examination, composed of essay and short-answer questions, which will account for 30% of the course grade. This requirement is flexible to the extent noted in 1) above.

3) Two typewritten reports on books read in addition to the assigned readings (see accompanying "Guide"). Students may report on any worthy and relevant work, but books not listed in the accompanying bibliography must be cleared with the instructor for worthiness and relevancy. One book report is due at the last class meeting prior to the midterm exam, and the other at the last class meeting prior to the final exam. Late book reports will be accepted at any time before the final exam at a discount of one letter grade.

Additional requirements for graduate students (LAH 5934)

Although the course is designed for undergraduates, graduate students are welcome. However, book reports by graduate students will be judged against higher standards of scholarly criticism than those applied to undergraduate work. Also, graduate students will be required to submit four one-page, single-spaced abstracts, each of a relevant scholarly article, at the last meeting of the class (see the accompanying sample abstract for guidance, and the accompanying bibliography for suggested titles). Each abstract will count 2½% toward the gradaute student's final grade; each book report, 10%; the midterm exam, 30%; and the final exam 40%--or 70% in case the graduate student misses the midterm exam.

Black, Jan Knippers, <u>United States Penetration of Brazil</u>

Bruneau, Thomas C., <u>The Church in Brazil: The Politics of Religion</u>

Conniff, Michael L., <u>Urban Politics in Brazil: Rise of Populism, 1925-45</u>

Dulles, John W. F., <u>Brazilian Communism, 1935-1945</u>

Fernandes, Florestan, <u>Reflections of the Brazilian Counter-Revolution</u>

Foweraker, Joe. <u>The Struggle for Land: Political Economy of the Pioneer Frontier in Brazil from 1930 to the present</u>

Holloway, Thomas H. <u>Immigrants on the Land: Coffee & Society in Sao Paulo, 1886-1934</u>

Leff, Nathaniel H., <u>Underdevelopment and Development in Brazil</u>

Malloy, James M., <u>The Politics of Social Security in Brazil</u>

Merrick, Thomas W. & Douglas H. Graham, <u>Population and Economic Development in Brazil: 1800 to the Present</u>

Weinstein, Barbara. <u>The Brazilian Rubber Cycle, 1850-1920</u>

BOOKS

Antoine, Charles, The Church and Power in Brazil

Baer, Warner, The Development of the Brazilian Steel Industry

Bastide, Roger, The African Religions of Brazil

Bello, José Maria, A History of Modern Brazil

Bethell, Leslie, The Abolition of the Brazilian Slave Trade

Bourne, Richard, Getúlio Vargas of Brazil, 1883-1954: Sphinx of the Pampas

Box, Pelham, The Origins of the Paraguayan War

Bruneau, Thomas C., The Political Transformation of the Brazilian Catholic Church

Burns, E. B., Nationalism in Brazil

_____, Perspectives on Brazilian History

_____, The Unwritten Alliance

Camara, Helder, Revolution Through Peace

Chandler, Billy J. The Bandit King: Lampiao of Brazil

_____, The Feitosas and the Sertão dos Inhamuns

Chilcote, Ronald, The Brazilian Communist Party: Conflict and Integration, 1922-1972

Conrad, Robert, The Destruction of Brazilian Slavery

Cortés, Carlos E., Gaucho Politics in Brazil: Rio Grade do Sul in Brazilian Politics

Costa, João Cruz, A History of Ideas in Brazil

Costa, Sérgio Correia da, Every Inch a King

Coutinho, Afránio, An Introduction to Literature in Brazil

Cunha, Euclides da, Rebellion in the Backlands

Dean, Warren, The Industrialization of Sao Paulo, 1880-1945

210

_____, Rio Claro: A Brazilian Plantation System, 1820-1920

Degler, Carl N., Neither Black nor White: Slavery and Race Relations in Brazil & the U.S.

Della Cava, Ralph, Miracle at Joaseiro

Dulles, J. W. F., Anarchists and Communists in Brazil, 1900-1935

_____, Castelo Branco: The Making of a Brazilian President

_____, Unrest in Brazil: Political-Military Crises, 1955-1964

_____, Vargas of Brazil

Eisenberg, Peter, The Sugar Industry in Pernambuco, 1840-1910

Erickson, Kenneth P. The Brazilian Corporative State and Workingclass Politics

Fernandas, Florestan, The Negro in Brazilian Society

Flory, Thomas, Judge and Jury in Imperial Brazil, 1808-1871

Flynn, Peter, Brazil: A Political Analysis

Freyre, Gilberto, The Mansions and the Shanties

_____, Order and Progress: Brazil from Monarchy to republic

Gauld, C. A. The Last Titan: Percival Farquhar

Graham, Richard, Britain and the Onset of Modernization in Brazil

Hahner, June E., Civilian-Military Relations in Brazil, 1889-1898

Hering, C. H., Empire in Brazil

Hewlett, Sylvia Ann, The Cruel Dilemmas of Development: 20th Century Brazil

Hilton, Stanley E., Brazil and the Great Powers, 1930-39: The Politics of Trade Rivalry

_____, Hitler's Secret War in South America: German Military Espionage . . . in Brazil

Holloway, Thomas H. The Brazilian Coffee Valorization of 1906

Jesús, Carolina María de, Child of the Dark

Leff, N. L., _The Brazilian Capital Goods Industry, 1929-1964_

_____, _Economic Policy Making and Development in Brazil, 1947-1964_

Levine, Robert N., _Pernambuco in the Brazilian Federation, 1889-1937_

_____, _The Vargas Regime: The Critical Years, 1934-1938_

Lima, M. de Oliveira, _The Evolution of Brazil Compared with that of Spanish & Anglo America_

Love, Joseph L., _Rio Grande do Sul and Brazilian Regionalism, 1882-1930_

_____, _Sao Paulo in the Brazilian Federation, 1889-1937_

Macaulay, Neill, _The Prestes Column_

McCann, Frank C., _The Brazilian-American Allience, 1937-1945_

Manchester, A. K., _British Preeminence in Brazil_

Margolis, Maxine L., _The Moving Frontier_

Martins, Wilson, _The Modernist Idea_

Marchant, Anyla, _Viscount Maud and the Empire of Brazil_

Morley, Helene, _The Diary of Helene Morley_

Morse, Richard M., _From Community to Metropolis: A Biography of São Paulo_

Nabuco, Carolene, _The Life of Joaquim Nabuco_

Parker, Phillis R., _Brazil and the Quiet Revolution_

Phelps, Gilbert, _The Tragedy of Paraguay_

Quartim, Joao, _Dictatorship and Armed Struggle in Brazil_

Rady, Ronald E., _Volta Redonda: A Steel Mill Comes to a Brazilian Plantation_

Rodman, Selden, _Genius in the Backlands: Popular Artists of Brazil_

Rodrigues, José Honório, _Brazil and Africa_

_____, _The Brazilians, Their Character and Aspirations_

Schmitter, Phillippe C., _Interest Conflict and POlitical Change in Brazil_

Schneider, Ronald M., The Political System of Brazil . . . 1964-1970

Simmons, G. W., Marshal Deodoro and the Fall of Dom Pedro II

Skidmore, T. E., Black into White

_____, Politics in Brazil, 1930-1964

Smith, Peter S., Oil and Politics in Modern Brazil

Smith, T. Lynn, Brazil: People and Institutions

Stein, Stanley J., The Brazilian Cotton Manufacturer

_____, Vasouras: A Brazilian Coffee County, 1850-1900

Stepan, Alfred, The Military in Politics: Changing Patterns in Brazil

Stepan, Nancy, Beginnings of Brazilian Science: Oswaldo Cruz,
    Medical Research & Policy

Thomas, Donald, Cochrane: Britannia's Last Sea-King

Thornton, Mary C., The Church and Freemasonry in Brazil, 1872-1875

Toplin, Robert B., The Abolition of Slavery in Brazil

Turner, C. W., Ruy Barbosa: Brazilian Crusader for the Essential
    Freedoms

Vellinho, Moyses, Brazil South: Its Conquest and Development

Wagley, Charles, An Introduction to Brazil

Williams, Mary W., Dom Pedro the Magnanimous

Wirth, John D., Minas Gerais in the Brazilian Federation, 1889-1937

_____, The Politics of Brazilian Development, 1930-1954

Wykeham, Peter, Santos-Dumont: A Study in Obsession

Young, Jordan, The Brazilian Revolution of 1930 an the Aftermath

The University of Alabama in Birmingham

History 460
Modern Brazil

Spring Q. 1982
Prof. Pang

Required Textbooks

Bruneau & Faucher, Authoritarian Capitalism: Brazil's Contemporary
    Economic and Political Development
Burns, A History of Brazil, 2nd ed.
Stein, Vassouras: A Brazilian Coffee County, 1850-1900.

Recommended Text

Pang, Bahia in the First Brazilian Republic: Coronelismo & Oligarchies
    1889-1934. (not required to buy)

Course Requirements

(A) Mid-Term: April 27, 1982
(B) Final Exam: May 28, 1982

Lectures and Discussions Schedule

A. The Neo-Colonial Legacy of Portuguese America (1808-1889)

3/26   1. Introduction: Colonial Heritage & Independence
3/30   2. Brazil's Political System: Who Ruled the Empire?
4/2   3. A Democratic Experiment in Government: The Regency Era
4/6   4. Sugar and Coffee Plantations: Twin Pillars of Brazil
4/9   5. Black Slavery and Abolitionism
4/13   6. Forces of Modernization: Immigration & Technology

readings: Burns, Chaps. 1-4; Stein, whole book
            Pang & Seckinger, "The Mandarins of Imperial Brazil," Com-
                parative Studies in Society and History (Sterne Reserve)
            Pang, "Modernization & Slavocracy in Nineteenth-Century
                Brazil," Journal of Interdisciplinary History (Sterne Reserv

A Select Bibliography

Leslie Bethell, The Abolition of the Brazilian Slave Trade.
Robert Conrad, The Destruction of Brazilian Slavery, 1850-1888.
Warren Dean, The Industrialization of São Paulo, 1880-1945.
Peter Eisenberg, The Sugar Industry in Pernambuco, 1840-1910.
C. H. Haring, Empire in Brazil.
Carolina Nabuco, The Life of Joaquim Nabuco.
Robert Toplin, The Abolition of Brazilian Slavery.

B. The Liberal Bourgeois Republic and Regionalism, 1889-1930

4/16   7.   Bourgeois Republic and Regional Oligarchies
4/20   8.   World War I, Middle Class, and Industrialization
4/23   9.   Popular Revolts: Tenentes and Urban Sectors

readings: Burns, Chaps. 5-6 (for Chap. 6, to p. 398)
            Pang, Bahia in the First Brazilian Republic, Chaps. 1, 5, 8

A Select Bibliography

Euclides da Cunha, Rebellion in the Backlands.
Billy Jayne Chandler, The Bandit King: Lampião of Brazil.
Ralph della Cava, Miracle at Joaseiro.
Robert Levine, Pernambuco in the Brazilian Federation, 1889-1937.
Joseph Love, São Paulo in the Brazilian Federation, 1889-1937.
Neill Macaulay, The Prestes Column: Revolution in Brazil.
John Wirth, Minas Gerais in the Brazilian Federation, 1889-1937.

MID-TERM: April 27, 1982

C. The Vargas Era and the Rise of Brazilian Populism, 1930-1954

4/30   10.   The Making of the Revolution of 1930
5/4   11.   Vargas, Estado Novo, & Economic Nationalism
5/7   12.   Post-WW2 Liberalism & Getulismo II

readings: Burns, Chaps. 6-7 (pp. 399-454)

A Select Bibliography

Carlos Cortés, Gaúcho Politics in Brazil, 1930-1964.
John Dulles, Vargas of Brazil
Stanley Hilton, Brazil and the Great Powers, 1930-1939.
Thomas Skidmore, Politics in Brazil, 1930-1964.

D. Brazil: From Democracy to Bureaucratic Authoritarianism (1954-1982)

5/11   13.   JK: "50-Year Progress in Five" & Developmentalism
5/14   14.   JQ, Goulart, and Radical Left
5/18   15.   The Military in Politics: From ESG to 1964
5/21   16.   Recipe for "the Brazilian Miracle": the State & MNCs
5/25   17.   Abertura in Brazil A Road to Chaos? (1974-1982)

readings: Burns, Chaps. 7-8 (from p. 454); Bruneau & Faucher
            Pang, "Brazil's Pragmatic Nationalism" Current History (Sterne)
            Pang, "Abertura in Brazil: A Road to Chaos?" Current History
                                                      (Sterne Reserve)
A Select Bibliography

Moreira Alves, A Grain of Mustard Seed.

Miguel Arraes, Brazil: The People and the Power.
Thomas Bruneau, The Political Transformation of the Brazilian Catholic
Church.
David Collier, ed. The New Authoritarianism in Latin America.
John Dulles, Unrest in Brazil, 1955-1964.
_____, Castello Branco: The Making of a Brazilian President.
Kenneth Erickson, The Brazilian Corporative State and Working-
Class Politics.
Peter Evans, Dependent Development: The Alliance of Multinational,
State and Local Capital in Brazil.
Octavio Ianni, Crisis in Brazil.
María de Jesús, Child of the Dark.
Riordan Roett, ed. Brazil in the Sixties.
_____, ed., Brazil in the Seventies.
Ronald Schneider, The Political System of Brazil (1964-1970).
Alfred Stepan, The Military in Politics: Changing Patterns in Brazil.
_____, ed., Authoritarian Brazil.

The Origins of the Brazilian State

rofessor Riordan Roett
all 1982-1983
ednesday, 8:30 - 10:30 am

rigins is a "great book" course in which we will read and critique a collection
f books that examine aspects of the development of the state in the Brazilian
atrimonial society from the discovery to 1930. Each week one book will be read
nd discussed in class. A set of discussion questions will be distributed the
eek before an assigned book is discussed. The questions will provide a general
ramework for class discussion.

or those who need to review basic Brazilian history, see E. Bradford Burns,
History of Brazil, second edition.

ither a term paper or a written final examination will be required.

ooks available in paperback are marked with an asterisk. From time to time, Kramer's
nd other bookstores will have discounted copies available; all paperbacks in print
ill be available at the International Learning Center. Copies of all assigned readings
ill be on reserve in the Library.

eptember 15 - Introduction

eptember 22 - Fernando Uricoechea, The Patrimonial Foundations of the Brazilian
Bureaucratic State

eptember 29 - Caio Prado, Júnior, The Colonial Background of Modern Brazil*(translated
by Suzette Macedo)

ctober 6 - C.R. Boxer, The Golden Age of Brazil, 1695 - 1750: Growing Pains of a
Colonial Society *

ctober 13 - Kenneth R. Maxwell, Conflicts and Conspiracies: Brazil and Portugal,1750-1808

ctober 20 - Warren Dean, Rio Claro: A Brazilian Plantation System 1820-1920

ctober 27 - Peter L. Eisenberg, The Sugar Industry in Pernambuco, 1840-1910: Modernization
Without Change

ovember 3 - Stanley J. Stein, Vassouras: A Brazilian Coffee County, 1850-1890*

ovember 10 - Richard Graham, Britain and the Onset of Modernization in Brazil, 1850-1914*

ovember 17 - Warren Dean, The Industrialization of Sao Paulo, 1880 - 1945

ovember 24 - Euclides da Cunha, Rebellion in the Backlands* (Os Sertoes), translated by
Samuel Putnam

ecember 1 - Joseph L. Love , Rio Grande do Sul and Brazilian Regionalism, 1882-1930

ecember 8 - Victor Nunes Leal, Coronelismo the Municipality and Representative Government
in Brazil

217

Contemporary Brazil

Fall 1984
Professor Roett

Contemporary Brazil examines the dynamics of political change in
Brazil from 1930 to the present. Attention will be given to the
Vargas regime, the populist politics of the 1946 Republic, the Revolution of 1964, the process of abertura and the political implications of the Brazilian debt crisis.

Readings will be on reserve in the library.

Paperback copies of Flynn, Roett, Stepan, Bruneau, Burns, Baer, and
McDonough are available at the bookstore; a limited number of copies
of Hewlett, Skidmore, Conniff, Bruneau, Humphrey, Levine are also
available.

The class will meet from 8:30 to 10:30 on Tuesday mornings.
The final exam will be given only once in December 1984.

Reading List

11 September - Introduction and Organization

Riordan Roett, "Brazil: Staying the Course," The Wilson Quarterly,
Summer 1983, pp. 47-61.

"Brazil's Debt Crisis", in R.E. Feinberg and V. Kalleb, eds. Adjust-
ment Crisis in the Third World, pp. 139-146.

18 September - The 1930 Revolution

T.E. Skidmore, Politics in Brazil, 1930-64, pp. 3-21

Peter Flynn, Brazil: A Political Analysis, pp. 28-69

E. Bradford Burns, A History of Brazil, 2nd ed., pp. 360-398

Michael L. Conniff, Urban Politics in Brazil: The Rise of Populism,
1925-1945, chaps. 1-7

Riordan Roett, Brazil: Politics in a Patrimonial Society, 3rd ed.
chap. 1, pp. 1-16

25 September - From Populism to Authoritariansm

Conniff - chaps. 8-10

Skidmore - pp. 21-47

Flynn - pp. 69-131

Burns - pp. 398-433

Roett - chap. 2, pp. 17-47

Stanley E. Hilton, "Brazilian Diplomacy and the Washington - Rio de Janeiro 'Axis', during the World War II Era," HAHR, 59 (2), May 1979, pp. 201 - 231

Thomas C. Bruneau, The Political Transformation of the Brazilian Catholic Church, chaps. 1 and 2, pp. 11-51

Robert M. Levine, The Vargas Regime: The Critical Years, 1934-1938

2 October - The 1946 Republic

Skidmore - pp. 48 - 186

Flynn - pp. 132 - 225

Burns - pp. 435 - 490

Frank D. McCann, "The Brazilian Army and the Problem of Mission, 1939-1964," Journal of Latin American Studies, 12(1), May 1980

Alfred Stepan, The Military in Politics: Changing Patterns in Brazil, Parts I and II, pp. 7 - 121

Werner Baer, The Brazilian Economy: Its Growth and Development, chaps. 3-4

Roett - chap. 4, pp. 78-94

Bruneau - Political Transformation, chap. 3

9 October - The Crisis: 1961-1964

Skidmore - pp. 187 - 302

Flynn - pp. 226 - 307

Burns - pp. 490 - 504

Stepan - Part III

João Goulart, "Address to the Sargents, March 30, 1964", in Richard Fagen and Wayne Cornelius, eds., Political Power in Latin America, pp. 182-6.

Baer - chap. 5

Roett - chap. 3, pp. 50-76

Bruneau - chap. 4

16 October - The Military and Authoritarian Rule: 1964-1967

Stepan - Part IV and Conclusion, pp. 213 - 271

Flynn - chap. 9, pp. 308 - 365

Skidmore - Epilogue, pp. 303 - 330

Stepan, "The New Professionalism of Internal Warfare and Military Role Expansion," in Alfred Stepan, ed., Authoritarian Brazil, pp. 47-65

Thomas E. Skidmore, "Politics and Economic Policy Making in Authoritarian Brazil, 1937-71, Ibid., pp. 3-46

Bruneau, Political Transformation, chaps. 5, 6 and 7, pp. 107-165

Roett - chap. 6, pp. 125-145

Baer - chap. 11 and 12

23 October - Organized Labor and the Authoritarian State

John Humphrey, Capitalist Control and Workers Struggle in the Brazilian Auto Industry

Roett, chap. 5, pp. 96-123

30 October - The Dilemma of Change and Reform

Sylvia Ann Hewlett - The Cruel Dilemma of Development: Twentieth Century Brazil

Flynn - chap. 10, pp. 366 - 471

6 November - The Regime Changes Course, 1974 - 1979

Peter McDonough - Power and Ideology in Brazil

Flynn - chap. 11, pp. 472 - 515

Roett - chap. 6, pp. 145 - 160

13 November - Abertura and the Elections of 1982

Flynn - Conclusion, pp. 516 - 522

Baer - chap. 6

Thomas C. Bruneau, The Church in Brazil: The Politics of Religion, chaps. 5 - 9 and Epilogue, pp. 69-160

Albert Fishlow - "The United States and Brazil," Foreign Affairs, Spring 1982, Vol. 60 (4)

Olavo Brasil de Lima Júnior, "Electoral Participation in Brazil (1945-1978): The Legislation, the Party Systems and Electoral Turnouts," Luso-Brazilian Review, XX (1), Summer 1983, pp. 65-92

Margaret J. Sarles, "Maintaining Political Control Through Parties: The Brazilian Strategy" Comparative Politics, 15 (1); October 1982

Riordan Roett - "Brazil" Vol. I 1981-2 pp. 233 - 255; Vol. II, 1982-3, pp. 286-307, Latin American and Caribbean Contemporary Record, Jack Hopkins, ed.

20 November - Brazilian Foreign Policy

Roett, chap. 8, pp. 188 - 210

Roett, "Latin American Foreign Policy," in Roy C. Macridis, ed., Foreign Policy in World Politics, 6th edition (1984)

Wayne A. Selcher, "Brazil in the World: A Ranking Analysis of Capability and Status Measures," in Selcher, ed., Brazil in the International System: The Rise of a Middle Power (Boulder: Westview Press, 1981)

Baer - chap. 7 and 8

27 November - The Debt Crisis

"Stabilization Policies in Brazil," in World Financial Markets (Morgan Guaranty Trust Company of New York), July 1984

Thomas O. Enders and Richard P. Mattione, Latin America: The Crisis of Debt and Growth (Washington, D.C., The Brookings Institution, 1984)

Riordan Roett, "Democracy and Debt in South America: A Continent's Dilemma," Foreign Affairs," America and the World 1983, pp. 695 - 720

4 December - <u>Adjustment and Political Liberalization</u>

Albert Fishlow, "The Debt Crisis: Round Two Ahead?" in R.E. Feinberg and V. Kalleb, eds., <u>Adjustment Crisis in the Third World</u> (U.S. - Third World Policy Perspectives, No. 1, Overseas Development Council, 1984)

William R. Cline, <u>International Debt and the Stability of the World Economy</u>, Institute for International Economics, Policy Analyses in International Economics, 1984 - <u>revised edition</u>

Baer - chaps 9 and 10

other readings to be assigned

UNIVERSITY OF WISCONSIN-MADISON
Department of History
Semester II, 1984-85

History 555   Brazil Since 1808   Thomas E. Skidmore

The lectures in this course will analyze topics, arranged within a
chronological coverage. Details on the latter can be obtained from
E. Bradford Burns, A History of Brazil, 2nd ed., which has been
assigned for the period up to 1930.

I.   Empire in the Tropics: 1808-1850

        January 21   Introduction: Why Study Brazil?
        January 23   Present day Brazil: The Issues and Their Origins

        January 28   Brazil: An Archipelago
        January 30   The Colonial Legacy

        February 4   A Slave Economy

        Required Reading:

            E. Bradford Burns, A History of Brazil, 2nd ed., 1-186.
            Werner Baer, The Brazilian Economy: Growth and Development,
                2nd ed., 3-29.
            Jorge Amado, Doña Flor and Her Two Husbands, entire

        Suggested Additional Reading (Optional):

            José Honorio Rodriques, The Brazilians: Their Character
                and Aspirations.
            A.J.R. Russell-Wood, ed., From Colony to Nation: Essays
                on the Independence of Brazil.
            Dauril Alden, ed., Colonial Roots of Modern Brazil.
            James Lang, Portuguese Brazil: The King's Plantation.
            John Hemming, Red Gold: The Conquest of the Brazilian
                Indians, 1500-1760.
            James Lockhart & Stuart B. Schwartz, Early Latin America:
                A History of Colonial Spanish America and Brazil.

II.   The Later Empire: 1850-1889

        February 6   The Governing of the Empire

        Feburary 11   Economic Dependence: Exports and England
                      (Title of book report due)
        February 13   The Rise of Liberalism

        February 18   Abolition: The Gradualist Approach
        February 20   The Fall of the Empire

223

February 25 SIX WEEKS EXAMINATION

Requiring Reading:

Burns, A History of Brazil, 187-276.
Richard Graham, Britain and the Onset of Modernization in
Brazil, 1850-1914, entire

Suggested Additional Reading (Optional):

Stanley J. Stein, Vassouras: A Brazilian Coffee County,
1850-1900.
Robert Brent Toplin, The Abolition of Slavery in Brazil.
Robert Conrad, The Destruction of Brazilian Slavery.
Gilbert Phelps, Tragedy of Paraguay.
Warren Dean, Rio Claro: A Brazilian Plantation System,
1820-1920.
Fernando Uricoechea, The Patrimonial Foundations of the
Brazilian Bureaucratic State.

III. Republic Brazil: 1889-1930

February 27 The New Republic in the 1890s

March 4   Rebuilding Rio: Civilizing the Tropics?
             (Book report due)
March 6   Guest lecture

March 11   The "Other" Brazil of the Interior
March 13   Intellectuals as Critics

March 25   1922: The Rediscovery of Brazil (Topic for paper
             due)

Required Reading:

Burns, A History of Brazil, 277-420
Baer, The Brazilian Economy, 31-57
Carl Degler, Neither Black Nor White, entire

Suggested Additional Reading (Optional):

Ralph della Cava, Miracle at Joaseiro.
Jorge Amado, Tent of Miracles.
Joseph Love, Rio Grande do Sul and Brazilian Regionalism,
1882-1930.
_____, São Paulo in the Brazilian Federation, 1889-1937.
Gilberto Freyre, Order and Progress.
Thomas E. Skidmore, Black into White: Race and Nationality
in Brazilian Thought.

224

Neill Macaulay, The Prestes Column: Revolution in Brazil.
Nancy Stepan, Beginnings of Brazilian Science: Oswaldo
    Cruz, Medical Research and Policy, 1890-1920.
John D. Wirth, Minas Gerais in the Brazilian Federation,
    1889-1937.
Victor Nunes Leal, Coronelismo: The Municipality and
    Representative Government in Brazil.
Thomas W. Merrick & Douglas H. Graham, Population and
    Economic Development in Brazil: 1800 to the Present.
Robert M. Levine, Pernambuco in the Brazilian Federation,
    1889-1937.
Thomas M. Holloway, Immigrants on the Land: Coffee and
    Sociey in São Paulo, 1886-1934.
Barbara Weinstein, The Amazon Rubber Boom, 1850-1920.

IV. The Vargas Era: 1930-1945

March 27   The Revolution of 1930

April 1   Political Awakening and Ideological Ferment,
            1930-37.
April 3   The Estado Novô: Vargas and Authoritarian Nation
            Building

April 8   Brazil and the World War
April 10   What happened in 1945?

Required Reading:

    Thomas E. Skidmore, Politics in Brazil, 3-47
    Peter Flynn, Brazil: A Political Analysis, 59-131
    Janet Lever, Soccer Madness, entire

Suggested Additional Reading (Optional):

    John D. Wirth, The Politics of Brazilian Development,
        1930-1954.
    Robert M. Levine, The Vargas Regime: The Critical Years,
        1934-1938.
    Philippe C. Schmitter, Interest Conflict and Political
        Change in Brazil.
    Frank McCann, Jr., The Brazilian-American Alliance, 1937-
        1945.
    Ronald H. Chilcote, The Brazilian Communist Party: Conflict
        and Integration, 1922-1972.
    Stanley E. Hilton, Brazil and the Great Powers, 1930-1939:
        The Politics of Trade Rivalry.
    _____, Hitler's Secret War in South America, 1939-45.

    Joe Foweraker, The Struggle for Land: A Political Economy
        of the Pioneer Frontier in Brazil from 1930 to the
        Present Day.

Michael L. Conniff, <u>Urban Politics in Brazil: The Rise of Populism, 1925-1945</u>.

V. Contemporary Brazil: 1945-1985

April 15   Economic Development: Accomplishments and Problems
            (Paper due)
April 17   Social Structure and Social Change

April 22   Parties, Populists and the Military
April 24   Nationalism and Foreign Dependence

April 29   Brazil Since 1964: A New Model of Development?
May 1   Attack from the Left: The Guerrilla Fails

May 6   The Economic Record Since 1964
May 8   The U.S. Role and Brazil's Future

Required Reading:

    Skidmore, <u>Politics in Brazil</u>, 48-330
    Baer, <u>The Brazilian Economy</u>, 59-151
    Skidmore, papers and draft chapters on Brazil since 1964
       (to be distributed)

Suggested Additional Reading (Optional):

    Alfred Stepan, ed., <u>Authoritarian Brazil: Origins, Policies
       and Future</u>.
    Peter Evans, <u>Dependent Development: The Alliance of Multi-
       national, State and Local Capital in Brazil</u>.
    Neuma Aguiar, ed., <u>The Structure of Brazilian Development</u>.
    Candida Procopio Ferreira de Camargo, <u>et. al.</u>, <u>Sao Paulo:
       Growth and Poverty</u> [A report from the São Paulo Justice
       and Peace Commission].
    Shelton H. Davis, <u>Victims of the Miracle: Development and
       Indians of Brazil</u>.
    Roger W. Fontaine, <u>Brazil and the United States: Toward a
       Maturing Relationship</u>.
    Charles Wagley, ed., <u>Man in the Amazon</u>.
    Joseph A. Page, <u>The Revolution That Never Was: Northeast
       Brazil, 1955-1964</u>.
    Alfred Stepan, <u>The Military in Politics: Changing Patterns
       in Brazil</u>.
    Riordan Roett, ed., <u>Brazil in the Seventies</u>.
    H. Jon Rosenbaum and William G. Tyler, eds., <u>Contemporary
       Brazil: Issues in Economic and Political Development</u>.
    Stefan H. Robock, <u>Brazil: A Study in Development Progress</u>.
    Martin T. Katzman, <u>Cities and Frontiers in Brazil: Regional
       Dimensions of Economic Development</u>.

John M. Connor, The Market Power of Multinationals: A
Quantitative Analysis of U.S. Corporations in Brazil
and Mexico.
José Comblin, The Church and the National Security State.
Thomas C. Bruneau & Philippe Faucher, eds., Authoritarian
Capitalism: Brazil's Contemporary Economic and Polit-
ical Development.
Simon Mitchell, ed., The Logic of Poverty: The Case of
the Brazilian Northeast.
Thomas C. Bruneau, The Church in Brazil: The Politics of
Religion.
Phyllis R. Parker, Brazil and the Quiet Intervention, 1964.
Janice E. Perlman, The Myth of Marginality: Urban Poverty
and Politics in Rio de Janeiro.
John Humphrey, Capitalist Control and Workers' Struggle in
the Brazilian Auto Industry.
Kenneth Paul Erickson, The Brazilian Corporative State and
Working-Class Politics.

Lectures and Discussions:

This course meets three times a week, Monday, Wednesday, and Friday
at 11:00. Normally there will be two lectures and one discussion
per week, with the discussion on Friday. Students can expect to
have ample opportunity to discuss the lecture and reading material.

Course Requirements:

Undergraduate:

There will be a six-weeks examination and a final examination.
(The format of the exam--take-home or classroom--will be
discussed in class.) Undergraduates will also be required
to write a book report and a short paper.

The book report should be a critical analysis of the author's
assumptions, line of argument, evidence used, and conclusions.
The book is to be chosen by the student and should be a significant work not included among the required reading for the
course. Titles listed under the "Suggested Additional Reading" for each section of this syllabus are examples of appropriate books. Additional ideas may be found in the supplementary bibliographies which will be distributed. The choice
of book must be approved by the instructor, who will be
happy to make suggestions of books that correspond to areas
of special interest. The book report should be approximately
4-6 pages long.

The paper is to be on a topic of student's choosing, and
should be approximately 10 pages long. The paper should

227

draw on several secondary sources and present an original interpretation of the topic discussed, i.e., it should not simply summarize the sources. Again, the topic must be approved by the instructor. Early choice of a topic is advisable in order to insure availability of books. Students may wish, in the paper, to expand upon a topic discussed in their book report. Or they may prefer to work on a completely different topic.

Title of book for Book Report due on February 11

Book report due on March 4

Topic for paper due on March 25

Paper due on April 15

Graduate Students:

Graduate students are required to take the six-weeks examination and the final examination. They will also be required to write a term paper (of approximately 20 pages) on a topic of the student's choosing. Students should feel free to pursue any special interest (political sociology, economic history, literary history, the Church, land systems, student politics, etc.) in choosing their paper topic. The instructor will be happy to suggest bibliography, of which there is a rapidly growing quantity in English. Graduate students are expected to use Portuguese-language sources, where such sources are relevant and available (the Memorial Library collection is excellent) and where the student's ability to read Portuguese is adequate. Those familiar with Spanish but pessimistic about their Portuguese should note that a little effort will yield surprisingly good results when attempting to read Portuguese.

If enrollment justifies, there will be a separate discussion section for graduate students, at an hour to be arranged. Attendance at these sections is required, since each graduate student will be asked to present an oral report to the section, which will then discuss the report. The topic will usually be in the area of the term paper and is to be agreed upon with the instructor at the beginning of the semester.

Graduate student term papers due on May 1

Professor Skidmore's History Department office is Humanities 5223 (telephone 263-1863 or 263-1800. His office at Ibero-American Studies is Van Hise 1470 (262-2811).

GRAN COLOMBIAN NATIONS

LAH 4520
Spring 1985

Professor Bushnell
Grinter 360

Course Objectives and Requirements:

The readings indicated below are intended to give the student a general grasp of the history of that part of Latin America which was once the Viceroyalty of New Granada, which attained independence as the short-lived "Gran" Colombia of Simón Bolívar, and then divided into the present Colombia, Venezuela, Ecuador, and Panama

The course will be conducted by means of informal lectures and discussion, with intermittent audiovisual aids. There will be a mid-term examination and a semi-comprehensive final; required readings as listed below; and one written report on a topic to be chosen by the student in consultation with the instructor.

Outline and readings:

All assigned readings except those at University Copycenter will be placed on reserve in the library. Lombardi and García Márquez may also be purchased in paperback.

1. ## Up to mid-term

   Osvaldo Hurtado, _Political Power in Ecuador_, pp. 1-166.

   John Lombardi, _Venezuela_, pp. 3-205.

   John Lynch, _The Spanish-American Revolutions, 1808-1826_, pp. 226-265.

   Selection of course readings available at University Copycenter

2. ## From mid-term to final

   Hurtado, pp. 169-311

   Lombardi, pp. 205-268

   Gabriel García Márquez, _No One Writes to the Colonel and Other Stories_

   Vernon L. Fluharty, _Dance of the Millions: Military Rule and the Social Revolution in Colombia_

History 464-Argentina

This course is designed to introduce students to the history and problems of contemporary Argentina. Classes will be held each Tuesday and Thursday, 9:30-10:45, and it is as important to attend classes as to do all the appropriate readings before coming to class. In addition to lectures, periodically classes will be devoted to class discussions of specific themes. All such discussions will be announced in the syllabus, and student participation will be evaluated by the instructor as part of the overall grade.

There will be one midterm exam and one final. In addition, each student will select a topic of interest to him/her related to the history of Argentina and write a term paper due November 20. It should be double-spaced, typed, proof-read, and have a bibliography of works consulted as well as footnotes to document quotes and opinions. If you do not know how to prepare a term paper, please consult the instructor. The maximum length of the paper, excluding footnotes and bibliography, will be 15 pages for undergraduates and 25 pages for graduate students. All topics must be approved by the instructor by October 4. All late papers will be penalized unless permission is granted by the instructor befor November 20. Any plagiarized paper, i.e. papers that quote directly from sources without quotation marks or footnotes and/or those that summarize opinions of others without acknowledging the source in a footnote, will be subject to penalities listed in the University Code of Conduct.

Four paperback books have been ordered for this class and are available at the bookstore: Scobie, Argentina, a City and a Nation; Sarmiento, Life in the Argentine During the Days of the Tyrant (Facundo); Imaz, Los Que Mandan (Those Who Rule); and Kon, Los Chicos de la Guerra. Additional reading assignments can be found on reserve in the Main Library and are indicated by an asterisk.

Assignments

Aug. 28-30   Introduction; Settlement of the La Plata Region

Scobie, Argentina, Intro. and Ch. 1-2

Sept. 4-6   Bourbon Reforms: Their political and social impact

Scobie, Ch. 3

Lynch, "Intendants and Cabildos in the Viceroyalty of La Plata, 1782-1810,"*

230

Sept. 11-13   Class discussion of   social   life in   Río de la
               Plata; Independence

               Readings for class discussion:

               Socolow, Susan, "Marriage, Birth and Inheritance:
               The Merchants of Buenos Aires,"*

               Johnson, Lyman, "The Entrepreneurial Reorganiza-
               tion of an Artisan Trade: The Bakers of Buenos
               Aires, 1770-1820,"*

               Johnson, "The Silversmiths of Colonial Buenos
               Aires: A Case Study in the failure of Corporate
               Social Organization,"*

               Sept. 13-Lynch, The Latin American Revolutions,
               Ch. 2

Sept. 18-20   The formation   of   a new order-Rivadavia and the
               Caudillos

               Scobie, Ch. 4

               Sarmiento, Life in the Argentine Republic During
               the Days of the Tyrant, begin

Sept. 25-27   The Rise and Fall of Juan Manuel de Rosas

               Finish Sarmiento

Oct. 2-4   The formation of   Argentine economic structures;
               The Dependency Debate--class discussion

               Brown, Jonathan, "Dynamics and Autonomy of a
               Traditional Marketing System"*

               Platt, D.C.M., "Dependency in Nineteenth-Century
               Latin America"*

               Goodwin, Paul,"The Central Argentine Railway and
               the Economic Development of Argentina, 1854-1881"*

Oct. 9-11   The formation of Argentine political structures

               McGann, Thomas, Argentina, the U.S., and the
               Interamerican System, Ch. 1-4*

               Rock, David, Politics in Argentina, Ch. 1-3*

Oct. 16-18   Immigration and the   growth   of Buenos Aires;
               discussion Oct. 20

Oct. 16-Scobie, Ch. 5

Oct. 18- Scobie, "Buenos Aires as a Commercial-Bureaucratic City, 1880-1910: Characteristics of a City's Orientation"*

Guy, Donna, "Women, Peonage and Industrializat Argentina, 1810-1914"*

Baily, Samuel, "Marriage Patterns and Immigrant Assimilation in Buenos Aires, 1882-1923"*

Oct. 23   Financial Crisis and Reconstruction

Oct. 25   MIDTERM

Oct. 30-Nov. 1 The formation of the modern military in Argentina and agricultural elites

Imaz, Los Que Mandan, Ch. 3-6

Smith, Peter, The Politics of Beef, Ch. 2*

Nov. 6-8   The Concordancia

Whitaker, "An Overview of the Period"*

Imaz, Ch. 10

Nov. 13-15   The Rise of Perón-Class discussion of Eva Perón

Nov. 13-Imaz, Ch. 9,11

Nov. 15-Bourne, Richard, "Eva Peron," in Political Leaders of Latin America*

Navarro, Marysa, "The Case of Eva Peron"*

Navarro, "Evita's Charismatic Leadership"*

Nov. 20   La Revolución Libertadora

Nov. 27-29   Non-Peronist Civilian governments; Military dictatoriship

Wynia, Argentina in the Postwar Era, Ch. 4-5*

Dec. 4-7   The rise of terrorism and the return of Peron

Silvert, "The Costs of Anti-Nationalism: Argentina"*

Start reading Los Chicos de la Guerra

Dec. 11   Two Dirty Wars

             Finish <u>Los Chicos de la Guerra</u>

Dec. 20   Final Exam 8-10a.m.

Grading System: Grades will be based upon class participation
and term paper (25%); midterm (25%) and final exam (50%).

Students are always welcome to come in during offic hours, Th. 3-
4 or by appointment, to discuss any problems or questions.   My
office is Social Science 129, and my office phone is 621-3737.
If I am not there you can leave a message in my mail box in the
History Department office or call them at 621-1586 to leave
messages.

CENTRAL AMERICA: THE STRUGGLE FOR CHANGE

History 8C   Winter 1985
Professor E. Bradford Burns

This historical analysis emphasizes first the economic growth and accompanying dependency of Central America from its independence until the Great Depression and then the turbulent consequences of that combination from 1930 to the present. The course will examine the causes of contemporary violence in Central America and pay particular attention to the Sandinista Revolution in Nicaragua, civil war in El Salvador, guerrilla warfare in Guatemala, and Honduras as a surrogate for the United States. Costa Rica will serve as an example of a reforming democracy — but is it a viable example? Of necessity considerable attention will focus on the relationship between the United States and Central America.

The principal goal of History 8C is to impart a better understanding of the events in Central America, a major tension area and a region of extreme importance for U.S. foreign policy today.

WEEK	TOPIC	READING
Jan. 7-9-11	Introduction. Colonial Heritage. Independence	Woodward, 1-119
Jan. 14-16-18	The National state Modernization, and Economic Growth	Woodward, 120-202
Jan. 23-25	The New Elite and Deepening Dependency	Diskin, 1-34
Jan. 28-30-Feb. 1	Costa Rica: Democracy and Reform	Gagini
Feb. 4-6-8	Guatemala: Revolution and Repression	Schlesinger & Kinzer; Diskin, 155-202
Feb. 11-13-15	Nicaragua: Intervention and Somoza	Woodward, 203-258; Diskin, 125-155
Feb. 20-22	Nicaragua: The Revolution Triumphs	Walker
Feb. 25-27-Mar. 1	El Salvador: The Dialectics of Change and Repression	Argueta; Diskin, 101-254
Mar. 4-6-8	Contemporary Crises in Central America	Diskin, 75-100; 203-124
Mar. 11-13-15	The Role of the U.S. in Central America	Diskin, 35-74

The Discussion Sections: Some Advice and Suggestions

Each student has enrolled in a discussion section and should attend that section regularly. Students can earn up to 10% of their grade through attendance and participation in the discussion sections.

The following remarks are made with the hope of making the discussions an important and meaningful experience for each student.

Classroom discussions are not the same as casual conversations, bull sessions or therapy sessions. Discussions often fail because students expect too much to come out of discussions too easily. Discussions also fail when students have not read the assignments and thus have nothing to contribute. Students should be aware that discussion is more demanding and frustrating than copying down lecture notes. The purpose of a discussion meeting is to interpret, analyze, organize, integrate and question the lectures and readings. Questioning is fundamental to participating in a discussion. Since the ability to ask the right question is an important part of education, the student should learn to ask them him/herself.

The discussion should not primarily be the place to present new material. However, it is the place for students to present their varying views on the subject under discussion.   The success of a discussion session depends to a large degree on the students' willingness to contribute   views and discuss those of others.

Learn the name of your teaching assistant, his/her office hourse, and the location of the office. Sometime during the first two weeks visit your teaching assistant in his/her office for a few minutes to become acquanted. You TA is an extremely valuable resource person.

Exams and Grades

During the quarter, students will take two exams, on January 25 and again on February 15. There will be a final exam. The final grade for the quarter will be computed as follows:

Discussion section	10%
First exam	20%
Second exam	20%
Final exam	50%

Please note in making your plans for this quarter that there will neither incompletes nor make-up exams given in History 8C.

I will hold office hours in Bunche 5361 on Mondays from 10:00 to 11:30 a.m. on Wednesdays from 2:00 to 3:00 p.m., or by appointment.

E. Bradford Burns

Texts

The following books are available from the Student

1. Ralph Lee Woodward, Jr., Central America. A Nationa Divided

2. Carlos Gagini, Redemptions

3. Stephen Schlesinger and Stephen Kinzer, Bitter Fruit. The Untold Story of the American Coup in Guatemalal

4. Thomas W. Walker, Nicaragua. The Land of Sandíno

5. Martin Diskin (ed.), Trouble in Our Backyard. Central America and the United States in the Eighties

6. Manlio Argueta, One Day of Life

Copies of these texts will be on reserve in the College Library Reserve Section.

Film Schedule

Jan. 7	Central America: A Human Geography (19 min.)
Jan. 11	Central America: Finding New Ways (17 min.)
Jan. 28	Turtle People (26 min.)
Feb. 13	Todos Santos Cuchumatan: Report from a Guatemalan Village (41 min)
Feb. 25	From the Ashes. Nicaragua Today, Part I (30 min.)
Feb 27	From the Ashes. Nicaragua Today, Part II (30 min.)
Mar. 4	Nicaragua: Report from the Front (32 min.)
Mar. 11	El Salvador: Another Vietnam (53 min.)

The University of Alabama in Birmingham

History 470
Fall Q. 1981

Professor Pang
401G Ullman

CARIBBEAN REVOLUTIONS

Course Description

This one-quarter course will focus on the study of social, economic, and political problems of the revolutionary movements and situations of the Caribbean in historical perspectives. The Caribbean Sea, surrounded by thousands of large and small islands between longitudes 59 and 85 west and latitudes 10 and 25 north, has been the incubator of various social, political, and economic revolutions. The first successful economic revolution took place in ca. 1640 ("the Sugar Revolution"); the first successful slave revolution occurred in 1792 in Haiti; and the first successful Marxist revolution in Latin America was the Cuban Revolution of 1959. In brief, the strongest revolutionary movements and situations in the hemisphere are found here. A composite of highly urban, extremely rural, and multiracial socities, the Caribbean region provides a scholar's treasure trove to study complex problems of nation-building, economic underdevelopment, political instability, and tensions of polyculture.

Required Books

Franklin W. Knight, The Caribbean.
Eric Williams, Capitalism and Slavery.
J. H. Parry and P. M. Sherlock, A Short History of the West Indies.
Carmelo Mesa-Lago, Cuba in the 1970s.

Course Requirements

(a) Mid-Term -- October 21, 1981 (two hours)
(b) Final Exam--December 2, 1981 (three hours)
(c) Graduate Credit--A short paper (consult the instructor)

Lectures and Discussions

Week 1: September 23

(A) The Caribbean Before Columbus

    1. Introduction: Defining the Course
    2. The Geography of the Caribbean
    3. Pre-Columbian Caribe Societies

readings
    Knight, Chaps. 1-2; Parry/Sherlock, Chaps. 1-2

A Select Bibliography
Eric Williams. From Columbus to Castro: The History of the Caribbean, 1492-1969.
Julian Steward and Louis Faron. Native Peoples of South America.
Jesse Jennings and Edward Norbeck, eds. Perhistoric Man in the the New World.

Gordon Willey, ed. Prehistoric Settlement Patterns in the New World.
R. H. Thompons, ed. Migrations in New World Culture.

Week 2: September 30
(B) The Making of the Spanish and Non-Iberian Colonies, 1492-1640

 1. The Establishment of Spanish Rule: Society and Polity
 2. Religion, Commerce, and War
 3. Bucaneers, Priests, and Smugglers

readings
 Knight, Chaps. 3-4; Parry/Sherlock, Chaps. 3-7

A Select Bibliography
Carl Sauer. The Early Spanish Main.
J. H. Parry. The Spanish Seaborne Empire.
C. R. Boxer. The Ducth Seaborne Empire 1600-1800.
Cornelis Goslinga. The Duch in the Caribbean and Wilde Coast, 1580-1680.
K. R. Andres. Elizabethan Privateering: English Privateering during
 the Spanish War, 1585-1603.
C. R. Boxer. "Piet Heyn and the Silver Fleet." History Today (June 1963).
Charles Gibson. Spain in America.
James Lang. Conquest and Commerce: Spain and England in the Americas.

Weeks: 3-6: October 7, 14, 21, and 28

(C) The Sugar Revolution and the Caribbean as Europe's Periphery,
 1640-1830

 1. New World Plantation Systems: Three Variations
 2. Slavery, Slave Trade, and Capitalism
 3. Slave Revolt and Resistance: Palenques and Maroons
 4. Abolition and the Economic Collapse in British West Indies
 5. Slave Revolution and Haitain Independence
 6. The Atlantic Revolution and New World Revolutions

MID-TERM EXAM: OCTOBER 28, 1981

readings
 Knight, Chaps. 4-5; Parry/Sherlock, Chaps. 8-12; Williams,
 Chaps., 1-6

A Select Bibliography
Philip D. Curtin. The Atlantic Slave Trade. A Census.
H. Hoetink, Slavery and Race Relations in the Americas.
William A. Green, British Slave Emancipation: The Sugar Colonies and
 and the Great Experiment, 1830-1865.
Barry W. Higman. Slavery Society and Economy in Jamaica, 1807-1833.
D. J. Murray. The West Indies and the Development of Colonial Govern-
 ment, 1801-1834.

238

Sidney W. Mintz. "Labor and Sugar in Puerto Rico and in Jamaica, 1800-1859." Comparative Studies in Society and History (1959).
Gwendolyn M. Hall. Social Control in Slave Plantation Soceities: A Comparison of St. Domingue and Cuba.
Ramiro Guerra e Sánchez. Sugar and Society in the Caribbean.
Lowell J. Ragatz, The Fall of the Planter Class in the British Caribbean.
Richard Price, ed. Maroon Soceities: Rebel Slave Communities in the Americas.
Eugene E. Genovese. From Rebellion to Revolution: Afro-American Slave Revolts in the Making of the New World.
_____. The Political Economy of Slavery.
Herbert G. Klein. Slavery in the Americas: A Comparative Study of Cuba and Virginia.
_____. The Middle Passage: Comparative Studies in the Atlantic Slave Trade.
Herbert S. Aimes. The History of Slavery in Cuba, 1511-1868.
Gordon K. Lewis. The Growth of the Modern West Indies.
Claude Levy. "Barbados: The Last Years of Slavery 1823-1833." Journal of Negro History (1959).
T. O. Otto, The Haitian Revolution, 1789-1804.
C. L. R. James. The Black Jacobins.
Marvis C. Campbell. "The Maroons of Jamaica: Imperium in Imperio?" Pan-African Journal (1976).
Orlando Patterson. "Slavery and Slave Revolts: A Socio-Historical Analysis of the First Maroon War, 1665-1740." Social and Economic Studies (1970).

Weeks 7-9: November 4, 11, and 28

(D) The Caribbean as a Periphery and World Revolutions, 1830-1981

1. The Political Economy of Sugar Plantations in Cuba
2. Manifest Destiny, "Cuban Colony," and the War of '98
3. Many Caribbeans: Problems of Nation-Building
4. U.S. Business Empire and Caribbean "Underdevelopment"
5. Cuban Revolution: From Batista to Castro
6. Fragmented Nationalism: British West Indies
7. The Caribbean in the 1980s: Past, Present, and Future

readings
   Knight, Chaps. 7-8; Parry/Sherlock, Chaps. 13-18; Williams, Chaps. 7-13; Mesa-Lago, Whole Book

A Select Bibliography
   Fernando Ortiz Cuban Counterpoints: Tobacco & Sugar.
   Franklin W. Knight. Slave Society in Cuba during the Nineteenth Century.
   Arthur F. Corwin. Spain and the Abolition of Slavery in Cuba, 1817-1886.

A. W. Singham, The Hero and the Crowd in a Colonial Polity.
Trevor Monroe, The Politics of Constitutional Decolonization:
    Jamaica , 1944-1962.
Selwyn Ryan. Race and Nationalism in Trinidad and Tobago: A Study
    of Decolonization in a Multiracial Society.
Howard Wiarda. Dictatorship and Development: The Methods of Control
    in Trujillo's Dominican Republic.
Abraham F. Lowenthal. The Dominican Intervention.
Carmelo Mesa-Lago, ed. Revolutionary Cuba.
Jorge Dominguez. Cuba: Revolution and Society.
Jerome Slater. Intervention and Negotiations: The United States and
    the Dominican Revolution.
Cole Blasier. The Hovering Giant: U.S. Response to Revolutionary
    Change in Latin America.
Rolando E. Bonachea and Nelson P. Valdés, eds. Cuba in Revolution.

Major Periodicals on the Caribbean

The Americas
Hispanic American Historical Review
Latin American Research Review
Caribbean Studies
Cuban Studies: A Journal
Journal of Latin American Studies
Journal of Inter-American Studies and World Affairs
Inter-American Economic Affairs

<u>Attendance</u>: Role will be taken by signing a sheet of paper. Atten-
dance is strongly recommended for those desiring to pass the
course. Experience teaches those who cut class get low grades.
<u>No cuts on exam days</u>. Each student is responsible, of course, for
anything and everything done, said, directed, or hinted at in
class, including any changes in deadlines, exam dates and so
forth. If you miss, find out what happened.

<u>Text and required readings</u>:
Ralph Lee Woodward, <u>Central America</u> (Oxford, 1976).
Walter LaFeber, <u>Inevitable Revolutions: The United States in Central
America</u> (Norton, 1983).

Feinberg, Richard E., "Central America: No Easy Answers," <u>Foreign
Affairs</u>, LIX (Summer, 1981), 1121-46.
Gallagher, John and Ronald Robinson, "Imperialism of Free Trade,"
<u>Economic History Review</u>, VI (1953), 1-15.
McCormick, Thomas, "Drift or Mastery? A corporatist Synthesis for
American Diplomatic History," in Stanley Kutler and Stanley Katz
(eds.), <u>The Promise of American History</u> (1982).
McCreery, David, "Coffee and Class: The Structure of the Development
in Liberal Guatemala, 1871-1885," <u>Hispanic American Historical
Review</u>, LXI (Aug., 1976), 438-460.
McGowan, Pat and Stephen Walker, "Radical and Conventional Models of
U. S. Foreign Economic Policy Making," <u>World Politics</u>, XXXIII
(April, 1981), 347-82.
Schoonover, Thomas, "Black Colonization in Mexico and Central America
during the Civil War: Foreign Relations and Imperialism," <u>Pacific
Historical Review</u>, XLIX (Nov. 1980), 607-20.
Sunkel, Osvaldo, "Big Business and 'Dependencia': A Latin American
View," <u>Foreign Affairs</u>, L (April, 1972).
Small, Melvin, "The Quantification of Diplomatic History," in Paul
Gorden Lauren (ed.), <u>Diplomacy: New Approaches in History, Theory
and Policy</u> (1979),
Williams, Williams A., "The Frontier Thesis and American Foreign
Policy," <u>Pacific Historical Review</u>, XXIV (Nov. 1955), 379-95.

Recommended reading: IN THESE TIMES, TIME, NEWSWEEK, THE NATION, or
some other newsweekly, or a good quality newspaper such as the
NEW YORK TIMES, WALL STREET JOURNAL, CHRISTIAN SCIENCE MONITOR,
etc. Questions about the contemporary American foreign policy are
valid since we are concerned with the historical context of how
our relations with Central America developed.

<u>Testing and grading</u>:
To receive your course grade earlier than normal University pro-
cedures, you must leave a stamped, self-addressed postcard or
envelope with me, or in my mail box in room 554, HLG.

Text assignments: W = Woodward, L = LaFeber

January	14	introduction	
	16	vocabulary, concepts for Central America-U.S. rel.	W, Chap 1
	18	geography, demography, culture of Central America	W, Chap 2,3
	21	Professor Robert Butler, guest lecture/discussion	W, Chap 4
	23	colonial Central America	W, Chap 5
	25	29th century	W, Chap 6
	28	20th century	W, Chap 7
	30	economic system	McCreery
February	1	political-social system	W, Chap 8
	4	Woodward's book; Central American themes	W, Chap 9
	6	Professor Ralph Lee Woodward, guest lecture/discussion	
	8	test	
	11	methodo; elite vs common people; social science	Small
	13	liberalism free trade; isolationism	Gallagher-R
	15	Prof. Richard Salisbury, lecture/discussion	
	22	imperialism (Marx and others)	McGowan
	25	open-door empire; informal empire; continentalism	Williams
	27	organized capitalism; political capitalism (Weber)	McCormick
March	1	developmental theory; dependency; interdependence	Sunkel
	4	theories of expansion (empire)	L, Intro, Chap 1
	6	test	
	8	Prof. Walter LaFeber, lecture/discussion	L, Chap 2
	11	U. S. Latin American policy overview	
	15	early U. S. Latin American policy overview (cont.)	
	18	sectionalism and Central America (the South)	

	22	sectionalism and Central America (the North)	Schoonover
	25	reconstruction, adjustment of the political economy	L, Chap 3
	27	depression, industrialization and the world system	
	29	expansion and communications	
April	1	Pan-Americanism and U. S. expansion	L, Chap 4
	3	foreigners in the American waistland	
	10	Panama, Nicarguan and other canals	
	12	World War I: U. S. excludes friends and foes	
	15	U. S. Caribbean security; intervention (fiscal/mil)	L, Chap 5
	17	U. S.-Central America 1930s: German challenge (compradores)	
	19	U. S.-Central America: World War II and cold war	
	22	transforming the Pan-American Union: Guat. Cuba	
	24	C. A. common market - creating investment/ market opp.	L, Epilogue
	26	Nicaragua/Salvador/Guatemala revolutions	Feinberg
	29	LaFeber's book; conclusions	
May	3	Final Examination, 7:30 a. m.	everything

FINAL EXAMINATION: Friday May 3, 7:30 a. m.

Central American-U. S. Relations bibliography
(in addition check the back of the books by Woodward and LaFeber

Anderson, Thomas P. Matanza: El Salvador's Communist Revolt of 1932
    (1971).
Arnson, Cynthia. El Salvador: A Revolution confronts the United
    States (1982).
Baker, George W. "Ideals and Realities in the Wilson Administration's
    Relations with Honduras." The Americas, XXI (July, 1964), 3-19.
--------. "The Woodrow Wilson Administration and Guatemalan Rela-
    tions." The Historian, XXVII (Feb., 1965), 155-69.
--------. "Woodrow Wilson's Use of the Non-Recognition Policy in
    Costa Rica." The Americas, XXII (July, 1965), 3-21.
Barry, Tom. Dollars and Dictators: A Guide to Central America
    (1982). HC141.B37 1982.
Biderman, Jaime. "The Development of Capitalism in Nicaragua: A
    Political Economic History." Latin American Perspectives, X
    (Winter, 1983), 7-32.
Black, George. Triumph of the People: The Sandanista Revolution in
    Nicaragua (1981). F1528.B53 1983.
Burbach, Roger and Patricia Flynn. Agribusiness in the Americas
    (1980). HD9005.B84.
Cardoso, Ciro F. S. and Hector Pérez Brignoli. Centro América y la
    economica occidental (1520-1930) (1977).
Castillo Rivas, Donald. Acumulación de capital y empresas trans-
    actionales en centroamérica. Mexico: Siglo XXI, 1980.
Crowell, Jackson. "The United States and a Central American Canal,
    1869-1877." The Hispanic american Historical Reviw, XLIX (Feb.,
    1969), 27-52.
Cook, Blanche Wiesen. The Declassified Eisenhower (1981).
Dinwoodie, D. H. "Dollar Diplomacy in the Light of the Guatemalan
    Loan Project, 1909-1913." The Americas, XXVI (Jan., 1970), 237-53.
Dominguez, Jorge I. "The United States and Its Regional Security
    Interests: The Caribbean, Central, and South America." Daedalus,
    CIX (Fall, 1980), 115-33.
Feinberg, Richard E. "Central America: No Easy Answers." Foreign
    Affairs, LIX (Summer, 1981), 1121-46.
Green, David. The Containment of Latin America (Chicago, 1971).
--------. "Paternalism and Profits: The Ideology of U. S. Aid to
    Latin America, 1943-1971," in Historical Papers, 1972 (Ottowa,
    1973).
Grieb, Kenneth J. "American Involvement in the Rise of Jorge Ubico."
    Carribean Studies, X (April, 1970), 5-21.
--------. "Guatemala and the Second World War." Ibero-Amerikanisches
    Archiv, New Series, III (1977), 377-94.
--------. "The Myth of a Central American Dictators' League." Journal
    of Latin American Studies, X (Nov., 1978), 329-45.
--------. The Regime of Jorge Ubico (1979).

--------. "The United States and the Rise of General Maximiliano Hernandez Martinez." Journal of Latin american Studies, III (Nov., 1971), 151-172.

--------. "The United States and Central American Federation." The Americas XXIV (October, 1967), 107-121.

--------. "La Conferencia Centroamericana de 1934." Latinoamericano, (1973), 85-106.

Griffith, William J. "Attitudes toward Foreign Colonization: The Evolution of Nineteenth-Century Guatemalan Immigration Policy." In Applied Enlightenment: 19th Century Liberalism. New Orleans: Middle American Institute, 1972, pp. 72-110.

Immerman, Richard H. The CIA in Guatemala (Austin, TX, 1982).

Karnes, Thomas. The Failure of Union: Central America, 1824-1975 (1976).

--------. Tropical Enterprise: The Standard Fruit and Steamship Company in Latin America (1978).

Kepner, Charles D. and Jay H. Soothill. The Banana Empire, a case study in Economic Imperialism (1935).

Kuhn, Gary G. "United States Maritime Influence in Central America, 1863-1865." The American Neptune, XXXII (1972), 277-286.

LaFeber, Walter, INEVITABLE REVOLUTIONS: THE UNITED STATES IN CENTRAL AMERICA (1983) F1436.8.U6L33 1983.

--------. The Panama Canal: The Crisis in Historical Perspective (1978).

Langley, Lester. The Banana Wars (1983) F 2178.U6L34 1983.

--------. The Struggle for the American Mediterranean, 1776-1904 (1978).

--------. THE U.S. THE CARIBBEAN IN THE 20TH CENTURY (1982).

LeoGrande, William M., and Carla Anne Robbins. "Oligarchs and Officers. The Crisis in El Salvador." Foreign Affairs, LVIII (Summer, 1980), 1084-1103.

Leon, Pierre. Economies et societes de l'Amerique Latine. Essais sur les problems du developpement à l'epoque contemporaine 1815-1967. Paris: S.E.D.E.S., 1969.

Lernoux, Penny. Cry of the People. Garden City, N.Y.: Doubleday, 1980.

Lowenthal, Abraham F., and Samuel F. Wells, Jr., eds. The Central American Crisis: Policy Perspectives. No. 119, Working Papers, Latin American Program. Wash.: Smithsonian Institution, 1982, 150 pp.

McCann, Thomas P. An American Company (1976). (about United Fruit)

McCreery, DAvid. "Coffee and Class: The Structure of the Development in Liberal Guatemala," Hispanic American Historical Review, LXI (Aug., 1976), 438-460.

--------. "Financiando el desarrollo en la America Latina del siglo XIX: el caso de Guatemala; 1871-1885. Revista del Pensamiento Centroamericano, CXLVII (April-June, 1975), 1-8.

McWilliams, Tennant S. "The Lure of Empire: Southern Interest in the Caribbean, 1877-1900." The Mississippi Quarterly, XXIX (Winter 1975-1976), 43-63.

Millett, Richard. The Guardians of the dyansty (1977).
Molina Chocano, Guellermo. Estado liberal y desarrollo capitalista in Hondouras. Tegucigalpa: Banco Central de Honduras, 1976.
Montgomery, Tommie Sue, Revolution in El Savador (1982).
Morris, J. A., and Steve C. Ropp. "Corporatism and Dependent Development: A Honduran Case Study." Latin American Research Review, XII (1977), 27-68.
Mosk, Sanford A. "The Coffee Economy of Guatemala, 1850-1918: Development and Signs of Instability." Inter-American Economic Affairs, IX (1955), 6-20.
North American Congress of Latin America, Yanqui dollar: The Contribution of U. S. Private Investment to Underdevelopment in Latin America (1971). HG4538.Y34.
Perkins, Dexter. The Monroe Doctrine--Its History and Value, (Harry S. Truman Library Institute, 1967).
Puhle, Hans-Jürgen. "Die Politik der USA in Mittelamerika: Eine self-fulfilling prophecy." Vorgänge. Zeitschrift für Gesellschaftpolitik, 54 (1981), 29-41.
Radke, August C. "Senator Morgan and the Nicaraguan Canal." The Alabama Review, XII (Jan., 1959), 5-34.
Rippy, J. Fred. "A Bond-Selling Extravaganza of the 1920s." The Journal of Business, XXIII (Oct., 1950), 238-47.
--------. "British Investments in Central America, The Dominican Republic and Cuba: A Story of Meager Returns." Inter-American Economic Affairs, VI (Autumn, 1952), 90-98.
--------. "French Investments in Latin America." Inter-American Economic Affairs, II (Autumn, 1948), 52-71.
--------. "German Investments in Guatemala." The Journal of Business, XX (Oct., 1947), 212-19.
--------. "German Investments in Latin America." The Journal of Business, XXI (April, 1948), 63-73.
--------. "The Inter-American Highway." Pacific Historical Review, XXIV (Aug., 1955), 287-98.
--------. "Investments of Citizens of the United States in Latin America." The Journal of Business, XXII (Jan., 1949), 17-29.
--------. "Italian Immigrants and Investments in Latin America." Inter-American Economic Affairs, III (Autumn, 1949), 26-37.
--------. "The Japanese in Latin America." Inter-American Economic Affairs, III (Summer, 1949), 50-62.
--------. "Relations of the United States and Guatemala during the Epoch of Justo Rufino Barrios." The Hispanic American Historical Review, XXII (1942), 595-605.
--------. "La Unión de Centroamerica, el canal por Nicaragua y Justo Rufino Barrios." Estudios (Guatemala), 4 (1971), 103-110.
Rodríquez, Mario. Central America (1965).
Ropp, Steve. "The Honduran Army in the Socio-Political Evolution of the Honduran State," The Americas, XXX (April, 1974), 504-528.
Rosenthal K., Gert. "La inversión extranjera en Centroamerica." Nueva Sociedad, 11/12 (March-June, 1974), 24-58.
Ross, Delmer G. "The Construction of the Interoceanic Railroad of Guatemala." The Americas, XXXIII (Jan., 1977), 430-56.

Ryan, Paul B. The Panama Canal Controversy: U. S. Diplomacy and Defense.

Salisbury, Richard V. "Costa Rica and the 1920-1921 Union Movement: A Reassessment." Journal of Interamerican Studies and World Affairs, 393-418.

--------. "Domestic Politics and Foreign Policy: Costa Rica's Stand on Recognition, 1923-1934." Hispanic American Historical Review, LIV (Aug., 1974), 453-478.

--------. "Good Neighbors? The United States and Latin America in The Twentieth Century." American Foreign Relations: A Historio-graphical Review. Edited by Gerald K. Haines and J. Samuel Walker. Westport, Conn.: Greenwood Press, 1981, pp. 311-333.

--------. "United States Intervention in Nicaragua: The Costa Rican Role." Prologue, IX (Winter 1977), 209-217.

Scheips, Paul J. "Gabriel Lafond and Ambrose W. Thompson: Neglected Isthmian Promoters." Hispanic American Historical Review, XXXVI (May, 1956), 211028.

--------. "United States Commercial Pressures for a Nicaragua Canal in the 1890's." The Americas, XX (April, 1964), 333-58.

Schlesinger, Stephen and Stephen Kinzer. Bitter Fruit (1982).

Schoonover, Thomas D. "Black Colonization in Mexico and Central America during the Civil War: Foreign Relations and Imperialism." Pacific Historical Review, XLIX (Nov., 1980), 607-20.

--------. "Central American Trade and Navigation: 19th Century Data Data Sources," Latin American Research Review IXV (1977), 157-169.

--------. "Costa Rican Trade and Navigation Ties with the United States, Germany, and Europe, 1840-1885," Jahrbuch für Geschichte von Staat, Wirtschaft und Gesellschaft Latein Amerikas, XIV (1977), 269-309.

--------. "Foreign Relations and Bleeding Kansas." The Kansas His-torical Quarterly, XLII (Winter, 1976), 345-52.

--------. "Imperialism in Middle America: United States Competition with Britain, Germany and France in Middle America, 1820s-1920s," in Rhodri Jefferys-Jones (ed.), Eagle Against Empire: American Opposition to European Imperialism, 1914-1982 (Aix-en-Provence, France: Universite de Provence, 1983), 41-58.

Smith, Carol A. Labor and International Capital in the Making of a Peripheral Social Formation: Economic Transformation of Guatemala, 1850-1980. No. 138, Working Papers, Latin American Program. Wash.: Smithsonian Institution, 1984.

Siman, José Jorge. The Impact of Monsignor Romero on the Churches of El Salvador and the United States. No. 135, Working Papers, Latin American Program. Wash.: Smithsonian Institution, 1983.

Stansifer, Charles L. "Application of the Tobar Doctrine to Central America." The Americas, XXIII (July, 1966), 251-72.

--------. "E. George Squier and the Honduras Interoceanic Railroad Project." The Hispanic American Historical Review, XLVI (Feb., 1966), 1-27.

Stone, Samuel Z. Los Cafeteleros. San José, C.R.: Universidad de Costa Rica, Facultas de Derecho, 1971.

--------. La Dinastía de los Conquistadores: La crisis de poder en la Costa Rica contemporanea. San José, C. R.: Editorial Universitaria Centroamericana, 1975.

--------. "Un Estudio de los Caficultores de Costa Rica." Universidad de Costa Rica, (1971), 167-217.

Tierney, John J. "U.S. Intervention in Nicaragua, 1927-1933: Lessons for Today." Orbis, XIV (1971), 1012-28.

Van Alstyne, Richard W. "American Filibustering and the British Navy: A Caribbean Analogue of Mediterranean 'Piracy'." American Journal of International Law, XXXII (Jan., 1938), 138-42.

--------. "British Diplomacy and the Clayton-Bulwer Treaty 1850-60." Journal of Modern History, XI (June, 1939), 149-83.

--------. "The Panama Canal: A Classical Case of an Imperial Hangover." Journal of Contemporary History, XV (April, 1980), 299-316.

Varas, Augusto. Soviet-Latin American Relations under United Sttes Regional Hegemony. No. 140, Working Papers, Latin American Program. Wash.: Smithsonian Institution, 1984.

Vivian, James F. "Major E. A. Burke: The Honduras Exile, 1889-1928." Louisiana History, XV (Spring, 1974), 175-94.

Walker, Thomas W., Nicaragua in Revolution (1982). F1528.N498 1982.

Webre, Stephen. José Napoleón Duarte and the Christian Democratic Party in Salvadorian Politics, 1960-1972 (1974).

Wehler, Han-Ulrich. "Handelsimperium starr Kolonialherrschaft. Die Lateinamerikapolitik der Vereinigten Staaten vor 1898." Jahrbuch für Geschichte Lateinamerikas, 3 (1966), 183-317.

--------. "Stutzpunkte in der Karibischen See. Die Anfänge des amerikanischen Imperialismus auf Hispaniola." Jahrbuch für Geschichte Lateinamerikas, 2 (1965), 399-428.

Wheelock Roman, Jaime. On the Nicaraguan Revolution. San Francisco: Center for the Study of American Militarism, 1984.

White, Alstair. El Salvador (1973).

Woodon, Drexel G. The Caribbean Presence: National and Local-Level Dimensions of Contemporary U.S.-Caribbean Relations. A Rapporteur's Report. No. 117, Working Papers, Latin American Program. Wash.: Smithsonian Institution, 1982, 20 pp.

Woodward Jr., Ralph Lee. "Guatemalan Cotton and the American Civil War," Inter-American Economic Affairs, XVIII (1965), 87-94.

--------. "Las Impresiones de un General de les Fuerzas Confederadas Sobre Centroamerica en los Anos Finales de Siglo XIX." Anuario de Estudios Centroamericanos (Costa Rica), IV (1979), 39-66.

--------. "Liberalism, Conservatism, and the Response of the Peasants of la Montana to the Government of Guatemala, 1821-1850." Plantation Society, I (February, 1979), 109-129.

--------. "Dr. Pedro Joaquin Chamorro (1924-1978), The Conservative Party, and the Struggle for Democratic Government in Nicaragua." Secolas Annals, X (March 1979), 39-46.

Books on U. S. Foreign Relations and theory of international
relations

Amin, Samir. Unequal Development: An essay on the social formations
of peripheral capitalism (1976).
Baran, Paul. "On the Political Economy of Backwardness," The Man-
chester School of Economic and Social Studies, XX (Jan., 1952),
66-84.
Chilcote, Ronald and Dale Johnson (eds.). Theories of Development:
Mode of Production or Dependency? (1983). HB 501.T4825 1983.
Edinger, Lewis J., "military leaders and foreign policy-making."
American Political Science Review, LVII (June, 1963), 392-405.
Gallagher, John and Ronald Robinson. "Imperialism of Free Trade."
The Economic History Review, 2d series, VI (1953), 1-15.
Gerschenkron, Alexander. "Economic Backwardness in Historical Per-
spective," in B. Hoselitz (ed.), The Progress of Underdeveloped
Countries (Univ. of Chicago Press, 1952), 3-29.
Hammond, Paul Y. "The National Security Council as a device for
interdepartmental coordination: an interpretation and appraisal,"
American Political Science Review, LIV (Dec., 1960), 899-910.
Kaplan, Morton A. "Balance of Power, Bipolarity and Other Models of
International Systems," American Political Science Review, LI
(Sept., 1957), 684-695.
-------- and Nicholas deB. Katzenbach. "The Patterns of International
Politics and of International Law," American Political Science
Review, LIII (Sept., 1959), 693-712.
McCormick, Thomas J., "Drift or Mastery? A Corporatist Synthesis
for American History," in Stanley Kutler and Stanley Katz (eds.),
The Promise of American History (1982).
McGowan, Pat, and Stephen G. Walker. "Radical and Conventional
Models of U.S. Foreign Economic Policy Making." World Politics,
XXXIII (April, 1981), 347-82.
Moran, Theodore H. "Foreign Expansion as an 'Institutional Neces-
sity' for U.S. Corporate Capitalism: The Search for a Radical
Model." World Politics, XXV (April, 1973), 369-86.
Schroeder, Hans-Jurgen. "Okenomische Aspekte der amerikanischen
Aussenpolitik 1900-1923." Neue Politische Literatur, (July-
September 1972), 298-321.
--------. "Amerika als Modell?: Das Dilemma der Washingtoner Aussen-
politik Gegenuber Revolutionaren Bewegungen im 20. Jahrhundert."
Historische Zeitschrift,   , 189-242.
Singer, David J. "The Correlates of War Project: Continuity, Diver-
sity, and Convergence." In Quantitative International Politics:
An Appraisal. Ed. Francis Hoole and Dina Zinnes. New York:
Praeger, 1976, pp. 21-41.
--------. "The Level-of-Analysis Problem in International Relations,"
in Klaus Knorr and Sidney Verba (eds.), The International System,
(Princeton Univ. Press, 1961), 77-92.
--------, and Melvin Small. "Patterns in International Warfare,
1816-1965." The Annals of the American Academy of Political and
Social Science, CCCLXLI (September, 1970), 145-155.

Small, Melvin. "The Applicative of Quantitative International Politics to diplomatic History." The Historian, (February, 1976), 281-304.

--------. "The Quantification of Diplomatic History." In Diplomacy: New Approaches in History, Theory and Policy. Ed. Paul Gordon Lauren. New York: The Free Press, 1979, pp. 69-96.

Sprout, Harold and Margaret. "Geography and International politics in an era of revolutionary change," Journal of Conflict Resolution, IV (March, 1960), 145-161.

Wallerstein, Immanuel. "Modernization: Requiescat in Pace." In The Uses of Controversy in Sociology. Ed. Lewis A. Coser and Otto N. Larsen. New York: The Free Press, 1976, pp. 131-35.

--------. The Capitalist World Economy: Essays. Cambridge, Eng.: Cambridge Univ. Press, 1979.

Weber, Henri. Nicaragua: The Sandinista Revolution (1981). F1528.W4213 1981.

Wehler, Hans-Ulrich. "Der amerikanische Imperialismus vor 1914." In Der moderne Imperialismus. Ed. Wolfgang J. Mommsen. Stuttgart: W. Kohlhammer, 1971, pp. 172-192.

--------. Der Aufstieg des amerikanischen Imperialismus. Gottingen: Vandenhoeck Ruprecht, 1974.

--------. "Industrial Gorwth and Early German Imperialism." In Studies in the Theory of Imperialism. Ed. Roger Owen and Bob Sutcliffe. London: Longman, 1972, pp. 71-92.

Weston, Rubin. RACISM IN U.S. IMPERIALISM (1972).

Williams, William Appleman. "The Frontier Thesis and American Foreign Policy." Pacific Historical Review, XXIV (Nov., 1955), 379-95.

--------. AMERICA CONFRONTS A REVOLUTIONARY WORLD (1976).

--------. THE CONTOURS OF AMERICAN HISTORY.

--------. TRAGEDY OF AMERICAN DIPLOMACY (2nd ed., 1972).